# Sovereign Jews

# Sovereign Jews

*Israel, Zionism, and Judaism*

Yaacov Yadgar

**SUNY**
PRESS

Cover image of the Israeli flag in front of the wailing wall / iStock by Getty Images

Published by State University of New York Press, Albany

For information, contact State University of New York Press, Albany, NY
www.sunypress.edu

Production, Diane Ganeles
Marketing, Anne M. Valentine

**Library of Congress Cataloging-in-Publication Data**

Names: Yadgar, Yaacov, author.
Title: Sovereign Jews : Israel, Zionism, and Judaism / by Yaacov Yadgar.
Description: Albany : State University of New York Press, [2017] | Includes
    bibliographical references and index.
Identifiers: LCCN 2016031432 (print) | LCCN 2016031634 (ebook) | ISBN
    9781438465333 (hardcover : alk. paper) | ISBN 9781438465340 (pbk. :
    alk. paper) | ISBN 9781438465357 (e-book)
Subjects: LCSH: Zionism. | Zionism and Judaism. | Jews—Identity—
    History. | Jews—Politics and government. | Jews—Israel—Identity—
    History. | National characteristics, Israeli. | Sovereignty. |Israel—
    Civilization.
Classification: LCC DS149.Y317 2017 (print) | LCC DS149 (ebook) | DDC
    320.54095694—dc23
LC record available at https://lccn.loc.gov/2016031432

10  9  8  7  6  5  4  3  2  1

# Contents

PART THREE
THE ISRAELI NATION-STATE AND JEWISH TRADITIONS / 161

# Acknowledgments

Several friends and colleagues offered me insightful commentary on earlier versions of the text, and for this I am grateful. I am especially indebted to Yehouda Shenhav and Lena Salaymeh for their support, guidance, and encouragement. I am also grateful to Eran Kaplan and a second reader, who preferred to preserve his/her anonymity, who have reviewed the manuscript for SUNY Press and offered me invaluable, constructive criticism. Thanks also to the staff at SUNY Press, and especially to Rafael Chaiken, Diane Ganeles, Anne Valentine, and Sharon Green, for their professional support. I am also grateful to the Office of the Rector at Bar-Ilan University for providing financial help for the publication of this book.

Chapter 3 is largely based on my previously published article, titled "Tradition," which appeared in *Human Studies*, 36(4), 2013: 451–470, with permission from Springer.

# Introduction

## A Jewish Sovereignty?

Sovereignty has always been a contested issue among Jews. Tellingly, the prototypical features of this historical debate can be found in the Hebrew Bible, specifically in I Samuel 8. There, the popular demand for the institution of political, earthly sovereignty (in the form of centralized Israelite kingship), a demand driven by growing concerns over security, is countered by the prophet's theopolitcs,[1] that renders political reality—including the earthly matters of security—a matter of Devine will, a derivative of obedience to God's laws, of His sovereignty.

The histories, traditions and laws of the Jews have maintained this tension between a sense of the inevitability of collective political agency, manifested in a form of sovereignty, and the just as inevitable sense of God's rule. Granted, this has mostly been a "theoretical" debate, as history—or God, if you will—positioned Jews as minorities among non-Jewish majorities. Nevertheless, the question remained: Should the Jews aspire—and actively strive—to gain sovereignty, or should they read their histories and traditions as bestowing them with a unique meta-historical role of ever being "diasporic" or "exilic," subjected, in the more immediate sense, to non-Jewish sovereignty, and, in the deeper sense, to God's sovereignty?

This exilic tradition, which has had the upper hand during most of rabbinical Judaism's history, famously relates the Talmudic story of the oaths adjured by God upon His people. The Jews are sworn to accept life in exile, and to obediently consent to a reality of living under foreign sovereignty.[2] Diaspora, in this regard, has been transformed from a spatial notion to a temporal and political one, denoting exactly the Jewish *lack* of sovereignty in "this world." The

1

absence of sovereignty has thus become a cornerstone of Jewish political thought.[3]

We must note that this does not mean that Jewish traditions—or Jewish life—were rendered apolitical. On the contrary, the same exilic, rabbinic tradition highlighted Jewish law as the foundation of Jewish identity. Law, which governs every aspect of the individual's and the community's life, *is* political. Moreover, paradigmatic codices of Jewish law, such as Maimonides's, for example, indisputably include also the "rules of the kings," which govern the political matters in the Jewish kingdom to come, once God redeems the Jews.

Nevertheless, if we view sovereignty as the constitution or dictation of law, and more importantly, the status of being above the law (through the ability to institute a "state of exemption,"[4] where the law is postponed), then it may be safely said that diasporic Jewish traditions tended to prefer the absolute assignment of sovereignty to God. Everyone else—including the kings and their states—has been ideationally subjected to His law, His sovereignty. In more practical terms this meant the acceptance of foreign political sovereignty as an historical existential Jewish feature.

Political-Zionism, the triumphant Herzlian thread of Zionist ideology, rebelled against this exilic tradition. Its success has tipped the scales of the historical debate decidedly toward the side favoring Jewish political sovereignty.[5] Significantly, Political-Zionism has won the debate using the conceptual framework and discourse of European modernity. Indeed, Zionism has celebrated itself as the modernization of the Jews, manifested in the dual revolution of allegedly secularizing Jewish identity and nationalizing, or politicizing it.

Zionism, then, introduced into the historical Jewish debate— or into the Jewish theopolitical traditions—a concept born out of a European, Christian, predominantly Protestant history and tradition: The modern European concept of the sovereign nation-state, that strives, beyond the state's monopoly over the use of violence and its status above the law, to create and preserve an absolute identification between sovereignty, territory, and identity. This "holy trinity" is served by the modernist discourse, which "subjects the concept of sovereignty to territory, war to international law, society to the sovereignty of the state, and civil rights to the national society."[6]

Zionist ideology was not the first to introduce the European-Protestant theopolitics of the sovereign nation-state into Jewish tradition; Moses Mendelssohn, who applied the category, or concept of "religion" born out of the nation-state's theopolitics to Judaism as a precursor to European-Jewish assimilation, preceded Zionism. But it was (Political-) Zionism, opposing the implications of Mendelssohn's apolitical reading of Jewish tradition, which made Jewish sovereignty—embodied in the concept of the modern European nation-state—the core of Jewish peoplehood, the foundation of Judaism itself. Thus, in the Zionist view, the sovereignty of the nation-state—and not, for example, Jewish traditions, laws, and practices that have developed in exile—is that which should define Jewish nationhood itself (which, in turn, dictates the application of civil rights in the nation-state of Jews).

However—and this, I would argue, is key to understating the history of Zionism and the sociopolitics of the State of Israel—Zionism has embarked on this project of establishing Jewish sovereignty as the very meaning of Jewishness, or Jewish identity, has been fundamentally put in question. Most significantly, while Zionist ideology takes central role in the debate over the meaning of Jewishness, rebelling against the rabbinical understandings and meanings of this identity, it nevertheless neglected, or failed to, offer a viable positive, meaningful understanding (or "definition") of Jewishness. In other words, Zionism's rebellion against Jewish traditions that have historically constructed or defined Jewishness was not complemented by the construction or invention of a viable alternative meaning instilled in Jewish identity.

The Political-Zionist project thus won the upper hand in the historical debate over Jewish sovereignty, but it lacked a clear answer as to the meaning of this adjective. Indeed, Zionist ideology was uneasy with the very term, "Jewish," which it identified with the malaise of exile. (Zionist ideologues preferred to use "Hebrew" as the adjective denoting their identity.) Zionism synonymized "Jewish" with a litany of negative traits, which were to be cured by sovereignty. Many have already noted the affinity—if not indebtedness—of this Zionist diagnosis, the "negation of the exile," to prevalent European anti-Semitic stereotypes of "the Jew." What sometimes goes unnoticed is the fact that the Zionist remedy, too, nourishes on a Christian (primarily Protestant) tradition; it understands sovereignty in historical-political Christian terms, and strives to apply it to Jews.

Zionist ideology and the sociopolitics of the State of Israel emanating from it, entail, then, somewhat of a paradox (in lack of a better term): First, propagating Jewish sovereignty, Zionist ideology would claim that it is this sovereignty—or, to be precise, its manifestation in the political form of a Jewish nation-state—that defines Jewish (national) identity. But the very struggle to achieve this sovereignty—and especially a campaign to achieve sovereignty over a land inhabited mostly by non-Jews—has been conducted and justified in the name of Jewish nationhood. There must be, then, a prior distinction—one that precedes sovereignty—that defines Jewishness. Even in the narrowest of nationalist understandings of the meaning of Political-Zionism—that is, a view of the State of Israel *not* as a Jewish state but rather as "simply" a state of *Jews*, the question remains: what is a Jew?

Failing (or neglecting) to offer a fully-fledged national identity that would be independent from rabbinical readings of Jewish identity, yet zealously rebelling against rabbinical authority and "religion" in general, Zionism was left with a racial notion of Jewish identity: Tautologically, echoing anti-Semitic notions of Jewishness, it would argue that a Jew, simply, is a Jew; that Jewishness is something someone is born with. One does not choose it, nor can one rid oneself of his Jewishness; it is in one's "blood."

This tautology, a markedly mythic, analogical reason, which has dominated pre-state Zionist ideology and shaped much of the Zionist ideologues' discussions on Jewish identity, proved insufficient in the framework of a nation-state that self-identifies as the state of Jews. The establishment of the sovereign nation-state of the Jews transformed the meaningful identification of what Jewishness is from a "cultural" matter to an existentially political one: it bore directly on the state's survival as the nation-state of Jews. This was specifically true since the state, following the logic of mainstream Zionist ideology, viewed itself as secular; it could not explicitly rely on what it viewed as "religious" elements of Jewish identity for its own identification as Jewish. To give but one obvious yet controversial example, the alleged secularity of the state meant that it could not rely on the constitution of Jewish law, which secularism renders a matter of "religion," as the law of the land to define its Jewishness.

The state chose not to (or maybe it was unable to, given its indebtedness to secularist epistemology and ideology) maintain a sovereignty that is *Jewish*, but rather to maintain the sovereignty of *Jews*. Indeed, as hinted to above, a dominant secularist-liberal reading has insisted that the secularity of the state means that it does not identify as Jewish at all (i.e., that the state does not carry a "religious" identity of its own; that its sovereignty cannot be meaningfully Jewish); rather, it is "simply" a state of those identified as Jews.

This, of course, necessitates the clear, legalist identification of Jews, and their differentiation from non-Jews. That is, the state itself must play an active role in drawing a clear distinction between Jews and non-Jews—specifically Palestinian Arabs, of course—and to mark the former as those whose state it is, and to make them a majority, while designating the latter a minority, who in effect cannot claim full, equal participation in the sovereignty of the Jews (and in civil rights).

Most importantly, this definition of Israel as embodying the sovereignty of Jews demands that the state takes an active role in the construction, maintenance and preservation of its majority's Jewishness. The state, in other words, needs sovereign Jews for it to obey its constitutive logic and exercise its sovereignty in their name. It thus devotes much attention and resources to the maintenance of those sovereign Jews—as *Jews*.

The aforementioned failure of the Zionist project and the State of Israel to construct and maintain a meaningful (that is, beyond the supposed biological trait of blood/race) non-rabbinical Jewish identity, meant that in practice, the state ended up relying on the (Orthodox) rabbinical establishment as the gatekeeper that would distinguish Jews from non-Jews. The state has also relied on the imposition of certain elements of Jewish traditions—which the secular logic itself marked as "religious"—for the maintenance of its majority's Judaism. This is famously expressed in the "status quo" and the entailed "religious coercion"—that is, the ("secular") state's imposition of a (nationalist interpretation of-) some aspects of Jewish traditions that preceded the state on the public sphere as well as on its citizens' private lives. This "religious coercion," the dictation by the state's ("secular") law that certain ("religious") practices are observed in public and private life, continuously draws the lines distinguishing Jews from non-Jews, maintain the former's Jewishness, and reaffirm them as sovereign. In other words, it creates and maintains those sovereign Jews.

This reality of Zionist history and Israeli sociopolitics had been obscured by a predominant discourse of modernization and secularization. Zionist ideology, and the historiography and social sciences servicing it, have put the matter of Zionism's unresolved relationship with its own Jewish, "religious" histories and traditions into supposed ease, by remaining loyal to the modern European discourse and presenting Zionism as the secularization of Judaism. The notion that the Zionist project (in its mainstream manifestations, of course) and the ensuing State of Israel are, as dictated by the conceptual and categorical distinctions of the modern nation-state, secular, has thus been a cornerstone of the dominant discourse. Even when the apparent "deviations" from the secularist European model are acknowledged, and as the very meaning of this "secularity" is put in question, the fundamental misguided binary of "religion" vs. "the secular," remains in place.

↩

This book is an attempt to re-problematize the very notion of the sovereignty of Jews by critically assessing the ways in which Zionism and the State of Israel have negotiated with Jewish traditions that preceded them.

This framing of the discussion comes as a direct confrontation with an obsolete yet still-dominant secularist discourse on "religion and politics" in Israel. Indeed, even though it may be safely stated that—epistemologically, at the very least—we are in a post-secular(ist) phase of the study of humanity, many still tend to accept, whether implicitly or explicitly, some of secularism's foundational binaries. Thus, while both organs of the most foundational binary of all—the secular-religion one—have been deconstructed, and critically put into the historical and political contexts from within which they arise as supposedly universal and transhistorical concepts, the discursive field abounds with references to the supposed complicated interaction of "religion and politics" (in Israel—and elsewhere, for that matter).

I argue that a central key to understanding the alleged convoluted relationship between "religion and politics" in Israel is the State of Israel's interest in maintaining its sovereignty as the nation-state of Jews. This, as I noted above, creates a need to mark a majority of its population as Jews and to distinguish them from non-Jews. Coupled with the failure or neglect of Zionist ideology and the Israeli state to formulate a viable, positive alternative national identity (either "Hebrew" or "Israeli"), this leads the sovereign, supposedly secular state, to apply a narrow and problematic interpretation of Jewish "religion" as a central political tool for maintaining a Jewish majority and its sovereignty.

This book harnesses the powerful epistemological critique of the still-prevalent secular epistemology to drive forward a reconsideration and reinterpretation of the Zionist-Israeli case. I argue that the conventional discourse obscures our understanding of Israeli politics by forcing both public debate and academic interpretation into distorted and biased conceptual frameworks. Utilizing a discourse on tradition, I also offer an alternative framework for understanding what I prefer to identify *not* as an issue of the interplay between "religion and politics" in Israel, but rather as the obviously political issue of the ways in which the nation-state's theopolitics negotiates with preceding Jewish traditions. Contrary to the secularist expectation, this relationship is far from being a resolved matter, as it fluctuates along a wide range of potential positions and attitudes—from indifference and negation, to assertive and conflictual reinterpretation, to explicit or implicit denial, to passive obedience, and even loyal dialoguing and observance.

The implications of this argument are not limited, of course, to the Zionist or Jewish-Israeli case. Indeed, in a certain sense this book, in the final analysis, is not about Israel, but about nationalism, political theology and the consequences of post-Westphalian sovereignty. Israel and Zionism—or the "Jewish problem," which in some readings is the essential meaning of the European nation-state's secularity— may indeed be seen as only the conduit through which this book establishes its argument.

This book thus highlights the distorting effect of the secularist (mis-)interpretation of sociopolitical reality in general. The secularist discourse is based on a foundational conceptual premise regarding an essential, categorical distinction between religion and politics. This involves matters of ontology, epistemology, and value-judgment. It assumes, as an essential preliminary consideration regarding the building blocks of human reality, that "politics" and "religion" are two ahistorical, universal (that is, culturally neutral), quasi-metaphysical realms (the historical manifestations of which are variations on the "ideal" concepts), which are mutually independent and distinguishable; It views and analyzes this reality inside a framework of understanding that emphasizes a list of binary distinctions (such as religion vs. secularism, modernity vs. tradition, and even the political vs. the non-political); And it conceives, or judges, the distinction between these two realms as proper—as a virtue that should be sought after and fought over, being that which guarantees the healthy coexistence of the two dichotomous organs: politics, as a realm of rational decision making, and religion, as a realm of private spiritual experience.

Most critically, this framework assumes the modern, liberal, supposedly secular nation-state, on its interests and normative worldview as ahistorical and acultural, thus camouflaging the Western, Protestant, sovereign-nation-state-centered political theology that underlies this phenomenon as an allegedly objective assessment of human reality. And, crucially, it is this interested imagining of the sovereign state that gives birth to the very modern concept of "religion" as the realm of the apolitical and spiritual.

The Zionist-Israeli case offers a fascinating explication of the fallacy of secularism, specifically since it implicitly or explicitly "reads" the European, Protestant traditions of the nation-state into a non-European and non-Christian context. This reading necessitates the explication of those hidden roots of what otherwise presents itself as a universal narrative of human progress. This book offers, in other words, a narrative of the European Other's attempt at adopting the European discourse of modernity, and the exposition of the hidden roots of this discourse that ensues.


## A Traditionist Stance

The interpretive exercise I wish to make in this book might be better understood if identified as a critical Jewish reading of the Zionist idea and the Israeli nation-state project or, more accurately, of the interested, manipulative (and often denied) ways in which Zionism and the state have negotiated with the histories of communities of Jews, manifested as they are in Jewish traditions that preceded the Zionist project and its culmination if the State of Israel. If I am not mistaken in this identification of my own work here, then this "local" aspect of my discussion, that which deals with the Israeli-Zionist case study, is far from being a groundbreaking novelty. A critical, Jewish reading of the ways in which the Zionist nation-state copes with preceding Jewish traditions has already received ample articulation, coming either from anti-Zionist Orthodox and Ultra-Orthodox circles,[7] or from intellectual and academic circles, which nourish on diverging understandings of the meaning of Jewish traditions, and adopt a wide range of attitudes towards Zionism.

What new perspective, then, do I wish to present in this book? I believe the main difference between previous Jewish critical readings and the interpretation I present herein is the traditionist stance that guides my critical interpretation. This stance focuses on our understanding of tradition, and our attitude towards it. In previous works[8] I described traditionism as a dialogical (yet surely not equal) stance in relation to tradition; an individual's or a community's loyal yet reflective—favorable and even sanctifying "in principle" yet interpretive, critical and selective in practice—attitude toward what they view as the tradition that constitutes their identity, that is: constitutes them as subjects. The traditionist stance is unique in its ability to stand outside of the binary structure of friend vs. enemy, upon which the dominant self-understanding of the West as secular, enlightened, and modern is constituted. It is thus further clarified by its independence from or critical appreciation of dominant Western epistemologies, conceptual frameworks, and narratives, which are usually headlined by the terms Secularism and Modernity.

As such, a traditionist stance can shed a unique light on various aspects of the dominant perception of reality, which are usually seen as self-evident and pass unexamined. Furthermore, a traditionist stance does so without necessarily adopting the Other's position, against which the dominant stance is shaped. A traditionist stance, in other words, can transcend the dichotomous binaries "religious vs. secular" and "modern vs. traditional," and offer an insightful perspective on the dominant interpretative framework, which is constituted upon these binaries. At the same time, this critical view nourishes on an intimate familiarity with these dichotomies and binaries, as they shape the political space in which traditionism exists. Chapter 3, in which I will offer a more elaborate explication of the way in which the notion of tradition should be understood—a notion that lies at the foundation of my interpretation in this book—shall also offer a more elaborate presentation of my traditionist stance.

## A Plurality of Judaism(s)

A clarification regarding my preference to use a plural form and speak of "Jewish traditions" and not simply of "Judaism" or a singular "Jewish tradition" would not be out of place here. Throughout this book I shall insist on highlighting the wide variety of forms of life that are commonly tagged as "Judaism." To put it simply, even if we could speak of a single constitutive meta-narrative of Jewish identity (this in itself is a questionable assertion), it is nevertheless a simple fact that history brought to life a rich variety of expressions, interpretations, and applications of this narrative. So much so that speaking of Judaism or Jewishness in the singular is misleading. The historical manifestations of "Judaism" or "Jewish tradition" are multifaceted, multi-vocal, varied and sometimes full of contradictions between competing interpretations and understandings of the essence of Judaism and its practical expressions.

This insistence on a plurality of "Judaisms" can rely on formidable precedents. Foremost among these is Jacob Neusner, who offers what another scholars describes as a "second order"[9] definition of Judaism, or, more accurately, of *a* Judaism. A Judaism, according to Neusner, "is composed of three elements: a world view, a way of life, and a social group that, in the here and now, embodies the whole."[10] According to this definition, it may be the case that, at times, varying, competing versions or understandings of Judaism are manifested simultaneously; or, at other times, there may be just one, dominant version/understanding. Ignoring the history of this variety would be gravely mistaken: "we cannot hope to define a single Judaism that sets the standard for all competing versions"[11]—simply because of the fact that a Judaism is dependent upon Jews to sustain it. Judaism does not have an "abstract" existence, one that is not rooted in the ways of lives of communities, who, by the very practice of their Judaism also constantly reinterpret and reconstruct it. José Faur, who offers a Sephardic-Jewish perspective for evaluating this argument, summarizes the implication of such an ethical understanding in a straightforward manner (quoting Neusner himself):

> Since there are "many communities of Judaism, and they differ from one another," we must speak of 'Judaisms'— in the plural. With one caveat, "there is no such thing as 'mine alone.'"[12]

Putting the emphasis on the notion of tradition, as I shall do in this book, immediately sheds light on this variety, and highlights our obligation to insist on a terminology and discourse that acknowledge this multiplicity, avoiding its coercion into a single, exclusive representation.

This is also the context in which one of the fundamental theoretical difficulties accompanying a discourse on Jewish politics comes to light. The "problem" with the Jewish histories, horizons of meaning, and traditions is that they do not fit easily, if they fit at all, into the commonly used categories, which originate in the modern Western discourse, such as nationalism, ethnicity, race, and religion. In many, meaningful senses "Judaism" is both and at the same time each of the above categories and neither of them. This is so since Jewish traditions offer full modes of living, touching upon various aspects, which are sometimes labeled by one of the abovementioned categories, and at times by another. They offer horizons of meaning, narratives, and behavioral codes that deal with the ways in which the individual and community are constructed, understand themselves, and cope with the surrounding world. And they are in a continuous, dynamic process of development.

## Structure of the Book

The main features of this book's arguments are discussed or revealed gradually: from the larger epistemological framework, through the Protestant history of religion, through Zionist ideology and to the sociology and politics of Israel. (A reader of an earlier draft suggested that the book offers the readers its argument in a Russian nesting doll structure). Sovereignty shall gradually emerge as carrying several meanings, which have to do with the state, the nation, society, civil rights, and more.

The book begins with an exposition of the theoretical, or epistemological foundation, of my argument. This is followed by an explication of my alternative analytical framework. The rest of the book deals with various issues that are often brought up into discussion under the heading of "religion and politics (or nationalism)" in Zionist ideology and the State of Israel, all of which touch upon, in one way or another, the ways in which the theopolitics of the Zionist project and the Israeli nation-state have negotiated with preceding Jewish traditions. This discussion involves aspects of the history of the Zionist idea, political arrangements in the State of Israel, and the Jewish identities of Israeli Jews. I both expose the shortcomings of the dominant discourse and explicate the ways in which the alternative interpretive framework I put forth illuminates these issues, and through them sheds light on the larger political project of the Israeli nation-state. The book is thus divided into three parts:

Part I lays the epistemological and theoretical framework upon which my discussion is based.

Chapter 1 offers a detailed presentation of the argument regarding the necessity to overcome the use of "religion" as an ahistorical and universal concept. This chapter presents some of the major arguments developed in an extensive field of critical interpretations of the issue (this includes works by, among others, William Cavanaugh, Wilfred C. Smith, Talal Asad, Daniel Dubuisson, and Jonathan Z. Smith), highlighting the misuses of the term as transhistorical and transcultural.

Chapter 2 shifts the focus of discussion to the Jewish case, studying the ways in which "Judaism" was transformed into a "religion," that is, the motives behind the reinterpretation (usually ascribed to Moses Mendelssohn) of Jewish traditions as corresponding to the modern meaning of the term "religion," and the political implications of this modern reinterpretation.

Chapter 3 discusses the notion of tradition, and—based on a sociopolitical reading of philosophical works by, among others, H. G. Gadamer, Ludwig Wittgenstein, Alasdair MacIntyre, and Charles Taylor—presents an understanding of the term that facilitates a better interpretation of the central issues discussed in the remainder of the book.

Part II is dedicated to a study of mainstream Zionist ideology's attitude toward preceding Jewish traditions.

Chapter 4 asks whether it is correct to view Zionism, as students of this movement and ideology often do, as a project of secularizing Jewish identity. The chapter offers a critique of this dominant reading (as formulated, for example, by Shlomo Avineri, Gideon Shimoni, and Yosef Salmon), and a general interpretive framework to replace it.

Chapter 5 studies the ways in which key Zionist thinkers most prominently associated with "secular Judaism" (mainly Aḥad Ha'am and M. Y. Berdyczewski) handled the project of rewriting their relationships with their "religious" traditions.

Chapter 6 is dedicated to a similar study of dominant streams of Zionist thought and praxis (Socialist, Revisionist, and Religious) and their relation to preceding Jewish traditions. It focuses primarily on the thought of Naḥman Syrkin, Yitzhak El'Azari-Volcani, Y. H. Brenner, and Jacob Klatzkin, as well as on the historical project of the

Socialist Zionist invention of Jewish-national tradition in Palestine. A discussion on Revisionist Zionism and Religious Zionism concludes the chapter.

Part III studies Israeli sociopolitics, or, more accurately, the political culture and Jewish identity of the Israeli nation-state.

Chapter 7 examines the complicated nature of Israeli national identity's relation to its own Jewishness. It does so through an analysis of the Israeli Supreme Court's denial of the very viability of Israeli national identity.

Chapter 8 offers a reevaluation of Israelis' Jewish identities, focusing on the theopolitics of Jewish sovereignty. It does so through a study of A. B. Yehoshua's formulation of this theopolitics.

Chapter 9 continues this reevaluation by focusing on the political arrangements that enforce a certain interpretation of Jewish traditions on the public sphere, and even on the private lives of Israelis, namely the "status quo."

I shall begin, then, with a critical assessment of the attempt to view "Judaism" as "a religion."

# Part I

# Religion, Judaism, Tradition

The theoretical, or rather epistemological ground upon which I wish to base the interpretive analysis I shall present in this book is encapsulated in the argument that in order for an understanding of the ways in which the Zionist project and the ensuing Israeli nation-state have coped with Jewish traditions that preceded them to be accurate, it must first be liberated from the shackles of the worldview, epistemology, and politics of a set of concepts and distinctions that constitutes the self-perception of the modern West. These include, among others, the binary couples of West vs. East, modern vs. traditional, enlightened vs. benighted, and also—or maybe first—religious vs. secular. These conceptual dichotomies form a complex array of mutual opposites, which constitute the Western, colonial subject as modern, secular, and enlightened. Although they present themselves as neutral, ahistorical, and universal, or cultural-context-independent conceptualizations of human life, these distinctions propagate a specific, power-driven, political-ideological agenda. Ultimately, they function to justify, if not simply necessitate, colonialism, while presenting the modern, sovereign nation-state as natural, and color its uses of power as rising above moral and ethical doubt.

The current section of the book presents this critique and offers an alternative. Chapter 1 discusses the problematic nature of the modern concept "religion." Chapter 2 studies the historical application of this concept to the Jewish case. And Chapter 3 discusses the notion of tradition as the foundation of an alternative interpretive framework.

# 1

# Religion—The History and Politics of an Ahistorical Concept

"Religion is a constructed category, not a neutral descriptor of a reality that is simply out there in the world."[1] A growing field dedicated to the study of the historical roots and development of the concept "religion" has convincingly shown that "there is no transhistorical or transcultural concept of religion. Religion has a history, and what counts as religion and what does not in any given context depends on different configurations of power and authority."[2] Indeed, in some corners of the wider field of the study of religion(s), the claim that we should forego the use of the term "religion" is an age-old convention. During the last few decades this claim has matured into a full-fledged deconstruction of the epistemology of the mainstream study of religion(s), coming from scholars such as Talal Asad,[3] Daniel Dubuisson,[4] Tomoko Masuzawa,[5] and Jonathan Z. Smith.[6] This list is far from being exhaustive.[7]

The critics all challenge (each in her or his way, of course) the universal use of the concept "religion." They often do so by deconstructing "the Western construction of religion,"[8] studying the history and politics of the evolution of the term and its contemporary uses. Moreover, the critics show that the main object of the field should be an exposition of the specific historical-political motives behind this construction, and a critical assessment of their implications to contemporary political reality.

Such a study focuses our attention on the modern, "secular" nation-state as the main generator of the Western invention/construction of religion:

> [T]he attempt to say that there is a transhistorical and transcultural concept of religion that is separable from secular

phenomena is itself part of a particular configuration of
power, that of the modern, liberal nation-state as it developed in the West. In this context, religion is constructed
as transhistorical, transcultural, essentially interior, and
essentially distinct from public, secular rationality. To con-
strue Christianity as a religion, therefore, helps to separate
loyalty to God from one's public loyalty to the nation-state.[9]

The definition of what is religious and what is secular touches directly
upon the configuration or distribution of power, since it dictates which
practices (and, specifically, what kinds of violence) are legitimate, and
which are illegitimate. Thus, as noted by the closing sentences of
Cavanaugh's quote above, in the Western, Christian context the conception of Christianity as a religion and of nationalism as secular
guarantees the Christian individual's fatal loyalty to the nation-state,
and not to the Church.

The construction of the concept "religion" necessitates that it
can be, at least theoretically so, distinguished from other historical
institutional powers; the term is meaningless unless it can be distinguished from that which is *not* religion. The critical historical readings mentioned above all show that such a transhistorical category
of religion, which is distinguishable from other political institutions,
is nowhere to be found. In premodern eras, the distinction between
(what is seen as) religion and other realms such as politics or culture
was meaningless.

This, it should be reiterated, is not a specifically novel argument.
Wilfred Cantwell Smith, whose 1962 book, *The Meaning and End of
Religion*, has become a "Modern Classic,"[10] shows that religion, as
a distinct category of human activity, such that it is separate from
culture, politics, and other realms of life, is an invention of the modern West. Smith shows that outside of the modern West there is no
equivalent, meaningful concept—not even a proximate one—to what
"we," in the West, understand as religion.[11] This argument is further
amplified if we keep in mind that the view of "politics" and "political
thought" as a distinct realm of human inquiry and practice—i.e., as
a category of human activity separate from religion—is also a clearly
modern notion.[12]

As we will see later on, this invention of religion as distinct
from the political—indeed, as apolitical "by definition"—is a central
move in the history of modern European-Jewish history; furthermore,

its negation is one of Zionism's central constitutive arguments. But let us not jump ahead too fast; the history of the concept "religion" demands further clarification.

## A Few Chapters in the History of Religion

While a full-fledged exploration of the history of the term "religion" is beyond the scope of the current discussion, a short review of some of the main chapters in the genealogy of the term can be highly informative, especially in explicating the dynamic nature of the history of a term that is currently widely misconceived to be ahistorical.

Pre-Christian Latin, from which the English term is commonly seen to be derived, used *religio* for identifying a social duty. Ancient Christianity tended to ignore the term *religio*, which had no equivalent concept in the Semitic, non-Latin world from which the early Christians originated. When the early Christians did use the term in their Latin writings (or translations), they used *religio* in several meanings, including "ritual practice, clerical office, worship (*religio dei*), and piety, or the subjective disposition of the worshipper toward God."[13] For Augustine, in the late fourth century, "*religio* means worship, the action by which we render praise."[14] This was an expression of man's natural inclination to worship, and could be directed equally either to the One True God or to false idols.

The term tended to be absent from the European-Christian discourse of the Middle Ages. As Smith notes, while this age is commonly viewed today as "the most religious" in the history of Christianity, "[d]espite this or because of it, throughout the whole Middle Ages no one, so far as I have been able to ascertain, ever wrote a book specifically on 'religion.' And on the whole this concept would seem to have received little attention."[15] When it was used, the term no longer denoted duty, but rather signified various rules, which had to do mainly with the covenantal life in Christian orders.

For Thomas Aquinas, in the thirteenth century, *religio* had to do with virtue; it is ethical, not theological, as "God is related to religion not as matter or object, but as end."[16] We may, following Cavanaugh, stress those meanings of *religio*, which are rather absent from the Christian understanding or usage of the term in the Middle Ages. First, *religio* does not denote a general notion, of which Christianity is supposedly a specific case; "for medieval Christians, religion was not a universal phenomenon: religion was a site on which universal truth was produced, and it was clear to them that truth was not produced universally."[17] Second, *religio* of the Middle Ages is not a set of statements of beliefs regarding reality. Third, *religio* is not some pure inner impulse, borne by the soul. And, fourth, it is not an institutional power that can be distinguished from the "nonreligious" powers. The distinction between the religious and the political is wholly absent from this world of thought: "*Religio* was not separable—even in theory—from political activity in Christendom. Medieval Christendom was a theopolitical whole [. . .] [T]he end of *religio* was inseparable from the end of politics."[18]

This, then, is the background for the modern invention of religion. The rise of modernity brought about a new concept, which carries a much wider and different meaning from those reviewed above. "Religion in modernity indicates a universal genus of which the various religions are species; each religion comes to be demarcated by a system of propositions; religion is identified with an essentially interior, private impulse; and religion comes to be seen as essentially distinct from secular pursuits such as politics, economics, and the like."[19]

Crucially, this concept renders Christianity apolitical, as it is now understood as a matter of the person's internal life, which has very little, if anything, to do with the political realm. This comes hand in hand with the emergence of "the secular," and is the basis of the (Western) notion of separation of state and church.

The invention of this modern notion of religion began in the Renaissance.[20] It is then that for the first time the notion that *religio* denotes the varying ways in which people worship God appears. *Religio* is a universal, inner impulse; rituals and ways of life are but an expression of it. God gave humanity various prophets, and they offered humanity various ways in which to study their insights. Thus, "there is, in spite of many varieties of rites, but one religion."[21] *Religio* is seen here is a constant, a timeless human characteristic: "all opinions of men, all their responses, all their customs, change—except *religion*."[22] It is, in other words, a Platonic ideal; the various manifestations of it, prevalent among human beings of all sorts, are its impure appearances.

Religion's transformation into a signifier of an inner, universal impulse—a "state of mind"[23]—was completed during the sixteenth and seventeenth centuries, as the emphasis shifted from practice and a way of life to belief as capturing the essence of religion; it is now understood as a set of propositions. This transformation was facilitated by the prevalence of a certain binaries, mainly those separating the inner (personal, apolitical) from the external (public, political), and belief from action or practice, which are also constitutive of the dichotomy separating those "Siamese twins"[24]—the secular and the religious.

Indeed, the story outlined above is not just the story of the invention—or birth—of religion. It is also, and maybe primarily, the story of the invention/birth of the secular. The history of this concept is wide, and it is the subject of a whole field of academic studies, often termed post-secularism.[25] This is not the place to retell this narrative. What is crucial for the current discussion is the historical fact that the secular, or its predecessor, *saeculum*, did not have an independent meaning or existence prior to the invention of the modern notion of religion. During the Middle Ages, *saeculum* had a spatial and temporal meaning: it referred to what we might call "this world"—the limitless whole of God's creation of the current epoch. It had not, then, referred to some specific realm outside of the interests of the Church. Modernity brought about the construction of the secular as the opposite of religion.[26]

The Reformation was, in this regard, a catalyst for the invention of religion, as we commonly understand it today. Moreover—this prevalent understanding of religion is a Protestant, Calvinist notion, which is taken to be a universal concept. It is the Reformation who put the emphasis on a "rational" understanding of Christianity and developed the notion of a list of core beliefs as essential to it. The seventeenth century thus witnessed a proliferation of books presenting "Christian religion," which were driven by the polemics of the competition between rival traditions and interpretations of Christianity.[27]

This, in other words, is a wholly Christian discourse. It is conducted among Christians, and understands Christianity as the highest, ultimate model of religion. Critically, it also imports the political history of a Christian notion of religion into the "general" discussion, and enforces this history on what it identifies as other "religions." Thus, the early seventeenth century also saw the publication of one of the first attempts at formulating that which is common to all religions. According to this, the religious common core is composed of five basic arguments:

1. That there is some supreme divinity. 2. That this divinity
ought to be worshipped. 3. That virtue joined with piety is
the best method of divine worship. 4. That we should return
to our right selves from sins. 5. That reward or punishment
is bestowed after this life is finished.[28]

Note that this understanding of religion cannot be disproved. If one
was to present a case of a certain society that has not held up to
the abovementioned five core principles, this will not amount to an
undermining of the universal claim; the specific case will be considered as "not normal." This understanding of religion creates its
own world, and defines its normativity. It is not a "discovery" of
the essence of religion, but rather a creation of a new reality, a self-
fulfilling prophecy—in which the eternal religion is inner, universal,
spiritual, and apolitical.[29]

This formulation encapsulates a universal vision: Once people
understand that all "religions" are, at root, the same, peace shall pre-
vail. It also manifests a basic sense of animosity and suspicion toward
tradition, as well as the complementary notion that the human mind
in its pure, uncorrupted state can grasp reality and arrive at the unbiased truth—two of the main building blocks of modernity.[30]

## A Political Conception of Apolitical Religion

The construction of religion as apolitical is rather ironic, since it lies
at the foundation of a new political order: "Attempts to construct religion as a universal, timeless, interior, and apolitical human impulse
in the early modern period are willy-nilly part of the creation of new
configurations of power, especially the subordination of ecclesiastical
power to that of the emergent state."[31]

This, then, is where the role of the modern, sovereign nation-
state in the invention of religion becomes clear. The transformation
of religion into a private, universal, and apolitical matter comes hand
in hand with the claim that the state is sovereign, and the church
its subject. What is presented as a scheme for encouraging tolerance
(of the inter-religious kind) is part of a larger scheme—that of the
creation of the sovereign nation-state with its monopoly over the use
of violence. The invention of religion as essentially composed of the

abovementioned five core notions justifies and enables the state's role as the neutral enforcer of mutual tolerance; it justifies the state's use of power against the church. Moreover, this identification of religion as apolitical was later also forced by the developing Western nation-state upon the non-European subjects of its colonialism.[32]

The Liberal construction of religion as apolitical, and the ensuing demand that it is excluded from the public realm, received ample attention in John Locke's thought. Religion, in Locke's political philosophy, is a state of mind. As such, it is "liberated" from the state's power, as the sovereign cannot force a certain mindset on its subjects; the human soul, where true religion lies, is beyond the reach of the sovereign. Locke does see value in religion, which he views as a driving force for the discovery of truth. But he sees a problem in the fact that people—or, more accurately, the differing churches—do not agree on the content and essence of the right way. Moreover, the "secular" ruler cannot help in this argumentation. This brings Locke to profess the privatization of religion, in which it becomes a personal, not public and surely apolitical, matter. Locke thus lays the foundation for the sharp separation of state, whose business is public by definition, and church, who deals with matters that are by definition personal. In other words, he delimits a public realm, which deals exclusively with "secular" matters. This is the foundation for a spatial separation between the religious and the secular.[33]

Locke, then, is not only an identifier of the supposed timeless essence of religion, but also a major contributor—through his construction of the necessary ideational foundation—of a new political order, a new distribution of power, at the center of which is the sovereign, modern state, which aims at confining the church under its authority. This is the context in which Locke invents the opposition between religious and civil matters:

> The very claim that the boundaries between religion and nonreligion are natural, eternal, fixed, and immutable is itself a part of the new configuration of power that comes about with the rise of the modern state. The new state's claim to a monopoly on violence, lawmaking, and public allegiance within a given territory depends upon either the absorption of the church into the state or the relegation of the church to an essentially private realm. Key to this

move is the contention that the church's business is religion. Religion must appear, therefore, not as what the church is left with once it has been stripped of earthly relevance, but as the timeless and essential human endeavor to which the church's pursuits should always have been confined.[34]

The rise of the modern concept of religion, then, is part of this "new configuration" of Christian societies, in which many claims to power where "migrated"[35] from the church to the modern, sovereign state. This new conceptualization was meant to "purify" the church from powers and claims which did not match its timeless essence and proper function. This new conceptualization, in other words, serves the superiority of the modern, sovereign (and, one must remember: colonial) state over the church.

William Arnal puts this argument in a succinct way as he clarifies that "[o]ur definitions of religion, especially insofar as they assume a privatized and cognitive character behind religion (as in religious belief), simply reflect (and assume as normative) the West's distinctive historical feature of the secularized state."[36] Moreover, they assume the state to be the normative, universal standard: "Religion, precisely, is not social, not coercive, is individual, is belief-oriented and so on, because in our day and age there are certain apparently free-standing cultural institutions, such as the Church, which are excluded from the political state."[37]

To summarize, the conclusions arising from Cavanaugh's critical interpretation outlined (selectively) above are far reaching. They show that religion has a history. It is not a transhistorical and universal concept, but rather a creation of the modern, sovereign nation-state, which has arisen out of a certain configuration of power and specific political interests, pertaining to the state's striving for absolute sovereignty and a monopoly over the use of violence. This means that the historicization of the concept does not simply aim to say that the meaning of the term has changed over time; rather, it aims to expose the political infrastructure of the invention of religion as such, as an organ in the binary distinction between the religious and the secular as the total sum of human life. Essentialist definitions of religion, which de-historicize religion, depict it as ahistorical and universal, and hide the ways in which power motivates the concept's meanings and its political usages.

## Religion and Colonialism

The discussion so far focused solely on the Christian West, that is, on the ways in which the history of the concept "religion" plays a central role in the West's evolving self-perception, and the construction of the modern, sovereign nation-state, on the Liberal concept of a "religiously neutral" public sphere. However, these institutions and concepts have never been a solely Western matter: the nation-state, Western modernity, and the accompanying notions of the religious and the secular are some of the central building blocks of the historical project of Western colonialism.[38] For the purpose of the current discussion, suffice it to note that the epistemology constructing religion as not only transhistorical but also as universal, that is as cultural-context-independent, has been central to the representation of the "East," the object of the Western colonial expansion, as primitive, that is, as deserving of Western redemption through colonization.[39]

"Religion"—the concept—played primarily two complimentary roles in the Western colonial project. First, the denial of the existence of religion among the Natives prior to colonial occupation of their lands was used to dehumanize them. Westerners tended to argue that the Eastern Natives do not have a religion; this implied that they are substantially backward, that they are not truly human. This legitimized depriving them of basic human rights. Then, post-occupation, religion was "discovered" among the Natives (or, to be accurate, the concept religion was forced upon native cultures, so as to render them applicable to the dominant Western understanding of the term). This "discovery" was used to depoliticize native cultures: viewed as essentially *wholly* religious, these cultures were taken to be not-political. The supposed apolitical nature of the Natives thus justified Western rule over them. In addition, this maneuver enabled the forcing of these cultures into a comparative framework, in which, measured against the "norm" of other religions (namely: Christianity), they were found to be missing and undeveloped, i.e., primitive.[40]

The implications of the usage of an historical and culturally contextualized concept as if it were universal must be stressed. Accepting, or rather forcing, religion as universal means that the Western subject is identified as universal, as transcending place and time, while the Other, the non-West, is identified as parochial, provincial, narrow-minded—by definition. This is an obviously political distinction:

religion has been constructed as universal, while it has been servicing specific political interests. It is not a neutral concept, but rather a tool in the hands of those who define it in specific historical circumstance and configuration of power. Thus, religion and its complementary concepts were used to compare Western practices to non-Western ones, and to find the latter inferior to the former. In addition, "[p]erhaps most important, the discourse of religion was also a tool of secularization, the cordoning off of significant elements of non-Western cultures into a personal, apolitical realm of belief."[41] We shall see in the following chapter how the invention of Judaism as a religion was aimed, from the outset, to do exactly this: to render it apolitical.

## Religion, Nationalism

Before we move on to discuss Judaism, we must note that the wider issue at hand touches upon matters of the philosophy (and politics) of science. The power to define the concept "religion" and to decide what counts as religion and what does not is a central element of the West's power to organize reality of both West and East. As Wilfred Cantwell Smith, who suggested that the term religion, which he judged as "confusing, unnecessary, and distorting,"[42] should be abandoned warned, the danger lies in the concept's reification; Indeed, Smith's work clearly demonstrates how the usages of the term help "finding"—or, more accurately: creating—religion where it had not existed.

As Cavanaugh is careful to note, this should not be read as arguing that there is no such a thing as "religion." Indeed, there can be no doubt that "[i]n certain cultures, religion does exist, but as a product of human construction."[43] The claim, then, is not against the relevant particular, historically and sociologically situated usage of religion, but rather against the presentation of the term as universal and transhistorical. The (academic) fact of a multiplicity of definitions for religion does not disprove the existence of the notion, but rather that it can be understood in multiple, conflicting manners: "There is no transhistorical and transcultural essence of religion, but at different times and places, and for different purposes, some things have been constructed as religion and some things have not."[44]

This encourages us to shift our focus of attention from religion to the ideology that constitutes the modern nation-state. It reminds us that the sovereign nation-state, which self-identifies as secular, has to deny the "religious" character of its nationalism:

> If nationalism is religious, why do we deny it? Because what is obligatory for group members must be separated, as holy things are, from what is contestable. To concede that nationalism is a religion is to expose it to challenge, to make it just the same as sectarian religion. By explicitly denying that our national symbols and duties are sacred, we shield them from competition with sectarian symbols. In so doing, we embrace the ancient command not to speak the sacred, ineffable name of god. The god is inexpressible, unsayable, unknowable, beyond language. But that god may not be refused when it calls for sacrifice.[45]

The question at hand, it must be stressed, is not whether nationalism is "really a religion"? The critical question is why are such immense efforts put into denying its "religiosity"? Why is the state taken to be essentially secular? Why is the violence inflicted in its name justified, while the violence inflicted in the name of some "religious" value unjustified and illegitimate by definition?[46]

The basic answer to this set of questions is to be found in the ways in which the "religious vs. secular" distinction functions as a central element of the conceptual infrastructure that legitimizes the modern, Western nation-state. Constitutive concepts such as "the West," "modernity," "liberalism," "secularity," etc., are not self-sustaining realities, but rather ideals, or projects, which are given to continuous debate. However, a central part of ideology's function is to present these projects as reality-based, essences that "simply exist," part of our surrounding world. The "religious vs. secular" distinction is thus presented as an organic part of the natural world.[47]

# 2

# Are Jewish Traditions a Religion?

The attentive reader must be aware of the fact that the first chapter, in a work that aims to be an interpretation of what is usually dubbed "religion and politics" *in Israel,* the "Jewish state," did not deal with Judaism, or Jewish traditions. Instead, the preceding epistemological discussion was focused on a specific—Western, Christian—history or genealogy of this discussion's basic concept, "religion," and its counterpart, "the secular." This preliminary theoretical step is acutely necessary, in part because it highlights the foundational conundrum with which any work dealing with a non-Western, non-Christian "case" (rather: history) must deal; namely the all-encompassing presence of the abovementioned concepts as the supposedly universal names of varying appearances of the same essence.

But this surely raises some serious misgivings: How can we, if ever, talk about Judaism as a religion? How, if ever, can we read and understand the traditions and histories of those who have self-identified (and have been identified) as Jews through a conceptual toolkit that is borne out of a Christian, Western sociopolitical history? Is it even possible to do so? Is it advisable? Does such a "translational" exercise (that is, a reading of Jewish traditions as a religion) have any positive value? Or may it bring about more distortion than elucidation?

The current chapter opens with a discussion of these matters. As we shall see from the outset, while the irrelevance of the Christian vocabulary for a study of Jewish traditions does not go unnoticed, Judaism is nevertheless largely discussed as a religion. This has to do, to a large extent, with a philosophical transformation that took place in eighteenth- and nineteenty-century Europe, in which Judaism was read, or invented, precisely as a manifestation of the apolitical, Protestant concept of religion. The main part of the chapter is accordingly dedicated to an historical-ideational study of this philosophical transformation.

## Judaism in a Protestant Straightjacket

The difficulty—or, indeed: distortion—brought about by the usage of "religion" and its more or less successful translations[1] to non-Latin languages and non-Christian traditions could in itself be a good enough reason to argue against the term's relevance to non-European contexts. Needless to say, the distortion at hand is not just a matter of semantics, but rather an importation, or imposition, of a whole worldview that is based on a misconception (encapsulated in the distinction between religion and the secular) on an alien context.

The difficulties brought about by the usage of a Christian conceptual infrastructure for the study of Jewish traditions and histories have not gone unnoticed. Such are, for example, José Faur's remarks regarding the clash between the "expectations" brought about by this conceptual infrastructure and apparent historical facts.[2] This involves the very foundational notions of the modern West, such as the distinction between science and religion: "The secularist notion, positing that 'science' and 'religion' are mutually exclusive is flawed, historically and conceptually. The reason for this misconception is that the secular concept of 'religion' is Christian—through and through."[3] Elsewhere Faur notes the distortion caused by the usages of the Christian notion of "scripture" for understanding the role of the book in the shaping of Jewish civilization. As he reminds his readers,

> Usually, Scripture is regarded as a 'religious' work—with all the semantic accessories that this term had acquired via Christianity. It is taken as a given, therefore, that it is proper to freely apply to the Hebrew Scripture ideas and insights gained from the teachings and disciplines associated with 'religion.' The method is flawed. This will be obvious upon considering that the plethora of concepts applied to Scripture, including those of 'religion,' 'spirituality,' and the like, originate in an analphabetic environment, fundamentally inimical to the culture of writing and Book.[4]

In other words: this is about the application of a wholly foreign (Christian, which Faur identifies as "analphabetic") conceptual framework to the study of what he views as the essence of Jewish identity, namely the book and its dialogical interpretation.

The obvious conclusion is that it would not be proper to treat Judaism as a religion. This conclusion sheds new light on adjacent concepts, such as "theology," "ethics,"[5] "philosophy," "canon," and others. This brings Faur to stipulate his principle position:

> I don't regard Judaism as a 'religion' in the standard, Christian sense of the term. For better or for worse, the primary structure of Judaism is not theological. The term does not exist and it cannot even be coined in classical Hebrew. This is not to say that the Hebrew Scripture and rabbinic texts are not bursting with concepts that one can treat theologically and philosophically. However, as with the 'philosophy' of science or law, the subject itself—science or law—is not philosophy.[6]

This also sheds light on the misrepresentation of Judaism as a "faith," which has become prevalent due to the dominance of a Christian reduction of religion into the belief it manifests; "In this regard it is instructive to notice that Maimonides [. . .] classified 'belief in God' as one of the 613 'precepts' of the Tora, which presupposes a primary political and judicial context, having nothing to do with theology."[7]

Another author whose comments on the matter deserve careful attention is no other than the well-known scholar of Jewish "mysticism,"[8] or *kabbalah*, Joseph Dan.[9] Dan voices certain misgivings regarding the application of "religion" to "Judaism." Given his central position in the study of "Jewish religion," these may indeed be seen as the seeds of heresy proper. Dan, like others, emphasizes the Christian hegemony encapsulated in the term "religion." He notes that this is a Christian category,[10] which forces "other religions" into a European-Christian framework of understanding, thus erasing their particularities and, ultimately, their meanings.

Following Jonathan Z. Smith,[11] Dan identifies several culprits responsible for the transformation of the study of religions into a field in which a Christian worldview is forced upon the entire history of humanity. In his formulation, these culprits—what others may simply identify as European colonialism—are an evolutionary conception of the development of human spirit, and the ultimate victory of European science, philosophy, military, and politics. The implications of this European-Christian hegemony are far reaching: "The very use of the concept 'religion' already sets the primary and basic parameters for every discussion, and these have already set Christianity as the center and standard of every spiritual being." Academia's "paternalistic generosity and norms of tolerance and courtesy" encourage the perpetuation of a rhetorical acceptance of all "religions" as equal. But this, Dan insists, is no more than a patina of pretense, easily exposed by notions such as " 'primitive religions.' Everybody pretends that all spiritual mode of beings are equal, but everyone knows that we are speaking about an evolutionary scale, in which each phenomenon has a position on a certain level, but the upper level belongs in whole to Christianity."[12]

If this may sound like a naïve complaint against a Christian sense of superiority caused by the misuses of the term "religion," Dan is quick to note the deep epistemological distortion caused by this Christian dominance:

> The term religion, in its various translations, such as *dat* in Hebrew and *din* in Arabic, expresses the belief that the contents are the same in all realms of the human spirit, while the lingual dress is accidental, and can be interchanged. The terms *dat* in Hebrew and religion in Latin must be identical in their meaning, since the spiritual phenomena are universal and meta-lingual. Hence, it makes no difference whether we use this or that sound to denote one of them. In other words, without the specifically Christian conception of translation, which lacks an equivalent in any other human culture, "the science of religions" is impossible. The very essence of the Christian translational conception set the ideational infrastructure regarding the internal uniformity of these phenomena, and the researchers dealing with the study of religions expose the examples and particularities, whose mutual identity in the varying cultures is inevitable, given the primary premise.[13]

The Hebrew translation of the term should be carefully addressed. It is doubly problematic, for it not only imports into the Hebrew-Jewish context a Christian concept (the point which Dan is focused on), but also uses a Hebrew term, *dat*, which carries along its own history of significations. In other words, like in the cases of "secular" and "secularism" (which, still carrying over their Western, Christian histories, are translated as *ḥiloni* and *ḥiloniyut* in modern, Israeli Hebrew[14]) so does the contemporary Hebrew usage of *dat* and *datiyut* (i.e., religiosity) carry over a double distortion. This has to do mainly with (a) the forcing of reality into distorted conceptual and epistemological frameworks (that is, the problematical modern usage of the Latin concept itself), and (b) a problematic translation of this same term into Hebrew, which ignores the history and politics of the Hebrew term itself.

Nevertheless, like others who articulate similar misgivings, so do Faur and Dan continue to use the term "religion" in a manner that seems to be "natural." At last count, they discuss Judaism as a "religion," using the term, with all due reservations, as it is understood in the common, distorting discourse. As attested to by the comments above, these scholars do not fail to address the problematic nature of this usage, but at the same time they also note the difficulty in pronouncing an alternative academic, analytical discourse (one that would make sense to its readers, of course), which will be liberated from the discussed conceptual Christian hegemony.[15]

## Apolitical Jewish Religion

What, then, are the implications of discussing Jewish traditions as if they fit into the Western-Christian (Protestant) concept of religion? In order to carefully assess these we must first trace the historical-ideational transformation, in which Judaism "became" (or was invented as) a religion. The ideational and political history of the forcing of Jewish traditions into the conceptual framework of "religion" is especially important for the purpose of the current interpretation, since it sheds an important light on the politics of the Zionist project and the State of Israel. Specifically, as we shall see in the succeeding chapters, it can be instrumental in reformulating the sociopolitical reality veiled behind the misnomers "religion and politics" or "religion and nationalism" in the Zionist-Israeli context.

Leora Batnitzky offers an insightful narrative of the transformation—or, as her title would have it, the "becoming"—of Judaism into a religion. This is a narrative of the de-politicization of Jewish traditions, so as to render them applicable to the Christian-Protestant concept and model of religion as a universal realm of private, spiritual life. This history, Batnitzky notes, is a specifically modern one.[16] It is also a specifically German-Jewish one.[17]

Jewish thinkers became interested in applying the category "religion" to Judaism in the eighteenth century. That was when a fundamental conflict between the apolitical character of the modern, Christian, European category of "religion" (a matter discussed elaborately in the preceding chapter) and the obviously public, political character of Jewish traditions became apparent: "Adherence to religious law, which is at least partially, if not largely, public in nature, does not seem to fit into the category of faith or belief, which by definition is individual and private."[18]

These thinkers sought to solve this tension by reconstructing Judaism as apolitical, that is, as a private, personal matter that does not touch upon the public sphere. The history of "Jewish religion" is thus a history of this reconstruction, its relative success, and the historical reactions to this transformation. To a large extent, this is also a key to understanding modern Jewish identity in general.

This history is driven, then, by a basic conflict between the modern category of "religion" and what is referred to as "Judaism." It comes hand in hand with the wider issue of trying to "fit" Jewish histories and traditions into other European conceptual frameworks, such as race, nationalism, culture, and ethnicity.

In Batnitzky's reading, the watershed line separating European-Jewish modernity from premodernity and leading to the invention of Judaism as a religion was European-Jewish Emancipation, that is, the granting of civil rights to Jews in certain European states. Prior to this, Batnitzky states, Judaism was not a "religion," and Jewishness was not a matter of culture or "nationality." Or, formulated in the positive: "Judaism and Jewishness were all these at once: religion, culture, and nationality."[19] Notably, this watershed also represents an epistemological rupture, which makes it difficult to discuss the matter at hand without falling into blunt conceptual anachronisms. In any event, what is of critical importance for our purpose is the rather obvious statement that Judaism cannot be easily, if at all, deconstructed into the theoretical and conceptual building blocks of the Protestant West.

The remainder of this chapter will offer, following Batnitzky's lead, a review of some of the main steps in the modern construction of Judaism as a religion, and some of the implications arising from this construction.

## Mendelssohn: De-Politicizing Judaism

Moses Mendelssohn is, in Batnitzky's reading, the first to explicitly and systematically formulate the notion that Judaism is a "religion." Mendelssohn's reading, or invention, of Judaism in terms of apolitical religion (that is, as a private matter that has nothing to do with the public sphere and politics) was aimed against anti-Semitic conceptions that viewed Judaism precisely as something that is more than just a religion—i.e., as public and political in essence. If this anti-Jewish thinking might be described as being correct in identifying Jewish traditions and Jewish law as having some obviously public dimensions, while being morbidly wrong in its racist judgment of these, then Mendelssohn's is not just a challenge against this judgment but against the very identification of Judaism as public and political.

The "invention" of Judaism as a religion is fed, then, by the modern tension that developed in the European context of the sovereign nation-state between the public/political status of the Jewish community and the status of Jews as individuals. For Mendelssohn, a reconstruction of Judaism as apolitical amounts to its modernization. He "moves Judaism into the modern world by contending that politically, but not theologically, the individual Jew is separate from the Jewish community. Mendelssohn defines the very category of Jewish religion by separating Judaism from politics."[20] He does so by defining Jewish law as "in no way political."[21] His, then, is a Protestant understanding of religion: religion is, by essence, not political; Judaism (or Jewish law) is religion; hence Judaism (and Jewish law) is not political.

Note that there are two diverging ways in which this exercise of a supposed modernizing of Judaism (either in Mendelssohn's formulation or in Batnitzky's interpretation of it) can be read: an apologetic one and a critical one. The apologetic reading would present this development as inevitable. It would acknowledge that the difference between the "premodern" ways in which Jewish traditions had been lived or understood and the apolitical character of Mendelssohn's modern Judaism may indeed be profound; Nevertheless, it would argue, this move is inevitable. Only through it could Judaism survive in the modern, Westernized world. The rules of the game have changed, and if Jews wish to continue living as such, they must adjust. According to this reading, the motivating change is primarily external to Jewish history, or Judaism. It might even acknowledge the Christian origin of this change. But it would nevertheless view this change as inescapably influencing Judaism, requiring it to adjust. Judaism cannot challenge this change or ignore it. This *is* modernity, then, and this is the way—the only way—for Judaism to survive in a modern age. As we shall see later on, the apologetic stance is dominant, and it is taken by many for granted. So much so, that it is sometimes hard to remember that there is also another way to read this exercise.

The alternative, critical reading would argue against the constraining of Jewish histories into a foreign conceptual splint. This reading would refuse to accept the Western, Christian epistemology as an unchallenged given, and will demand a Jewish reading that remains dialogically loyal to the particularities of Jewish histories.[22] Needless to say, such a reading may be driven by varying ideologies and arrive at a wide range of conclusions. Crucially, for the purpose of the current discussion, it would seek to mark what goes unmarked and taken-for-granted in the modern, Protestant invention of "Jewish religion."

## Jewish Religion and the Sovereign State

The constitutive duality of religion and the secular/politics/the state (discussed in the previous chapter) receives a rather straightforward explication in Mendelssohn's thought.[23] The state, he argues, is by definition the party that deals with power and violence, while religion, in the true sense of the term, does not. That is, Judaism (signified by the name "Jerusalem") does not deal with power; hence, it does not inhibit the successful incorporation, or assimilation, of Jews (as individuals) inside the non-Jewish political communities, i.e., the modern, secular European nation-states.

Mendelssohn also claims that Judaism is not about faith, but rather a matter of practice. This claim is aimed at presenting Judaism as a *rational* religion. Since Judaism does not require belief of the religious, nonrational kind, it does not conflict with rationality; the two are complementary. Crucially, being a rational system, Jewish religion, again by definition, cannot be forced upon the individual. In other words, it is exactly the property of lacking power, the absence of a political dimension (that of "coercion") that renders "Jewish religion" unintimidating for the non-Jewish public sphere, or "secular" politics.[24]

Mendelssohn's main goal, then, is not a philosophical analysis of Judaism and Jewish law, but rather a *political* argument: his aim is to deny the anti-Jewish claims, and enable the inclusion of Jews inside the political order of the sovereign, modern nation-state.[25] This turns out to be overridden by self-contradiction:

> Mendelssohn's definition and description of Judaism are in a fundamental sense at odds with themselves. Mendelssohn claims that Judaism is not a religion like Christianity because Judaism demands action, not belief. But Mendelssohn also defines Jewish law in completely apolitical terms—that is, precisely in contrast to the laws of the state [. . .] Mendelssohn wants to have it both ways: Judaism is a religion of law requiring action and stimulating contemplation. But when it comes to questions of universal action—that is, state law—and when it comes to universal contemplation— that is, the eternal truths of philosophy—Judaism remains separate and dispensable, except insofar as Judaism calls for obedience to the state's law.[26]

## Religion and Law

Mendelssohn's construction/invention of Judaism as a religion was not complete. Even though he sought to distinguish, politically so, between the Jewish individual and the Jewish community, he nevertheless failed to construct a *theological* distinction between the two. Nevertheless, his political-intellectual exercise carried some devastating consequences for Jewish law. As Batnitzky notes,

> Mendelssohn offers no philosophical or theological justification for why Jews should obey the law, and by virtue of his own definitions, he cannot supply any philosophical or theological justification for Jews to follow the law, because

he argues that Jewish law is a temporal, historical truth whose legitimacy rests on neither the universally accessible dimensions of philosophical truth nor the dogmas of particular theological belief.[27]

Mendelssohn's successors tended to solve this tension by formulating a redefinition of Judaism in which law does not play a major rule.[28]

Even though Mendelssohn rejects, at least rhetorically so, the limits put by Protestant thought on the concept of religion (after all, Mendelssohn did claim that Jewish law fits perfectly into the category of religion), he also denies that there may be a conflict between Judaism and universal truth. This comes hand in hand with his denying that there may be a tension between Judaism and the state. He does so by arguing that in both cases what appears as conflict is a result of a categorical mistake, a confusion between distinct concepts: Judaism is separate from universal truth and does not threaten it, just as it is separate from state law and does not pose any threat to it.[29]

## Law, Tradition, and Science

Mendelssohn's pioneering ideational exercise instigated a wide-ranging reorganization and reinterpretation of the meaning of Judaism in Europe. He "functions as an axis of sorts, defining the new paradigms of the modern Jewish discourse."[30] Differing on a variety of issues regarding Judaism, history, philosophy, and law, German-Jewish thinkers nevertheless tended to accept Mendelssohn's assertion that Judaism is a religion that does not come into conflict with the sovereignty of the modern nation-state.[31]

As Amnon Raz-Krakotzkin notes, the reverberations of Mendelssohn's thought constitute a genuine revolution in the development of Jewish thought. Whether by agreeing or arguing with Mendelssohn, Jewish thinkers,

> all—except for the Orthodox circles—wished to construct a worldview in which Jewish identity will no longer be based on an exilic consciousness [which Raz-Krakotzkin identifies as the essence of Jewish tradition], but rather on one's belonging to society and accepting the values of the dominant [non-Jewish] culture. The meaning of this movement was to match the definition of Judaism not only to

the language of modern culture, but also to its foundational principles—which were conceived as neutral, that is, indifferent in terms of religious identity.[32]

In a wider sense, Mendelssohn initiated the dispute regarding the question whether Judaism is a "religion" or a "nationality"; seen as two supposedly mutually contradictory possibilities, these two concepts do have a crucial common denominator: "a definition of Jewish existence which is based on a detachment from the exilic principle, and on full acceptance of the concept of modern nationalism, that is an acceptance of the guiding principle of the dominant culture."[33]

This was formulated in the context of a debate on whether Judaism has an "essence" that constitutes it and sets it apart from other "religions." For, "[i]f Judaism has no essence from a scientific-historical point of view, then there is no such thing as Judaism. Rather, there are many Judaisms, all of which, from a historical perspective, are equally valid or invalid."[34]

Mendelssohn's answer to this question is at root a "halachic" one, as he sees Jewish law as Judaism's unchanging historical essence. But Mendelssohn does not deny the role of tradition in understanding the meaning of the law. He acknowledges that the interpretation and practice of the law changes over time, as demanded by human historical reality; for him, tradition plays a positive role in understanding the essence of Judaism.

By the beginning of the nineteenth century, with a growing field of a "scientific" study of Judaism, based as it was on the antinomy pitting science and tradition as opposites, Mendelssohn's equation was untenable. A traditional understanding of Judaism (which, at last count, Mendelssohn tries to uphold, by reinventing it as a religion) came to be seen in this modern framework of thinking—either in its political iteration (i.e., the sovereign nation-state) or the scientific one—as obstructing the "true meaning," or "essence" of Judaism. It thus becomes an object of either confrontation (in the case of the state) or deconstruction (in the case of science). [35]

## Jewish "Religion" and the
## Denominationalization of Jewish Identity

Mendelssohn's interpretation/construction of Judaism as a religion influenced the formation of practically all streams of modern European

Jewish thought, and the ultimate division of (European) Jewry into separate "denominations."

Perhaps most immediately, his thought was the driving force behind Liberal Judaism and the Reform movement. Liberal Judaism sought to solve the tension between the Jew's commitment to Jewish law and her commitment to the "secular" law of the state by giving up, in practical terms, on Jewish law. Staunchly loyal to the sovereign state, the Liberal/Reform stance presented Judaism as wholly apolitical. It also sought to reinterpret, or reconstruct, Judaism as a modern religion by utilizing the dominant culture's conceptual toolkit. It views Judaism's essence as exactly the "universal-religious element,"[36] that is, its being a (Protestant) religion. In other words, this worldview understands modernity primarily in Protestant terms and seeks to show that this modernity is rather the essence of Judaism itself.[37]

In the Liberal reading, the history of Judaism can only be the history of "spiritual" achievements, specifically because of Judaism's apolitical nature, which has guaranteed its historical continuity, its very survival. This means that the only truly essential value of Judaism is the religious, the apolitical. This argument is directly connected to the political argument for Jewish assimilation in the German culture—that is, in the modern, sovereign, German nation-state—which is seen as the privatization of Jewish belief inside a "neutral" political order. The main move that would enable the "spiritualization" of Judaism (that is, the transformation of Judaism so as to remain loyal to its spiritual essence, while shedding anachronistic additions, which inhibit cultural and political assimilation) is the release of Judaism from its "fixation" on Jewish law.

In other words, the invention of Jewish religion in its Reform/Liberal formulation argues exactly against the Jewish "*dat*" (as "religion" is commonly translated to Hebrew today), in its original meaning, that is, law. While Mendelssohn sought to nevertheless preserve the essence of "Jewish religion" as Jewish law (a supposedly apolitical law, at that), in the Liberal/Reform context this paradox is resolved rather straightforwardly: the invention of internal-spiritual, apolitical Jewish religion demands its negation as law.[38]

One of the clearer signs of the overwhelming power of this invention of Judaism as a religion is another invention—that of Orthodox Judaism, which came as a counter reaction to the Liberal/Reform maturation of Mendelssohn's original exercise. Seeking to reject Reform, and to counter some of the more apparent consequences of

Mendelssohn's invention of "Jewish religion," the Orthodox stance nevertheless accepts Mendelssohn's basic premises. That is, it accepts the very condition of a discourse it hopes to negate: "[O]rthodoxy is actually predicated not on a rejection but rather an intensification of Mendelssohn's premise that Judaism is a religion that in no way conflicts with the sovereignty of the modern nation-state."[39] Moreover, Orthodoxy's commitment to this notion is what renders it "like Jewish religion more generally," a "modern invention."[40]

Significantly, the Orthodox stance claims to be opposed to the forcing of Judaism into Christian-Protestant frameworks of understanding, emphasizing instead Judaism's all-encompassing nature, i.e., its being a total way-of-life. This would appear to be based on exactly a denial of the argument that Judaism is a religion: "Judaism is not a religion, the synagogue is not a church, and the Rabbi is not a priest."[41]

However, this stance's reliance on the foundational premises laid by Mendelssohn is quite apparent. It argues that Judaism, and especially Jewish law, are by definition not political. Orthodoxy is revealed here as being built exactly on those same modern concepts used by others to deny traditional Jewish identities: "Drawing on the very modern concepts that have usurped traditional Jewish identity and authority," the Orthodox stance "agrees with Mendelssohn in arguing that Jewish religion is not coercive but instead concerns only the heart and mind."[42]

How, then, should we understand the Orthodox claim, quoted above, that Judaism is *not* a religion? Batnitzky offers a rather categorical judgment of this: "Despite [Orthodox] protestations to the contrary," this stance nevertheless "understand[s] Judaism as a religion."[43] It holds on to an apolitical notion of Judaism, accepting the very epistemological framework that separates the theological from the political. Moreover, it sees this apolitical, un-coercive conception of Judaism and Jewish law as the *true* Judaism, distinguishing it from false claims to Jewish identity.

To put this in the context of a Zionist-Israeli discourse, Orthodoxy relates directly to the invention of Jewish religiosity/religiousness ("*datiyut*"), which is identified in Israeli political culture (following Zionist ideology's lead) with Orthodox Judaism, and in effect also with Jewish authenticity. It should be stressed already at this early point of my discussion that Zionism holds a rather complicated relationship with this Orthodox identity: rejecting Reform

Judaism, Zionist thought accepted, often implicitly but nevertheless forcefully, Orthodox Judaism's claim to Jewish (religious) authenticity. Of course, it had done so out of a negation of certain essential elements (those it deemed "exilic") of this identity; Nevertheless, it has remained critically indebted to Orthodoxy's definition of Jewish identity. I shall elaborate this point in the second part of the book.

It is also important to note the degree to which this Orthodox identity, on its sectarian nature, is indebted to Reform Judaism and European-Jewish secularism (as formulated by the *haskala*, or Jewish Enlightenment movement) as its significant "Others." Its self-imposed sense of separation from the larger world of Jewish identities is based on a distinctly Christian, Western conceptual framework, one constituted on notions of "belief," "spirituality," and a distinction between "theology" and "politics."[44]

This irony cannot be ignored: "[O]rthodoxy is not only modern but rather in a certain sense the most modern of modern Judaisms in molding itself as a religion on the German Protestant model."[45] Furthermore, it is this conservative stance, and its notion of a fundamental distinction between the "religious" and the "political" that enables a sense of inter-religious pluralism. After all, the Orthodox stance accepts the supposedly secular, modern, sovereign state as the embodiment of the political (which is external to Judaism); this leaves room for "secular politics" and a certain sense of religious tolerance.[46]

To sum, European Orthodox Judaism is revealed to be another invention of Judaism as a religion, which presupposes the political order of the sovereign nation-state and the distinction between the secular (identified with the political), and the religious (which is now identified as sectarian by nature). The essential disagreement between Liberal/Reform and Orthodox Judaism is about the content of this "Jewish religion"; both sides accept the Protestant-German conceptual bed as the constitutive foundation of their worldview.

In Batnitzky's reading, what is now referred to as Conservative Judaism—or, in its original iteration, the Positive-Historical School—comes closest to a full, rich understanding of Jewish tradition as dynamic and evolving. In this reading, it is also the most successful in avoiding the implications of a definition of Judaism as a religion. Critically, Conservative Judaism does so inside a Hegelian framework of historical understanding.

Unlike the Reform and Orthodox "denominations," the Positive-Historical stance views Judaism as an active force in the history of Jews. It acknowledges the dynamic nature of Jewish law, but—contrary to the Reform argument—sees the changes brought about by this dynamism as resulting from Jewish creativity and historical activity, which should be adapted to modernity, and not simply neglected.

Rejecting Hegel's dismissing assessment of Judaism yet nevertheless holding on to an understanding of Judaism in terms of Hegel's philosophical history, the Positive-Historical stance brings Jewish politics back to the forefront. It sees Judaism as in essence presenting a dialectical relationship between theology and politics in which the transcendental gains a political presence. This dialectic demands that Judaism is not a religion, which by definition is limited to the private realm. Judaism is public, communal, and political. Thus, while accepting the epistemology that separates religion from politics, this stance nevertheless does not accept the historical separation of the two realms. Judaism and Jewish history, it argues, have always been simultaneously characterized by both political and religious elements.[47]

∼

The ideational passages reviewed above are far from exhausting the philosophical discussion at hand. Such a review is surely beyond the scope of this book. What is important for our purpose here is the way in which the invention of Jewish religion drives and solidifies the Zionist idea. As will be discussed shortly, Zionism's stance in relation to the ideational developments reviewed above has been complicated. As a matter of Jewish politics, it argues against the construction/ invention of Judaism as a religion, but as an ideology aiming at the establishment of a European-like nation-state it is, in actuality, constituted upon this construction. It is my contention that a focus on this matter will enable us to better understand the issues commonly labeled under "religion and politics" and/or "religion and nationalism" in Zionist ideology and the State of Israel.

The next section of the book will develop this argument. It will suggest that we focus on Zionism's relation to preceding Jewish traditions while paying close attention to Zionist ideology's rather peculiar stance: rejecting the notion that Judaism is an apolitical religion while at the same time relying on the same epistemology that gives birth to it in the first place, and accepting as a natural given the very concept of "religion." But before dwelling into the matter of Zionism, I wish to present a more detailed interpretation of the concept of tradition, which, I argue, can be a more fruitful alternative to the epistemology of the secular-religious dichotomy. This I shall do in the succeeding chapter.

# 3

# Tradition as Language and Narrative

As aforementioned, I am presuming here not only to highlight the devastating lacunae and failings of the dominant epistemological framework that is most commonly used to understanding what is usually dubbed "religion and politics" in Israel, but also to offer at least the outline of an alternative epistemology. This would be a "traditionist" stance, as it has to do with the concept of tradition. This chapter is dedicated to an interpretation of the concept and a study of our relation to our traditions. The chapter will first note the prevalence of a misguided suspicion toward tradition, as well as an overt misunderstanding of the very notion of tradition in certain academic circles. It will then outline some of the basic tenets of an alternative understanding of tradition, based on a "sociological" reading of several major philosophical works. It does so by revisiting and synthesizing some well-known, highly influential conceptual arguments that, taken together, offer a compelling, comprehensive interpretation and understanding of tradition, which manages to avoid and overcome the false dichotomies that have dominated social-scientific thought. I will suggest two corresponding analogies that capture the complex nature of tradition: tradition as language and tradition as narrative. The chapter then goes on to discuss the main implications these analogies carry to our understanding of tradition.

## Tradition as Antimony to Liberty?

In a 1955 address to the Congress on Cultural Freedom, at a Conference on the Future of Freedom, Edward Shils cautioned his audience not to discount tradition as an absolute antinomy of freedom. Although stating that liberal belief "correctly points" to the "inherent antinomy between *tradition* and *liberty*,"[1] Shils nevertheless insisted on a more nuanced understanding of tradition, one that highlights both the inevitability and limitedness of its authority, and its complex relationship to individuality (indeed, this has been one of the major projects of his life work as an intellectual). For this he used a rather ingenious analogy, that of tradition as a gardener:

> Tradition is not the dead hand of the past but rather the hand of the gardener, which nourishes and elicits tendencies of judgment which would otherwise not be strong enough to emerge on their own. In this respect tradition is an encouragement to incipient individuality rather than its enemy. It is a stimulant to moral judgment and self-discipline rather than an opiate.[2]

Shils is speaking here against a background of a general disregard of tradition as something that is, at best, of relevance only for understanding the past, surely lacking relevance for understanding the present or the future. To an extent, this sentiment has become foundational in the construction of the modern, Western self.

This sentiment owes much to an Enlightenment-born "scientistic" (ontological) sense of an inherent antinomy between tradition and individual sovereignty and liberty, hence, ultimately, an epistemological opposition between tradition and (scientific or artistic) truth. This sense of suspicion was best captured by Descartes in his opening remarks to his first meditation, where he argues that the constitutive act, the very basis of his ability to acquire true knowledge, has to be his self-liberation from his past, or tradition, which had imposed its untruths on him.[3]

Descartes's remedy for his "anxiety"[4]—that is, his solution to his fear that he might be believing that which is false (due to tradition's authoritative imposition of its questionable dictates on the unsuspecting young Descartes) to be true—was to (allegedly) disengage himself from everything he knows, as well as from any system of knowledge that lacks a methodical and systematic "proof" component, and to return to a supposedly "pure" stage of a clean but nevertheless rational and logical mind acquiring truths through a methodical search and analysis.

This ideal has become a formative stage in the construction of the modern subject, or self, as a sovereign, independent, self-reflective and willful agent who is liberated from the hold of tradition and authority; hence, as Charles Taylor[5] notes, the charged ethical implications encapsulated in what might otherwise seem to be rather technical considerations pertaining to the philosophy of science. It brought to life a conception of a human being who is detached from her past, or at least is potentially so; at a minimum, this rational, disengaged agent is surely perceived to be *sovereign* in relation to her past—that is, she can approach it independently and judge it "from the outside," as it were.

Now, while there are some obvious flaws in Descartes's notions of knowledge, truth, and agency,[6] this conception of the disengaged subject or "mind," and the implied antinomy between traditional knowledge and truth have nevertheless been enshrined as foundational notions of "true" science.[7] Indeed, in some readings, the philosophical project that Descartes initiates *is* what we mean by our modern use of the word "science." This is also the background against which arguments to the contrary—most notably those of Polanyi[8] and Kuhn[9] have been viewed as "controversial" if not outright "revolutionary": convincing as these arguments are, they were nevertheless "shocking" in their undermining of the foundational ideal of a disengaged, ahistorical mind seeking truth and knowledge through methodical, systematic observations and analysis.

The dominance of this scientific ideal might explain why Shils's call seems to have been left largely unheeded during the heydays of positivist behaviorism in the social sciences. Accepting the dichotomous distinction between "modern" ("man," society) and "traditional" as a paradigmatic axiom of the scientific study of society (part of the more comprehensive narrative of secularization and modernization), a dominant self-image of the modern, liberal West has tended to discount tradition as a matter of the bygone past. Viewing the Modern, rational, epistemologically secular individuals as sovereign over their pasts, these social sciences tended to view tradition as a taken-for-granted, authoritatively unchallenged and rather unambiguous element of the "premodern" (indeed, "tradition*al*") sociocultural setting. They thus tended to view tradition as a restraint on individual liberty, on rationality and on reflectivity. The liberation from tradition thus became a precondition of one's ability to view reality in an unbiased, truthful, rational manner.

Those rare attempts by social scientists to discuss tradition in ways that transcend the false dichotomy between tradition/history and modernity/change or at least to facilitate a more nuanced consideration of the concept of tradition, while illuminating in themselves, also point to the obvious fact that such attempts at "rehabilitating" the discourse on tradition are a revisionism offered against the backdrop of a general "orthodoxy" that disregards the notion of tradition as irrelevant for the understanding of the supposedly liberated, secular modernity, if not an outright enemy of it.

This truism plays into a well-maintained argument that pitches rationalists/secularists against conservatives/traditionalists as the two exclusive, exhaustive opposites of a historical and ethical argument regarding the worth and value of tradition in modern life. However, fierce as the arguments along this opposition tend to be, it is quite apparent that both sides hold on to a fundamentally similar notion, or imagery of tradition as a sealed "package" transferred to us, contemporaries, from the past, carrying authoritative dictations as to what we should believe to be true and how we should behave in the present. Both sides seem to agree that the past is a given, unchanging and univocal "fact"; The only argument between the two sides, so it seems to be, is whether we should abide by the dictations this past entails, in a conservative/traditionalist manner, or ignore them (if not rebel against them) in a rationalist/secularist act of intellectual independence and individualist sovereignty. This argument, constitutive as it is of so much sociophilosophical discussion, is especially regrettable, since it is based on a grave misunderstanding of tradition.

To a large degree, this misunderstanding and the ensuing disregard of (if not outright hostility toward) tradition nourishes on a regrettable disciplinary schism, which separates the social sciences from the humanities, especially from philosophy. For philosophy both lies (although often unacknowledged) at the core of the positivist social science's suspicion and disregard of tradition, and offers some thoughtful alternative understandings of tradition, such that can surely shed an illuminating light on the study of society. For one thing, as hinted at earlier, it is rather obvious to anyone even only partially attuned to the philosophical study of epistemology that this skeptical attitude toward tradition is a manifestation of what must be labeled, paradoxical as it may sound, a "traditional" Cartesian and Kantian epistemology.[10] And as the criticism of this epistemology gains coherence and credence, so does an explication of an alternative understanding of tradition become urgent.

Moreover, as I mentioned earlier, one of the strongest, revisionist currents in contemporary social science (or, more broadly, the human sciences) has been an overwhelming deconstruction and discrediting of the almost-paradigmatic secularization narrative, the ultimate social-scientific harbinger of the abovementioned antimony between tradition and freedom and its derivatives (contrasting tradition with truth, rationality, modernity, reflectivity, neutrality, objectivity, and other foundational concepts of the dominant self-image of the academic-scientific profession). This turn highlights the urgency in Shils's abovementioned call, even more than half a century after it was first made public: a careful, nuanced, non-ideologically-secularist evaluation of tradition is essential for the development of our self-understanding. It is surely critical for understanding the subject matter of this book, namely the ways in which Zionist thought and Israeli sociopolitics cope with Jewish traditions that preceded them.

## An Alternative Epistemology

The remainder of this chapter seeks, then, to outline some of the basic tenets of such an alternative understanding of tradition, based on a "sociological" reading of several major philosophical works (needless to say, the alleged disciplinary distinction is challenged by practically every author concerned). It does so by revisiting and synthesizing some well-known, highly influential philosophical works that, taken together, offer a compelling, comprehensive interpretation and understanding of tradition, which manages to avoid and overcome the false dichotomies that have dominated social-scientific thought, such as that of the abovementioned allegedly inherent antimony between tradition and individuality or between tradition and modernity, between truth and authority, between science and tradition, etc.

At the core of this understanding of tradition is an emphasis on tradition's foundational, or constitutive, nature. Seen from this perspective, tradition emerges as a rather dynamic meta-structure into which one is born and within which and through which one acquires her sense of the world, and develops her sense of agency, subjectivity, or selfhood: in short, her individuality. Tradition is thus viewed as the infrastructure that both enables our self-understanding *and* sets its limits, even when this self-understanding comes to be defined by its rebelliousness against tradition.

This view also stresses that tradition is meaningless without its actual, contemporaneous interpretation-application by individuals and communities, thus highlighting the rather dynamic nature of tradition. In other words, this understanding of tradition is closely

attentive to the continuous formation and reformation of our constitutive past. It rejects the conservative/secularist consensus that the past
is an inflexible given, arguing instead (tautological as this may sound)
that the very meaning of these meaning-instilling infrastructures of
our being human is never fixed, but rather being interpreted and
reinterpreted as it is being applied, practiced.

Indeed, this can be seen as yet another formulation of what some
logical schemes may see as a paradoxical attempt at stressing both
and at the same time the past's authority over us and our agency in
constructing and shaping this very past. Still, "[t]hinking about it [the
past, or 'public memory'] is as close as we can get to reflecting on
the conditions of our thought"[11]—as undetermined and inconclusive
as this may sound.

Needless to say, this understanding of tradition, or at least strong
currents of its main notions (bearing various, divergent labels), is not a
sociophilosophical novelty. Without offering a systematic, comprehensive explication of this claim (this, I suspect, must be left to a much
longer monograph), I would argue that strong currents of a fundamentally similar understanding of tradition can be found (to name-
drop but the most notable) in Ludwig Wittgenstein's[12] discussion of
"forms of life," "inherited background," and "rule governed" behavior; in Clifford Geertz's[13] post-Wittgensteinian argument that human
thought is inherently public and in his corresponding reconstruction of "culture"; in Michael Polanyi's[14] notion of "tacit knowledge";
in Thomas Kuhn's[15] idea of "paradigm"; in Michael Oakeshott's[16]
highlighting of the role of "traditional knowledge"; and in Charles
Taylor's[17] emphasis on "intersubjective meaning" and "language" for
the understanding of humanity; It also receives a most comprehensive
and systematic formulation in the thought of Hans-Georg Gadamer[18]
and Alasdair MacIntyre.[19] And as the abovementioned quote from
Shils demonstrates, this understanding of the notion of tradition can
be also found in the works of major social scientists. (In addition to
Shils,[20] S. N. Eisenstadt[21] is probably the other most notable sociologist
in this regard). But, I suspect, it has failed to penetrate the common
Western discourse on tradition.

Granted, as anyone even slightly familiar with the thought of
the abovementioned thinkers can tell, the very act of identifying several of them and their modes of thinking as alleged members of a
single, coherent "school" is clearly misguided. Nevertheless, since my
aim here is an attempt at offering an interpretive understanding of

one of humanity's most fundamental notions, and not the narration of a history of philosophy, I would argue that a careful, attentive consideration of some of the main themes developed by these various authors can be highly productive in facilitating a much needed reconsideration of tradition.

Hence, although the aforementioned thinkers emerge from diverging philosophical schools and employ various modes of investigation, their conceptualizations of tradition seem to be complementary. They all aim at a rather similar notion of tradition as what can be termed background, textual and constitutive, *contemporary* precondition of both community and self. And, as noted above, they stress that tradition, which is inherently collective, is not only unavoidable but also vital to the shaping of individual, private identity. Tradition, in other words, both enables and limits our ability to comprehend reality, stressing our situatedness as a precondition of our very cognition; and it is in itself a reflection of present, contemporary understandings of the meaning of the past.

Two corresponding imageries, or analogies capture this complex nature of tradition: tradition as language and tradition as narrative. In what follows, I will present these analogies, and discuss the main implications they carry to our understanding of tradition.

## Tradition as Language

This analogy would stress the view of tradition as a practical system of significations, much like language is a textual and verbal one. Most importantly, this imagery captures both the inevitability of tradition's influence (which is, of course, inherently public, or collective) on the individual, and, in a sense, the limits of this influence, or the speaker/bearer's agency in maintaining and reshaping language/tradition. It does so, first, by stressing that tradition is a precondition of our individuality; that much like language, tradition is a substructure, primarily of practice and meaning, that is the nurturing bed from within which we develop and through which we conduct ourselves as individuals and members of society. It also points to the fact that just like the varying human languages, so does each tradition have a unique meaningful structure, a certain way of signification (with its own history, its own particular way of representing reality, its own set of guiding values, etc.).

At the same time, this analogy also highlights the individual's role in "maintaining" tradition, underscoring the dialogical (although not equal) nature of our relation to tradition. Thus, this analogy can help us both to appreciate the inescapable nature of tradition's constitutive role in shaping our "dialogical" agency, or individuality (as against rationalist-individualist notions of a "monological" agent[22]), and to contextualize this role so as to expose its inherent dependence on the practice, application, and interpretation of language/tradition by the individuals and communities who speak/carry, or practice them (as against the conservative inclination to underestimate human agency).

To begin with, just as we do not choose the language into which we are born, so do we not choose the tradition into which we are born and through which we are shaped as individuals. ("Socialization" has been so overused a term as to have rendered it almost meaningless, but it might nevertheless be suitable here.) And this rather circumstantial fact carries heavy, decisive implications: for language is not just a medium or a tool of our thought, but the very precondition of one's ability to think.

There are various ways in which we can conceive of this: we can, for example, stress that thought is inherently public or dialogical. But what is probably more important is that we cannot even conceive of such a "monological," or, to use Wittgenstein's famous phrasing, "private" language. In other words, language—*inherently public* language—can be seen as a precondition of one's consciousness. If there is something like consciousness without language, it is simply beyond our ability to know or comprehend.[23]

Now, it may very well be the case that tradition, with its emphasis on practice, should be viewed as somewhat "less all-encompassing" than language: For one thing, while we cannot conceive of a conscious person who does not have a (public) language, we can at the least conceive of a viable person who is nevertheless so ignorant of her tradition—that is, ignorant of the way of life it constitutes, ignorant of how to practice the tradition of which she is a part—that it would be correct to assume that she "cannot speak" its "language" and in a certain sense is "traditionless." Needless to say, this hypothetical person is the kind of person whom we usually view as missing a crucial element of her identity, as inauthentic. Moreover: given the view of tradition with which I began this discussion, it would be also correct to argue that this person, if she is an at least minimally active member of society, is not truly without tradition—that in order to function sensibly in a social setting one has to share in a tradition-based social practice, the very "grammar" that enables social communication. This hypothetical person would thus be viewed as "doubly ignorant": that is, as being unaware of the fact that she does indeed follow the guidelines of a tradition-based practice (say, as she has acquired from watching representations of reality on TV). Nevertheless, the fact that we can conceive, and be critical of such a person hints that this potential person is not a total figment of academic imagination. Hence it would be wise to keep in mind the limits of the discussed analogy.

This analogy is especially illuminating since it captures the "silent," inevitable nature of tradition's "hold" on us. Tradition, like language, precedes us, not just chronologically, but also—being the "modus vivendi," or "the way things are done" in our sociocultural habitat—meaningfully, in setting the (practical) grammar through which and by which we develop as individuals. In other words, this analogy captures the public, or collective, constitutive infrastructure of our individual agency, of our consciousness and self-understanding.

Second, this analogy addresses our attention to the historical and particularistic nature of this infrastructure, thus shedding a critical light on the universalistic pretense of rationalistic notions of an independent, rational mind freely examining reality by its use of the (abstract) rules of logic. Just as that inevitable foundation of our consciousness, language, is particularistic in nature—that is, it has a certain past, a certain way of viewing reality and describing it, a certain way of conducting one in her/his world, etc., enabling us to express ourselves in certain ways and preventing us from doing so in others (a fact of which we can be intellectually aware and nevertheless unable to articulate), so does tradition "impose" its "practical grammar," if you like, on us. It enables us, its bearers, to conduct ourselves in certain ways—and prevents us from doing so in other ways. It would be simply misleading to assume that "one is liberated to do whatever one wants to do": not only does practice and the authority it manifests directly encourage us to do things in certain ways, they also (somewhat indirectly) prevent and forbid us from doing things in other ways.[24]

But, as I hinted to earlier, this emphasis of tradition's authority over us is far from being the whole story: for our dialogical relation to tradition also means that tradition—again, much like language—is dependent on us, its bearers, for its interpretation, application, practice and, ultimately, its very survival.

We commonly refer to a language that is not spoken as a "dead" language. Its remnants may reside in books and dictionaries, and some academics who are dedicated to the study of this language might still know how to speak it. But once the community of people who speak this language ceases to be, once this language is no longer in daily use, its very existence as an actual system of signification is viewed as something that had ceased to be. This points to the fact that as long as this language is indeed spoken, alive, it is in a constant, dynamic process of formation and reformation. The people who speak a certain language, its "practitioners" in the present, are also its applicators, its interpreters, and they—as a community—constantly shape and reshape it.

Thus, to state but the obvious, while a certain language is spoken and has a history, it takes on varying forms of life in different communities and different periods of time. The English spoken today in the United States, to give but a rather banal example, is quite different from the language bearing the same name that Shakespeare used in sixteenth-century England for writing his plays; and the introduction of certain technologies encourages new plays on the same set of signification "tools," so much so that a generational divide is transformed into a lingual one. And we still refer to all of these varying instances as manifestations of one language, English. This, then, highlights the fact that the speakers of a certain language are also its shapers and reformers. They, as individuals and as a community, live it, they live by it, and they change it as they do so.

The same is true of tradition. The practice of tradition means its interpretation. A living tradition is never set or frozen, but is rather "a moving image of the past [. . .] Parts of tradition may wither and die while other continue to move and flourish."[25] To understand this we must pay attention to the unique sense of knowledge upon which tradition is based. Practical knowledge, or traditional knowledge, is quite different from that form of "technical" or formal knowledge that has come to dominate our sense of intelligence. Tradition lives in practice, in the "experiential," or "intersubjective" meanings[26] it signifies, and not in formal articulations of it. Indeed, as Oakeshott notes on political traditions, such attempts at formalizing these traditions into formal sets of "political doctrines" or "ideologies," are but caricatures of the traditions upon which they are based: they capture a certain authentic element of tradition, and stress it so much as to overtly distort the original tradition from which it was derived.[27] In Rabinow's phrasing, this is indeed the opposite of tradition, namely, alienation: "the attempt to maintain a fixed sense of symbols once other conditions have shifted."[28] This might have an intellectual value, but it obviously fails on the practical level. The same can be said of other traditions—say, legal or religious—and of the attempts at inscribing and codifying them: once completed, these codifications immediately call for interpretations in order for them to be actualized, practiced, and applied in changing circumstances.

This last matter also addresses our attention to the institutional and organizational aspects of both language and tradition. Both have been the objects of attempts by sovereign powers (especially the modern nation-state and what we commonly refer to as "religious" authorities) to "regulate" the practice—and indeed, the very meaning in some cases—of these systems of significations. The history of these attempts tell us both of the potentiality of institutional organization to influence the way we perceive and practice language/tradition (the "standardization" of "national" languages and the accompanying "invention" and forceful dissemination of national traditions is too immense to disregard), but also of their limits. In a sense, the same allegedly "non-logical" argument I presented earlier is to be reiterated here: Even in cases when these powers are successful in establishing a "standardized" tradition (i.e., present programmatic, interested renditions of the past and its meaning) or language (as antinomous this notion is to the essence of tradition and language), once these standardizations are "alive," carried by their speakers/practitioners, the ability of these powers to control the way this practice is carried about (including the possibility of revisiting the past and rejecting the official rendition of it) is rather limited.

The likening of tradition to language thus sheds an illuminating light on the kind of relationship we—bearers of tradition or speakers of language—have with these social-historical preconditions of our individuality. It brings to the fore both sides of the story: that we are forever "captured" in the web of meanings weaved by tradition (as manifested in our practice, our way of life, that "given" or "taken for granted" medium in which we conduct ourselves), and that we—bearers of tradition—are also its interpreters, who not only maintain it but also constantly reshape it.

Now compare this view of tradition and language to the logical-positivist attempt at "overcoming" what is seen as the limited nature of human language as a tool with which to approach reality. This project that has peaked with Russel, Ferge, and the early Wittgenstein, tended to view human language as a weak, biased tool, that tends to encourage us to err: it enables us to state rather easily and naturally that which is obviously false as if it were true. Instead, they sought to replace human language with mathematical symbols, replacing discourse with logic, as a means of "forcing" the mind into comprehending reality "as it is." In the social sciences this would take on the shape of a behaviorist attempt at constructing a "neutral," "scientific" (i.e., jargon laden) language that is based on "theorizations" and "models" that are supposed to overcome the multiplicity of meanings associated with symbols (whether discursive or practical) by detaching scientific language from, well, human language.

The analogy between tradition and language would also shed a critical light on conservative notions regarding the rigidity, or timelessness, of tradition, for it highlights tradition's dynamic, contemporaneous nature. I will get back to this point later.

## Tradition as Narrative

According to this analogy (developed most fully by MacIntyre), tradition is, quite simply, our story: it is the historical-yet-ever-developing narrative of which we are a part. This can be a narrative of a certain practice or profession, of a certain ethnicity or nationhood, a certain religion, a certain moral philosophy, and so on. According to this view, every human institution has—or in a sense maybe even *is*—a narrative. And, most critically, individuality and human agency are accordingly viewed as constituted by these social narratives. As MacIntyre puts it:

> I can only answer the question "What am I to do?" if I can answer the prior question "Of what story or stories do I find myself a part?" We enter human society, that is, with one or more imputed characters—roles into which we have been drafted—and we have to learn what they are in order to be able to understand how others respond to us and how our responses to them are apt to be construed [. . .] [T]here is no way to give us an understanding of any society, including our own, except through the stock of stories which constitute its initial dramatic resources [. . .] Narrative history of a certain kind turns out to be

the basic and essential genre for the characterization of human actions [. . .].[29]

One immediate implication of this analogy, very much like in the case of the former one, is the simultaneous emphasis of the inevitability of both tradition and agency. Put differently, this analogy embodies the interplay and interconnectedness between change, development, and continuity in the clearest of senses. For, "[t]o be an adherent of a tradition is always to enact some further stage in the development of one's tradition."[30] Narrativity—having a narrative framework that instills reality with meaning—is a precondition for our ability to do that which makes us human, that is: to understand. "Our story" is what enables us in the first place to comprehend reality and conduct ourselves in the world. As MacIntyre puts it in the quote above, tradition, or the narrative that is tradition, "drafts" us into a "role" whose basic features are already set. We do not choose this role, nor do we choose these constitutive features. But we are the ones who enact these roles. Each individual "plays" her various roles, and—as in every case of play—interprets these roles, and their features, as she does so.

It is not a coincidence that the concepts of "play" and "game" have such a decisive role in several of the philosophical works mentioned above. Much like MacIntyre's notion of agents playing their "roles" in an ongoing play/narrative, both Wittgenstein's notion of "language games" and Gadamer's discussion of "play," to mention but the two most striking examples, point directly to the core of the complex relation between rule-governed behavior (i.e., the power of tradition over us) and an active, conscious agency or individuality. To understand this we must first forsake rationalistic notions of human subjectivity, according to which an independent human subject "knows" that she is just playing, and "reflects" on the game while enacting it (indeed, such "conscious" acting or playing is a recipe for a manifestly bad performance); Instead, we are dealing here with a "mode of being"[31] in a setting that seems to have a life of its own but is nevertheless fundamentally dependent upon the actor-player in order to be.

Hence, a study of play clearly reveals what might be considered its supremacy over the human being playing it:

> The players are not the subjects of play; instead, play merely reaches presentation (Darstellung) through the players [. . .]
> Play clearly represents an order in which the to-and-fro

> motion of play follows of itself [. . .] [A]ll playing is a being-
> played, [. . .] the game masters the players [. . .] The real
> subject of the game [. . .] is not the player but instead the
> game itself. What holds the player in its spell, draws him
> into play, and keeps him there is the game itself.[32]

But, at the same time, the most obvious fact that we must bear in
mind is that without players or actors to preform it, play does not
have an actual existence; and that no two performances of the same
play are identical: every enactment is also an act of interpretation, an
"individual" case of performance.

How are we—whether as players enacting a role in a narrative
or as researchers studying their behavior—to decide which narrative
is the "right" narrative to be enacted? In other words, how are we
to answer MacIntyre's above-quoted constitutive quandary, "Of what
story or stories do I find myself a part?" For it is rather obvious that
the answer to this—let's call it the issue of "selectivity" in the phenomenology of bearing tradition—is never a set, clear and determi-
nate one. It is "I" who "finds" (choice seems to be indeed too strong
a term here, but agency is far from being mute) myself in a story, and
then goes on to enact the next chapter of this narrative.

One forceful answer would argue that it is precisely this unde-
terministic—indeed, "relativistic"—hermeneutic that preserves the
core notion of democracy; that the insistence on dialogue encapsulated herein enables hermeneutics to "claim to be a possible philosophy of the social transformation, which would be based [. . .] on the
affirmation of cultural identity as a weapon in the struggle against
capitalism and the imperialist world order."[33]

But this still leaves us with the unresolved matter of "authenticity": One can easily think of instances where agents, or "actors,"
seem to try and enact a role in a narrative that smacks of inauthentic-
ity, clearly not "theirs" (varying instances of "Americanization" are
probably the most obvious examples of this)—that they try to carry
a tradition that is, at base, foreign to them. This gains an even more
urgent impetus in the context of an ethos of authenticity, in which
one is expected to be what one "essentially" is.[34] I suspect that this is
one of those matters that demand to be left unresolved: that beyond
those obvious cases of outright, often ignorant mimicry, we are left
with a wide range of potential, "relativistic" readings and enactments
that are open to differing judgments regarding their "authenticity."

This last matter of selectivity and authenticity is further complicated if we take into consideration those unique instances in history, namely revolutionary moments, in which the acting agents proclaim to be disserting an "old" tradition/narrative, and to be writing a novel, indeed: revolutionarily new, narrative and tradition. While it is clear that these are instances of heightened agency, in which the dialogue between tradition and its carriers becomes assertive, if not combative, it can still be argued that perception of such revolutionary moments as wholly "new," as having nothing to do with their pasts, is simply wrong. As MacIntyre[35] makes clear in his criticism of the unlikely duo Kuhn and Burke (and see below), a "revolutionary" (as opposed to evolutionary, developmental) conception of the progression inside and between traditions (or paradigms) fails to see that these "new" traditions/paradigms contain an essential narration of the failure of their predecessors, hence an understanding of their past. There is, in other words, an important element of "carrying over" even in cases of revolutions: "What is carried over from one paradigm to another are epistemological ideals and a correlative understanding of what constitutes the progress of a single intellectual life."[36]

Tradition, "a flow of sympathy,"[37] is ever challenged and might indeed be understood as misguiding, but even this challenge and the potential ensuing crisis/revolution should be seen as, in an important sense, a "traditional" move:

> [Tradition] may be temporarily disrupted by the incursion of a foreign influence, it may be diverted, restricted, arrested, or become dried-up. And it may reveal so deep-seated an incoherence that (even without foreign assistance) a crisis appears. And if, in order to meet these crises, there were some steady, unchanging, independent guide to which a society might resort, it would no doubt be well advised to do so. But no such guide exists; we have no resources outside the fragments, the vestiges, the relics of its own tradition of behaviour which the crisis has left untouched. For even the help we may get from the traditions of another society (or from a tradition of a vaguer sort which is shared by a number of societies) is conditional upon our being able to assimilate them to our own arrangements and our own manner of attending to our arrangements.[38]

A second central implication of the "tradition as narrative" analogy is that these narratives are *open* narratives. Their endings have yet
to be written. Our interpretations of them are stages in their development, and these interpretations play a role in determining the future
development of the narrative.

This points us directly to tradition's dynamic, contemporaneous nature. Contrary to both rationalist-secular and conservative perceptions of tradition as a rather firm and unchanging set of beliefs
and practices, a "narrative understanding" of tradition shows it to
be essentially dynamic and ever changing. Seen as a narrative in
the process of being written and rewritten, a story that is not only
told and retold but also, in the same process, as it is enacted, being
constantly reshaped by the various interpretations of it enactors (i.e.,
individuals and communities who carry this tradition), tradition is
revealed to be as much contemporary as it is ancient (or at least as
much as it is viewed as rooted in the past).

This emphasis on tradition's dynamic character is so profound as
to bring MacIntyre, who is often taken to be a "conservative" thinker,
to criticize the man usually seen as the father of conservative thought,
Edmund Burke, in the harshest of words, calling him at one point
"an agent of positive harm."[39] Thus, while the notion of tradition
as narrative facilitates an argumentative, conflictual, and discursive
notion of tradition,[40] a conservative a-la-Burke notion of tradition, in
which stability and truthfulness beyond criticism are seen as essential
characteristics of tradition, is, in the best of cases, a misunderstanding:
"Traditions, when vital, embody continuities of conflict. Indeed when
a tradition becomes Burkean, it is always dying or dead."[41]

## So, What Do These Analogies Point At?

The view of tradition manifested in the analogies discussed above has
several implications for our self-understanding as rational, tradition-
constituted agents. Again, this is far from being a novelty. Rather, this
view of tradition and its implications echo several themes, which are
common to all or most of the aforementioned thinkers, and might
help us in evaluating these themes. In what follows I will sketch the
very crude outlines of some of the more pressing of these.

Epistemologically, the notion of tradition outlined above challenges the Enlightenment-born, empiricist, positivist rationalism,

with its general disregard for tradition and practice and its exclusive emphasis on abstract reason, method, and technical knowledge. Instead, this view of tradition highlights the essential role of practical reason or traditional knowledge. This amounts to a challenge against the alleged antinomy between tradition and reason that characterizes rationalist epistemology, highlighting instead the role of tradition and authority as constitutive elements of reason and thought. At the same time, this view would stress tradition's dynamic nature and the role of the individual agent and of the relevant community in interpreting and maintaining tradition, arguing against conservative notions of tradition's alleged rigid, "eternal" and overtly authoritative nature—to the degree of almost celebrating tradition's supposed irrationality.[42]

This challenge against Enlightenment notions of rationalism comes hand in hand with a heightened sensitivity to the role of practice. Tradition is, by its very "essence"—ontologically and phenomenologically, that is—realized only when it is comprehended, interpreted, loaded with meaning (which is ever "contemporary"), internalized and applied or practiced by its bearers. In other words, the practical understanding of tradition (always requiring its interpretation and affirmation) is a precondition of its existence. Practice is thus imbued with heightened importance, as the carrier of reason itself.

Given that the empiricist/positivist/rationalist epistemology has been the intellectual nurturing bed of the secularization thesis, the insistence on exposing the blind spots of this dominant epistemology, which is entailed in the understanding of tradition summarized here, and the various attempts at overcoming its limits via an emphasis on alternative modes of knowledge can prove to be highly fruitful in facilitating a post-secular outlook and epistemology.

Crucially, such an alternative epistemology would overcome the allegedly exclusive choice between, on the one hand, objectivism, realism and truth, and, on the other hand, relativism. It would offer a careful, nuanced insistence on a view of reality in which ontological truth is acknowledged and can surely be the subject of discourse, but at the same time it would be obviously weary of the empiricist absolutism. Instead, it would stress the limited nature of our ability to grasp this truth, and the historical, communal and dynamic (i.e., tradition-bound) nature of our knowledge of this truth.

This view of tradition also refutes the supposed antinomy between (collective) tradition and (personal) liberty, stressing instead that the very ability to conceptualize subjectivity and to view the self as an independent agent is itself dependent upon a constitutive tradition in which such a formulation is possible in the first place. As practically all of the aforementioned works of philosophy argue, it would be gravely mistaken to discount the constructive role played by preconceptions and inherited perspectives of sociohistorical reality in shaping our understanding of this reality.

Understanding tradition's constitutive role also sheds light on the nature and role of authority, highlighting it as a precondition for accumulating knowledge and for enabling us to reflect upon reality. Indeed, this can be seen as yet another critical reflection on the rationalistic suggestion that any precondition to knowledge is inherently wrong and misleading.

Another central theme captured here is a careful assessment of tradition's developing, dynamic nature. Given its constitutive role, "traditional change"—that is, development—is relatively slow and gradual in nature. But we should nevertheless insist that since tradition lives only through the individual's and the community's practical interpretations of it, it is bound to change over time. This also opens up the potentiality for conflict in tradition, and, in a wider historical timeframe, also for contesting tradition altogether. Acknowledgment of the constitutive nature of tradition should also lead us to a careful assessment of our ability to acquire new traditions, which are originally alien to us, our ability to translate traditions, and the nature of the eventual mutual influence, correspondence, or conflict between traditions.

Admittedly, this interpretation nevertheless leaves several matters unresolved. Primarily, I cannot argue to be offering a straightforward understanding of the way tradition is transmitted and appropriated. What "exactly" happens when I stand next to an experienced cook as her apprentice and gain the practical knowledge of cooking in a certain tradition? This, indeed, is one of the fundamental questions of the study of humanity, and it touches upon our being social and historical. Beyond noting the obvious: that tradition is transmitted and appropriated—much like language and narrative—in its very practice (and only partially and often misleadingly, it should be noted, in its formal "study" and codification), I suspect that this is one of the aspects of our humanity that evade a clear articulation and formulation. It is not a coincidence that the philosophical works upon which the current discussion is based all focus on an interpretation of the phenomenon of tradition, and do not pretend to offer a schematic "explanation" of the way tradition "in actuality" works and is transmitted and appropriated. Similarly, it seems both urgent and ultimately futile to pin down the "nature" of the (social) power of tradition. This, simply, is a matter of our humanity.

# Part II

# Zionism and Jewish Traditions

The current part of the book focuses on Zionism's relation to Jewish traditions that preceded it and continued to live alongside it. In order to do so we have to, first, reconsider—and, as I shall argue, overcome—the rather naïve and overtly misleading one-dimensional notion that Zionism entails, simply, a secularization of Judaism. Chapter 5 captures this alleged truism, and discusses its shortcomings. It then goes on to present the outlines of an alternative understanding of Zionism, posited in terms of its relation to those preceding Jewish traditions. I would suggest that attentiveness to Zionism's position vis-à-vis the European-Jewish reinterpretation of Judaism as a "religion" may entail some important keys to understanding Zionism's relation to its Jewish past. Chapter 6 applies this reconsideration to the thought of several key Zionist thinkers. Chapter 7 focuses on three main streams—Socialist, Revisionist, and Religious—of Zionism. Part III of the book moves on to discuss the Israeli political culture and its negotiation of tradition, Jewishness, and Israeliness.

# 4

# Zionism, Jewish "Religion," and Secularism

### Religion, Secularization, and the Nation-State: The Zionist Narrative

In many, important senses the notion that Zionism amounts to a "revolution" in the Jewish world—a revolution that entails a reformulation of Jewish identity, meaning, and politics so as to render them more attentive and adaptable to a "modern" and "secular" context—is taken for granted, an obvious argument indeed, in public and academic discourses in and about Israel. This alleged truism argues, in varying formulations, that Zionism is mainly a project of a modernization, secularization, and politicization of Judaism, so as to adapt it to the modern, dominant sociopolitical framework, namely: the nation-state. This modernization and secularization come after "religious" eons, in which Jewish religion—or, in some formulations, religious tradition—dominated the Jewish world and subdued the spirit of the Jewish people in "exile," encouraging as it did a passive, essentially apolitical thought.[1]

An important, authoritative and representative formulation of this argument can be found in Shlomo Avineri's review of Zionist thought,[2] which can be seen as an authorized biography of Zionist ideology.[3] Avineri's interpretation is noticeable not only for its straightforward presentation of the "Zionism as secularism" narrative, but also for its explicit, overtly ideological celebration of the nation-state as the epitome of this process. His is hence also an iteration of the substitution of "religion" and "religious" theology by the political theology of the (allegedly secular) nation-state. As such, his analysis of Zionist thought demands a careful consideration.

Avineri, who is one of the more prominent authors to identify Zionism as a (Jewish) revolution—a "permanent revolution"[4] at that—describes Zionist thought as a "*modern* answer to the question who are [the Jews] and what is their identity."[5] This answer was an urgent remedy to a modern predicament: The necessity to offer a "secular" formulation of Jewish meaning. (The early seeds of this have already been planted with the *haskala*, preceding the solidification of the Zionist idea.) And this, quite clearly, is key to understanding Zionism:

> Zionism is the most fundamental revolution in Jewish life. It substituted a secular self-identity of the Jews as a nation for the traditional and Orthodox self-identity in religious terms [. . .] Zionism is not just a reaction of a people to persecution. It is a quest for self-determination and liberation under the modern conditions of secularization and liberalism.[6]

This secularization means primarily the "decline of the status of religion in the Jewish community"[7] and a gradual "liberation" from the shackles of "religious tradition."[8] "Secularization" emerges here as an unchallenged, natural historical development; With the coming of modernity, religion declines and the individual's and community's commitment to tradition weakens, as sort of a preordained universal phenomenon, independent from specific historical, political, cultural, and local contexts.

Moreover, this very obvious secular fact brings up important questions: How is it that Zionism emerges as a Jewish national movement exactly "in a generation characterized for both Jews and for non-Jews by liberation from religious tradition and deepening secularization?"[9] "Why was it precisely in the secularized atmosphere of the nineteenth and twentieth centuries that a link [between the Jewish People and The Land of Israel], which was originally religious, became a potent force for action?"[10]

Note how these questions create, in the background, a matter-of-factual identification between "Judaism" and "religious tradition": The decline of the latter, i.e., of Jewish "religion," is naturally expected, so these questions suggest, to bring about the weakening of Jewish identity, of Judaism or Jewishness itself. In other words, the celebration of the "modern," and "secular" Zionist answer to the question of the meaning of Jewish identity—an answer that is seen as challenging the identification between "Judaism" and "Jewish religion" (or

"Jewish religious tradition")—assumes this identification as a given basis for any ideational and historical development. This identification echoes "The Myth of Past Piety"[11]—or the misguided historical conception of "the Age of Faith," which identifies the past with the religious, and argues that in the past everything was about religion, and everyone was religious.[12]

This narrative, then, revives the dichotomous conceptualization that conflates or synonymizes the "modernity—premodernity" binary with the "secular—religious" one. The big surprise, the alleged "paradox"[13] that must be explained, is hence the essential tie between Zionism (which is "secular" by definition, being a modern movement aimed at the establishment of a nation-state) and Judaism (which is at root "religious" or at least primarily about "religion").

This view of secularization presupposes, then, also the complementary organ in this binary, namely religion: The identification of "Jewish religion," or even "Orthodoxy," as a supra-historical category appears here as an unchallenged given. This religion appears to be dealing with practice and belief, but it is hard to know how it is different from, for example, the supposedly secular politics of the Zionist nation-state, which constitutes its own elaborated system of practice and belief, and, ultimately, as is the case with virtually all nation-states, demands its subjects'/citizens' self-sacrifice for securing the state's own interests.

This must be reiterated: Avineri's narrative portrays secularization as a meta-historical phenomenon, a teleological evolution of sorts (that is, it is driven by a preordained *telos* or purpose), of the human race toward reason, rationality, and enlightenment. As such, secularization goes unquestioned, a normatively neutral phenomenon, which compels the Jews to redefine their identity. Yet it is also clear that for Avineri, this meta-historical phenomenon is necessarily positive, for it amounts to the emancipation of both individual and community from the shackles of tradition, i.e., restrictive "religiosity."

But this freedom also entails a crisis: a loss of identity. With the coming of secularization, "Jewish identity lost [. . .] its normative and public standing"[14]; "Religion and the *kehila* [Jewish community]," who served in pre-Emancipation period as the "normative focus"[15] of Jewish existence, could no longer do so post Emancipation and *haskala*. A redefinition of the meaning of modern Jewish existence was critically needed. The Jews, who were, at least in part, "liberated from the traditional religious framework in matters of practice [*mitzvoth*] and belief,"[16] were compelled to "instill new public meaning in their being."[17]

For Avineri, Zionism's single most monumental achievement is exactly its success in answering this need, that is, building a secular alternative to Jewish collectivity, in the form of the Jewish (or, more accurately, the Jews') nation-state. Hence his proclamation that "the State of Israel put the public, normative dimension back into Jewish life. Without this having ever been defined, and maybe it cannot be defined, it can be said that to be Jewish means—more than anything else—feeling attachment to the State of Israel."[18]

This, the author stresses, is not a matter of value judgment; rather, it is an an objective identification of an empirical fact: The Israeli nation-state, the modern, secular offspring of Zionist politics, is the ultimate substitute for traditional Jewish religion:

> This is not an ideological claim or the expression of a pious wish that this is how it should be, but a statement of fact. It is a fact that religion does not unite the Jews today as it did in the pre-Emancipation past. It is a fact that the majority of the Jewish people, both in the Diaspora and in Israel, defines itself in terms that are basically secular—ethnic, national, cultural—and the life style of most Jews in the world today is utterly secularized. Jewish religion itself is split into at least three major trends (Orthodox, Conservative, and Reform), and the relationship between these trends sometimes divides Jews more than it unites them [. . .] Today there does not exist one idea or one institution around which all Jewish people can or do unite—with the exception of Israel.[19]

The author's dominant Zionist imagery is of note: it echoes the "negation of exile," painting the Jewish traditions that preceded Zionism as having lost their contact with history and with the external, non-Jewish world, and "froze" in a closed system of self-reinforcement.

It is difficult to overlook the theological and teleological dimensions assigned to the nation-state in this analysis. The state emerges as positioned at the very heart of the Jewish people's existence, as the only agent instilling a meaningful content into this collectivity, and enabling it to remain a cohesive "people." Jewish unity emerges as dependent upon the State of Israel.[20]

Moreover, the collectivity centered around the state normatively supersedes all other Jewish communities:

> This, then, is what distinguishes Israel from other Jewish communities. Other Jewish communities are merely aggregates of individuals, and as such they have no normative standing as a public entity. Israel, on the other hand, is conceived not only as an aggregate of its population, but its very existence has immanent value and normative standing.[21]

At its peak, the mostly implicit identification of the nation-state as a theological-yet-secular entity becomes rather explicit:

> Israel is thus the new public dimension of Jewish existence, the new Jewish *parhessia*. As such it replaces the old religious-communal bonds that circumscribed Jewish existence in the past. Today, due to modernization and secularization, Israel is the normative expression of this collective existence of the Jewish people, of *klal Yisrael*.[22]

Moreover, Avineri's clarifying note explicates that the theopolitics of the nation-state is larger than mere "religious" theology. As he stresses, his argument should not be understood as saying that "the state of Israel replaces Jewish religion, but functionally it fills today a similar existential role;"

> Clearly, for those Jews who are religious in the traditional sense even today, religion has a deep collective existential meaning. But since not all Jews, or even the majority of Jews, self-identify with religious tradition, religion has become, purely and simply, one of the partial symbols of identity. Only the State of Israel, and not religion (or any other agent) can function today as the common denominator that incorporates the totality of heterogeneous elements of Jewish being.[23]

The bottom line is simple, then: Zionism is a secular substitute—a superior one at that, as it is more suitable for the challenges of modernity—to Jewish religion, as the agent unifying the Jewish people and instilling Jewish identity with meaning. Zionism, and especially its culmination if the State of Israel, is the superior alternative to religious Jewish politics. "This is the meaning of the Zionist revolution from a historical perspective: the renewal of the Jewish public aspect, replacing the community and its religious institutions."[24]

It is also interesting to note that this narrative does not deny the "foreign" dimension in the Zionist endeavor to fit Jewish traditions into Christian frameworks. Needless to say, this endeavor is not viewed as alienating. Quite the contrary: The Zionist reading of Judaism in Christian terms is seen here as a most successful move. In a manifestly Hegelian manner the author explains that the "new assessment of Jewish history" that lies at the root of the Zionist idea is no longer satisfied with the "traditional-internal" account of the essence of Judaism; Contrary to "Jewish tradition," which "did not feel compelled to tie this essence to external factors," Zionism did indeed feel compelled, and was even actively interested in doing so, i.e., "to define Judaism in the terms of Christianity [. . .] to find even a small thread that will enable the tying of Judaism to the world of general history [and to seek] meaning and essence to the existence of Jews by the criteria common among the nations of the world."[25]

## A Zionist Revision:
## Modern but Not Exactly "Secular"

This constitutive narrative of Zionism as the secularization of Jewish tradition and identity has won its share of criticism and revision.[26] Such, for example, is Yosef Salmon's assessment of the interaction between "religion" and "nationalism" in the early Zionist movement.[27] Salmon is critical of the dichotomous worldview of certain scholars, who contrast religion, which they see as a "conservative, medieval [agent], both politically and normatively" with nationalism, which they see as "a modern [and] secular" agent. Accompanied by its corresponding presupposition, that secular nationalism aims to replace religion and "give both society and individual an identity they have lost with the loss of religious identity," this worldview is "a stereotypical and one-dimensional understanding of human history in the last two-hundred years."[28]

Salmon's more nuanced view feeds his harsh criticism of this worldview. Relying on contemporaneous research (which, in the most part, has not dealt directly with Zionism) from the 1990s he reminds his readers that "national identity uses elements of religious tradition to form its image, and sometimes it is wholly justified by the religious difference of a certain national group from others." At the end, he writes, nationalism and religion are tied together in a "Gordian knot, which holds the potential for continuous conflict between the two components."[29]

Moreover, for Salmon the Zionist case clearly exemplifies the intensity of what he identifies as mutual co-dependence between religion and nationalism: "In Jewish nationalism, there was not a single thinker or influential person who demanded separation between religion and nationalism or believed in it. Even those who call for a separation of religion and state did not extend this demand to the national Jewish movement in its whole."[30]

Salmon accepts that there are those who believe that Jewish nationalism, or Zionism, has substituted Jewish religion; but such views, he writes, "were more prevalent among historiographers and sociologists of Jewish nationalism than among its main thinkers." Salmon mentions Ben-Zion Dinur, David Vital, and Baruch Kimmerling as offering similar formulations of the worldview he judges as a "stereotypical understanding" of the nature of the interaction between nationalism and religion. This worldview is so committed to the idea that Zionism is "in essence a movement that has rebelled against tradition in general and Orthodoxy in particular,"[31] that it takes the notion of "religious Zionism" to be an incoherent and seemingly illogical abnormality. Such historiographers and sociologists, Salmon cautions, "have cast on Zionist historiography a subjective axiomatic model, that is conflicted with the historical substance."[32] Salmon notes that at the very least, while there is no doubt that Zionism "is the Jewish answer to the challenges of modernity," it is also true that it would be wrong to assume that this answer is "identical to secularization."[33]

Zionism, then, is for Salmon a "modern yet not secular movement." Accordingly, he reframes the decisive issue as referring to religion's role and its degree of influence inside the national movement. Salmon's view of the matter thus becomes "revisionist," as it challenges the simple notion that Zionism equals secularization: religion, he concludes, "on its various aspects, is a component in the historical manifestation of Jewish nationalism, but not its subject."[34]

This nuanced revisionism has been widely acknowledged. Thus, for example, in Avineri's own insistence (some two decades after the publication of the work discussed earlier) that Zionism and the State of Israel should *not* be viewed as the outcome of a simple process of a secularization of Judaism. Remaining firmly inside a Hegelian frame of analysis, this discourse now frames the discussion as having to do with "The *Dialectics* of Redemption and Secularization."[35] A simplistic narrative of secularization is no longer deemed applicable:

> The thesis I would like to propose in dealing with the question of Zionism and religion is that there exists a much more dialectical relationship between religion and nationalism. The secularization thesis, to my mind, has to be tested, and in testing it I suggest that it will be found wanting.
>
> [. . .] [F]ar from being a clear break with the past, national movements are essays in reinterpretations of the past and its retrieval. And since one element of this past has to deal with religion, every national movement has to deal in an innovative and transformative way with the religious dimension of its past. Far from being imagined communities, national communities relate to a past made usable, reinterpreted and retrieved.[36]

This clarification comes as a programmatic introduction to an edited volume titled *Zionism and Religion*[37] that as a whole manifests one of the more comprehensive attempts at studying the various aspects of the narrative told under this headline. Avineri's cautionary introductory notes notwithstanding, most authors in the volume tend to nevertheless accept the secularization thesis in its simplistic form. More importantly, the underlying epistemology guiding Avineri, as well as the volume's editors and contributing authors—and apparently shared by scholars such as Yosef Salmon, who call for a more nuanced view of sociohistorical reality—is exactly the epistemology that identifies religion and nationalism as two discrete concepts, which may, indeed, be found in a complex relationship of mutual influence, but are a priori distinct and essentially different; And, to begin with, they exist as independent conceptual entities.

As discussed in chapter 1, this foundational conceptualization is part of the wider secularist epistemology, which is constitutive of the modern social and historical sciences. This epistemology presents us with a whole litany of dichotomous binaries as the constitutive axes of human reality (these include, among others, the distinctions between modernity and premodernity/tradition, reason and belief, science and religion, and rationality and belief/prejudice). Moreover, its worldview nourishes on an acultural and ahistorical conception of modernity, viewing it as a universal phenomenon of the triumph of instrumental rationality, utilitarianism, technology, science, and bureaucracy;[38] all of which it identifies with secularization. Even when it is attentive to the complex relationship between the two organs of the distinction at hand (i.e., between religion and nationalism) it is nevertheless loyal to the basic notion of the essential distinction between the two, and to the identification of nationalism with the secular.

This distinction is of special importance, since it establishes the ontological, essential separation between the nation-state (on its legitimizing ideology) and religion, which is delegitimized by this very act of distinction; it is in essence alien to the nation-state. It may serve the nation-state, but it cannot present political claims. This essential distinction is echoed in Avineri's aforementioned introduction, as well as in the collection of essays that follow it. Its traces can also be clearly detected in Salmon's abovementioned work,[39] which aims to challenge the simplistic notion of Zionism as secularization, but remains loyal to the conceptual distinction between religion and nationalism.

For Salmon, the issue at hand is the nature of the complicated interaction between the two essentially distinct organs; the changing "balance" between them is what differentiates, in his reading, religious Zionism from mainstream ("secular") Zionism. Moreover, he seems to be torn between the arguments denying the historical narrative of secularization and the master narrative of secularization. Thus, for example, he opens another article, whose very title ("Religion and Secularity in the Zionist National Movement") already testifies to the presence of this conceptual dualism, with the following determined statement:

> The Zionist national movement has been a secularizing phenomenon. Many of those joining it, mostly among the young, experienced through it the change in their way of life and belief from observance to nonobservance. From belief in a higher power overseeing and guiding reality to a human being responsible for his own fate and deeds. Many symbols taken from religious tradition have gone through a process of secularization.[40]

At the very least, this distinction sheds light on the "problematic" nature of the secularist discussion on the relationship between religion and nationalism (or, in the same vein, between religion and politics in Israel). For, as noted by the editors of the volume *Zionism and Religion*, "Jewish nationalism [. . .] lacks some of the distinguishing marks of nationalism more generally,"[41] and the role of Jewish "religion" in it seems to be more significant than in other cases.

## The Persistence of the Secularization Narrative

But the secularization narrative persists. All reservations from identifying Zionism as a simple act of a (or the) secularization of Judaism, which are quite prevalent today, notwithstanding, it is still a matter of common practice to view Zionism as a project of redefining Jewish identity as secular. "Zionism as Secular Jewish Identity"[42] is, for Gideon Shimoni, in a book that offers the most comprehensive analysis of Zionist ideology, one of the two fundamental issues of this ideology (the second is "The Right to the Land"). "Zionist Ideology involved far more than an innovatory political program for the material welfare of Jews,"[43] Shimoni clarifies. He reads the essence of this program to be a reinterpretation of Judaism in terms of secularism, which was instigated by the Enlightenment, rationalism, modern science, and modernity in general. Note how this historical-ideational narrative takes for granted the dichotomous distinctions that lie as the foundation of the secularist epistemology: tradition vs. modernity, rationality vs. belief, religion vs. science, and, at the end, also religion vs. politics—all in a few short sentences:

> [Zionist ideology] redefined the nature of Jewish identity in nationalist terms. It was the legacy of emancipation and enlightenment, [. . .] that made this nationalist redefinition possible. Exposure to modernism in respect of the application of scientific criteria in order to expand the frontiers of knowledge about man, his society, and its history inevitably challenged the traditionalist understanding of Jewish identity. Belief in the transcendental origin of Jewish identity, that is to say, its creation by a divine force outside nature, was placed in question. An alternative understanding presented itself, according to which Jewish identity as the immanent, evolving product of natural, scientifically expli-

cable developments within an ethnic group that came to be known as the Jews.[44]

Zionism and Jewish traditions that preceded it are, according to this narrative, to be found on the opposing sides of an epistemological rupture: "The schism between the traditionalist, transcendental self-understanding on the one side and the modernist, immanent self-understanding on the other side is the great divide in modern Jewish identity."[45] This schism, Shimoni clarifies, preceded Zionism: Zionist thought was born into it, and accepted it as the lens through which it views reality. Moreover, inside Zionism itself two opposing stances, each relying on one of the opposing poles of this schism (i.e., "religious" Zionism and "secular" Zionism), have coexisted.

In other words, Shimoni, much like Salmon, views the tension between religion (or theology, metaphysics, and the transcendental; the terminology varies, the arguments are essentially the same) and politics (or "state"), which is by this very definition secular, as the main line of division separating "the national-religious Zionists" and "the secularized Jewish intelligentsia."[46] As for the religious Zionists, Shimoni states that "although accommodating the modern concept of the nation" (and note the evolutionary tone here), they have nevertheless "clung to the traditionalist belief that this unique nation had been brought into existence by the terms of an essentially religious covenant emanating from God." In contrast, that "secularized Jewish intelligentsia" represented a political-secular-national stance, in the context of which "religion" was incorporated into—but surely was not equal to—nationalism.[47]

The crucial matter for understanding Zionism, then, is what Shimoni, following Zionist thinkers, identifies as religion's exilic, "inordinate" dominance and its corrosive influence over the wellbeing of the nation:

> The aspiration toward a renaissance of Jewish culture that was to be accomplished by Zionism was predicated on the secularized understanding of Jewish identity as an outcome of immanent processes in the history of the nation. Religion was neither wholly coextensive with Jewish culture nor its original source; it was merely one of the ingredients of Jewish national culture. It was the condition of *galut* that had

endowed religion with so inordinate an influence on Jewish existence, enabling it to consume, as it were, the nation.[48]

The secularization narrative, then, persists.

## Zionist Ideology and the Invention of Jewish "Religion"

It is my contention that a more accurate appreciation of contemporary Israeli political culture demands that we overcome two hurdles: One is the argument recognized by Avineri and others, whether implicitly or explicitly, as naïve, yet nevertheless enjoying widespread circulation and influence, that Zionism is a rather simple, one-directional project of the secularization of Judaism. The other, an epistemological and higher hurdle, overlooked by most authors (or, to be precise, accepted as their taken-for-granted, unchallenged premise, as an "objective" tool for the analysis of human reality) is the secular epistemology, which gives birth to the categorical and conceptual distinction between religion and politics (or nationalism). We must challenge the very distinction between religion and politics (whether of the nationalist kind or otherwise), and to question the epistemological value of these categories.

This, of course, is far from being a novel argument, and it bears a universal character—it is not limited to the particularities of the Jewish or Zionist case. Its introduction into the Zionist case is especially illuminating, since it reminds us that the construction of Jewish histories and practices, or "Judaism" as a "religion" is in itself a rather recent effort (see chapter 2), which bears a wide variety of implications for the study of Zionism.

One of the more fruitful ways to understand Zionism is, then, to identify it not necessarily as a (or the) secularization of Judaism or of Jewish tradition through the invention of a national tradition, but rather as a counter-reaction to another project of invention, which preceded Zionism. This preceding invention entails the transforming of Judaism into a religion, or, in other words, the invention of "Jewish religion."[49]

The driving force of Zionism I wish to focus the discussion on is, then, a forceful *negation* of the argument that Judaism is a religion. Zionism, as a political ideology, one that adopts its constitutive ideas from modern, European nationalism, argues against an apolitical interpretation/reading of Judaism, upon which the historical project of the invention of Jewish "religion" is based. Against this apolitical notion of religion, Zionism seeks to promote an understanding of Judaism as a nation, in terms of the ideological discourse and epistemological framework of modern European nationalism.

In other words, while Mendelssohn and his successors have "invented" Judaism as an apoloitical "religion," the Zionist idea is focused on an "invention" of Judaism as a politicized "nation." If the main (political) motive driving Mendelssohn was his hope that a redefinition of Judaism as a religion will enable the social, cultural and political assimilation of Jews within the German political community, then the force driving the Zionist idea is exactly the opposite aspiration: to prove that assimilation is impossible, and to demand the political expression of the collective identity of Jews inside the nationalist, statist European discourse.

But Zionism does not negate the epistemology from which the invention of Judaism as a religion nourishes. Moreover, it shares the constitutive notions of this invention; yet it offers a different reading of history and reaches different conclusions. Zionism, in other words, is established on that same duality from which Mendelssohn's "invention" emerges, namely the distinction between apolitical religion and secular politics, and between the modern and the traditional. Like Mendelssohn and his successors, Zionism, too, adopts its philosophy, language, vocabulary, and ideological grammar—upon which and by which it formulates its negation of the reading of Judaism as a religion—from the contemporaneous European political ideology, culture, and language.

In its dominant formulations, Zionism adopts the ideology of the sovereign nation-state as the ideational infrastructure for the development of a Jewish nationalist ideology. This idea has, of course, seen varying formulations, and it would be wrong to identify Zionism as a homogenous, wholly unified body of ideas. But it is safe to argue that at the root of all varying formulations of the Zionist idea lies a basic consensus: that Jews are a nation, as this term is understood in modern Europe, under the sovereignty of the nation-state. The main, dominant stream of the Zionist movement also formed a tight linkage between the argument that the Jews form a nation and the demand for the nation's self-definition in a sovereign nation-state, and stated that Jewish nationalism must be expressed and materialized in the political framework of a nation-state, in which the meaning of Jewish identity as nationalism will be reconstituted.[50]

We must bear in mind that the two sides of this supposed argument ("Judaism is a religion" vs. "Judaism is a nationality") were born together. Their common origin is the attempt to force histories and traditions of Jews into the modern European discourse, on its particularistic (Christian) roots. It is worth repeating here that what is commonly titled "Judaism," "Jewishness," "Jewish identity," and "Jewish traditions" (the very fact of this multiplicity of names is in itself a testimony to the conceptual misperception that characterizes the discussion) have always presented those who wished to locate them inside modern, Christian, European categorical frameworks with a daunting challenge. Judaism, or, to be precise, the histories, practices, and traditions of those identified as Jews could, with some adjustments and in varying levels of screeching mismatch, be seen as applicable to each and every one of the supposedly distinct and mutually exclusive categories: nationality, ethnicity, race, faith, culture, folklore, and religion. Or, if we should prefer the negative formulation of the same argument, Judaism does not fit well with either of those categories.

Indeed, as chapter 1 makes clear, these categories face a devastating critical deconstruction also inside the Christian, European context from which they emerge and within which they develop. But their importation—and especially that of the religion and nationalism duo—to a Jewish context expresses, either knowingly or unknowingly, a deep epistemological rupture. The reading of Judaism as a religion (or, for that matter, as any one of the abovementioned categories) entails a comprehensive redefinition of the meaning of Judaism, in the terms of a foreign tradition that in many, deep senses is alien to the traditions and histories of Jewish communities.

In certain readings of these two competing arguments—that is, the view of Judaism as a religion vs. the view of Judaism as a nationality—they may appear to be negating each other. As discussed in chapter 2, one of the arguments entailed in the notion that Judaism is a religion, and that as such, and *only* as such it should be understood, is that Judaism is not a nationality, as this term was understood in European politics of the sovereign nation-state—that is, exactly in the sense in which Zionism views Judaism as a nationality. Indeed, it is not far-fetched to view Mendelssohn's claim that Judaism is not a nationality as driven exactly by his wish to enable the successful (national) assimilation of Jews among non-Jewish nations. For Mendelssohn and his contemporaries, the identification of Judaism as a religion was supposed to solve the obvious tension entailed in the identification of Jews as an alien nation, living among a nativist host nation. Mendelssohn enabled the Jews, as the famous idiom stated, to become "German (or French, etc.) nationals of the Mosaic faith"; loyal citizens and servants of the nation-state, patriots beyond doubt, an integral part of the (majority non-Jewish) nation, who differ from other members of the nation only in the inherently limited, private realm of religious faith, which is essentially apolitical.

Zionism sought to negate this argument.[51] Leading Zionist figures presented this nationalism as a wider, more inclusive—indeed, the *most* inclusive—framework of meaning that contains Jewish "religion," but is surely not subservient to it, and essentially not identical to it.[52] This perception is also a constitutive notion of the Sate of Israel's identification as the (secular, or at least "not-religious") state of the Jewish nation.

As in other cases of emerging national movements and the articulation of a nation-statist claim, the Zionist project also comprised a wide-ranging mission of an "invention," or construction, of national tradition. Zionism was required to instill meaningful content in the notion of Jewish national identity, and Jewish thinkers were required to rewrite Jewish history and to offer a new interpretation of Jewish meaning and content, such that would correspond positively with the nationalist meta-narrative of (political) affinity and concurrence between territory and identity (whether ethnic, national, lingual, and so on).

Needless to say, Zionism found the building blocks for this reinterpretation and retelling of the Jewish collective story in the histories of Jews, that is: in Jewish traditions, and has done so through varying degrees of dialoguing with these traditions. But it has arrived at this dialogue and reinvention as it has already been positioned deeply inside the context of European "secularization," presenting a local, or particularistic conception of a Jewish secularity that has preceded the Zionist project.

In other words, Zionism does not offer an alternative epistemology for understanding Jews than the one that directed Mendelssohn's thought; Zionism, too, accepts the dominant European discourse, on its secular epistemology, and adopts as taken-for-granted the distinction between religion and the secular. From the outset, the Zionist idea is based on that same distinction between Jewish "religion" and other aspects of Jewish identity (political, national, cultural, lingual, and so on), which are, at root, "secular." In its dominant iterations, the Zionist idea stresses this distinction to clarify that the secular, national aspect of this identity must gain precedence over the religious, or theological aspect of Judaism, in order to remain loyal to the notion of a nation-state of Jews. Similarly, influential streams in Zionist ideology tended to view that same Jewish "religion" as essentially negative, being, in their reading, an inhibiting agent that suffocates the national vitality. Indeed, for them, Jewish religion is responsible for what they viewed as the diminishing of the Jewish people in "exile."

This distinction between what is presented as the "religious" or "theological" aspect and the political-national one of Judaism is not limited to thinkers who adopt a "secular" ideology and identity. It also reverberates from the arguments posed by those who are identified as religious Zionists. In other words, the epistemological distinction between religion and politics (and not, it should be stressed, the demand to separate the two in the constitutional-legal and political-practical levels) lies at the very core of the Zionist idea, including its streams that are identified as "religious." As Salmon notes,

> the controversy between those identified as holding on to a religious-public stance and those identified as holding to a secular stance revolves mainly around the relationship between these two entities [that is, religion and politics]; those demanded to make religion an instrument of the nation, while the others wanted to make the nation an instrument of religion.[53]

What tends to evade even Salmon, who is very careful to note the shortsightedness of the discourse that simplistically identifies Zionism as secularism, is that the very distinction between religion and politics goes wholly unchallenged, and is taken for granted by all sides in this debate. Religious-Zionism too, in other words, assumes secularism as a taken-for-granted fact.

Now, as Yehouda Shenhav notes, the gap between Zionist ideology or rhetoric and political practice is noticeable. A careful examination of the interplay between "religion" and "nationalism," "the religious," and "the secular," and other such binaries in modern nationalism clearly reveals that the intersection between the suppos-edly mutually exclusive opposites "is simultaneously produced and obscured." Studying Zionist discourse, Shenhav finds it to be exhib-iting "both of these seemingly contradictory principles." It is both and at the same time religious and secular, manifesting what Bruno Latour[54] finds to be a quintessentially modern trait: hybridization and purification.[55]

If we remain attentive to the epistemological argument with which the current discussion opened, we must, then, transcend the secular discourse on its constitutive epistemology and reexamine the question of Zionism's relation to preceding Jewish traditions. The following chapters shall offer some insights that arise from this consideration.

# 5

# Zionism and Jewish Traditions

How, then, has Zionist ideology constructed its stance in relation to Jewish traditions that preceded it (and were, so the argument common among Zionist ideologues went, stained with the mark of exilic religiosity)?

Some Zionist ideologues, including, to the embarrassment of many, Theodor Herzl, tended to largely ignore this issue; or, at the least, they suspended its treatment, focusing instead on the notion of Jewish political power by imagining the Jews' state as a European-like nation-state,[1] ruled by Europeans of Jewish descent. Other Zionist thinkers were severely critical of this tendency to ignore what they saw as the most fundamental issue. Foremost among them is, of course, Aḥad Ha'am (Asher Ginzburg), who flung at Herzl the rather simple yet damaging question (in paraphrase): What exactly is Jewish in your *Judenstaat*? He notes that in Herzl's utopia, *Altneuland*, "there is no trace" of questions regarding the "essence of Judaism." Herzl's imagined state, which could be, in "few and minor" changes not the Jewish but the Nigerian nation-state is nothing but "an imitation of monkeys," without any authentic, particularly Jewish "national trait."[2]

Critics such as Aḥad Ha'am argued that the Zionist project must focus on the historical undertaking of "secularizing" Judaism, understood via the prevalent European nationalist interpretive framework, that is, to reinterpret Judaism so as to adapt it to a rationalist, modernist, and utilitarian worldview that would function as a basis for (secular) Jewish life in the ultimate form of a nation-state. Such ideologues present a quintessentially historical sensitivity; they understand that "a revival of [the People of] Israel that will be genuinely the *revival of Israel*, not the revival of Nigerians, cannot appear instantaneously [. . .] An historical ideal demands a historical *development*."[3]

But how are we to understand the meaning of this "history"? In order to answer this question we must remember that in the confines

of the common, dominant narrative, the said historical development
was framed inside the "secular vs. religious" and "modern vs. primitive (or traditional)" binaries. Accordingly, the Zionist thinkers identified by Shimoni as the "ethnicist intelligentsia"—the central and most
important group in the formulation of Zionist ideology—argued that
the task of Zionism was to "revive the secular dimensions of Jewish culture while incorporating only those elements of the religious
heritage that were malleable and consonant with modernity."[4] The
formative narrative, then, projects the quintessentially modernist distinction between the secular and the religious on Jewish history in its
entirety. Put differently, the invention of Jewish religion is projected
backward, to the Jewish past, as this religion, or what is identified as
belonging to its realm, is distinguished from all that is "not-religion,"
i.e., the wider realm of national identity, ethnicity, culture—and more
generally: history—which are, "by definition," secular.

This intellectual exercise merits a careful consideration. As aforementioned, critics of secularism have already outlined the Christian
roots of the notion of the secular, as well as the "Enlightened" transformations it has gone through. These should not be retraced here.
Suffice it to note that the ideological move instigated by the "ethnicist
intelligentsia" is set against the background of a distinctly European,
Christian history of an evolving relationship between two realms first
outlined by the Church (namely: the religious and the secular) and
later on transformed by the politics of the nation-state.[5] These Jewish
(mostly East-European) ideologues adopted, following their successors in the *haskala* movement, that same secular/secularist perception
of history, painted in noticeably nationalist colors. In order to do so,
they have reconstructed and reinterpreted not only the meaning of the
histories of Jews in immanent (as opposed to transcendental) terms,
but also further developed the very notion of Jewish "religion" to
correspond to the prevalent (Protestant) concept.

The nature of this exercise of distinction, in a projection backward, of the "secular vs. religious" dichotomy on the histories of Jews
can now be better appreciated. The Zionist thinkers concerned have
cast on the histories of Jews a modernist gaze, distinguishing secular realms of this past (i.e., nationality, culture, politics, etc., namely:
"real" history) from "religious" ones (i.e., the spiritual, belief, the apolitical, etc., namely: "religion"). To borrow Amitav Ghosh's (studying
a supposedly totally different case) brilliant formulation, the Zionist
intelligentsia was "laying claim to the future, in the best tradition of
liberalism, by discovering a History to replace the past."[6]

This exercise is based, primarily, on an importation of concepts, perceptions, and categories that are in themselves the products of specific European-Christian history, political interests, and ideological developments. First among these are, of course, the concept "religion" and its "secular" opposite (which, at least in the formative years of Zionist ideology, still lacked an agreed-upon Hebrew translation).[7] This importation is not exempt from the a priori problematic nature of the distinction, and further complicates it by arguing that the histories of Jews could, and should, be read through the same historical-narrative framework used by the European Enlightenment to tell the story of the distinction between religion and politics. These Zionist ideologues are thus able to project the modernist distinction between the religious and the secular, problematic as it is, on the pasts, identities, and ways of lives of Jews, and to read these concepts (religion/religiosity/orthodoxy and secularity/secularism, etc.) backward—that is, to find them to be relevant to sociohistorical contexts in which they and their objects of signification were, quite plainly, meaningless.

This, then, is an anachronistic exercise that combines two complementary inventions: Jewish "religion" and Jewish "secularity." The infrastructure enabling this invention is a third invention, that of nationalism (also constituted on anachronistic narrativity, projecting the constitution of the modern nation, under the sovereignty of the nation-state, onto a distant past[8]).

## "Judaism as Culture" versus a Nietzschean Rebellion Against Tradition

It goes without saying that those Zionist intellectuals who have indeed endeavored to offer substantial rewritings and reinterpretations of Jewish history and identity so as to fit them into an allegedly secular nationalistic framework do not present a single, unified stance vis-à-vis preceding Jewish traditions.[9] One possible way to outline the multiplicity of Zionist stances on this matter is to identify two main pillars upon which it is established. One pillar is represented by Ahad Ha'am. The second, in varying formulations, is represented by Micha Yosef Berdyczewski, Yosef Haim Brenner, Nahman Syrkin, Yitzhak El'azari-Volcani, and others.[10]

Ahad Ha'am represents the stance labeled nowadays as "Judaism as culture." His principal position vis-à-vis tradition is loyal yet confrontational; he demands a reinterpretation of Jewish tradition,

guided by manifest loyalty to its "essence," and driven by a rebellion against the rabbinical authority over its interpretation. One of
the most important aspects of this stance is its tendency to be firmly
based on a deep, extensive knowledge of the building blocks—mainly
texts, but also (Eastern-European) Jewish practices—from which this
tradition is built. The second position is essentially a Nietzschean
rebellion against tradition—indeed, against the "past" itself.[11]

It should be noted that the prevalent way of mapping these
sometime conflicting ideological positions and the ensuing arguments and controversies they entail tends to conflate the two positions, and to endow both Aḥad Ha'am and those Zionist disciples of
Nietzsche with the title of "rebels." However, in this common reading[12] the object of rebellion is not exactly Jewish tradition but rather
Jewish "religion." This prominent reading of Zionism does note, of
course, the differences in both rhetoric and substance characterizing
those rebellious positions. But located firmly inside the secularization narrative—that is, inside secular epistemology as the framework
constituting the historical-ideational reality we encounter—it is often
hard to fully appreciate the nature of the differences distinguishing
the varying position. Yet at other times, it is quite hard to see how
these different ideologues are conflated with each other, presented
to be occupying the same principle position, while they themselves
argue and negate each other in both the most personal and ideological of manners conceivable. (Such, for example, is the controversy
surrounding Brenner's "rebellious" essays of 1910, which won him
Aḥad Ha'am's vehement opposition, resulting in the latter's attempt
to censure Brenner.[13]) The bipolarity "religious vs. secular" enforces
a one-dimensional view of all those ideologues as adopting a "secular" or "secularist" position, which by definition is expected to mean
the opposite of a "religion/religious" position. The differences among
them dissolve into the binary scheme.

Zionist's historiography encourages a misunderstanding of the
issue discussed here, since it adopts the ideological discourse of secular nationalism as the taken-for-granted infrastructure for analyzing
its objects of study (see chapter 4). This is apparent, for example,
in Shimoni's work: while carefully outlining Aḥad Ha'am's complicated position toward Jewish tradition, he nevertheless sums it up
in the crude terminology of the religious-secular, traditional-modern,
and benighted-enlightened dichotomies. Traditional Jewish elements
and enlightened modernism appear as standing, by definition, on

the opposite sides of a formidable divide.[14] This dichotomous think-ing paints Aḥad Ha'am's project not as a dialogue, but rather as an unfinished, somewhat lacking project of secularization: "The seminal importance of Aḥad Ha'am's thought for the inner development of Zionism lay [. . .] in the implications of his approach for shaping the identity of the new national Jew. It was to be a secularized identity *but* one bound by certain norms rooted in the religion-saturated cultural heritage of the Jewish nation."[15] The important word here is "but"; the tying together of secularized identity with "religion-saturated" tradition is not a matter of "and" or "also"—that is, of an interpreta-tion that combines "new" readings (European, Positivist ones) into a continuous process of dialoguing with tradition; Rather, it is a matter of "but"—that is, an association of contradictory, opposing elements.

The issue I wish to focus on herein is the implications of this Zionist "secularization" on the Jew's position in relation to her Jew-ish tradition.

## Aḥad Ha'am: "Secularization" or a "National Theology"?

Aḥad Ha'am[16] is commonly identified as the main spokesperson for those wishing to reinterpret Jewish tradition as a "culture" as opposed to "religion."[17] Indeed, the conceptual distinction between "religion" and "culture" is critical for comprehending Aḥad Ha'am's understanding of Jewish tradition. His cultural project outlines a reinterpretation of tradition through an imported conceptual lens; he adopts his constitutive, critical concepts from European Empiricism and Positivism, relying on thinkers such as John Locke, David Hume, John Stuart Mill, and Herbert Spencer.[18]

### A Universal Secularization in a Jewish Guise

In certain readings, the aforementioned European men are among the most pronounced articulators of modern, "scientistic" atheism.[19] Their scientific worldview is premised on the thesis of secularization, and especially on the modern, apolitical concept of "religion," discussed in chapter 1. Inspired by Spencer, for example, Aḥad Ha'am finds a supposedly non-metaphysical anchor for understanding the history of the Jewish people: the life instinct, or "will to life" (*ḥefetz ḥaqiyum haleumi* in Aḥad Ha'am's Hebrew) of the collective organism (which he views, of course, in terms of nationalism).[20] By this he is able to transform the traditional argument regarding the importance of tradition in preserving the group's vitality, and to argue that the group survives by its own life-instinct (like any other organism); tradition, religion, belief, practice/observance—and maybe most important than all, culture—are mere functions of this supposedly natural instinct, or "Will." Seemingly, this ideational exercise is the root of Aḥad Ha'am's secularization of Judaism. It "enabled him to relegate religion to the status of a subsidiary aspect of culture and to shift his Jewish self-understanding from the traditionalist transcendental basis to a secular immanent basis."[21]

Aḥad Ha'am adopts the secularization narrative in its whole. As Kurzweil notes,

> Out of concern for the continuity and survival of Judaism, Aḥad Ha'am made an effort to save it, on the one hand, from total assimilation, and, on the other hand, from a purely political-national interpretation, as it was expressed after Herzl's emergence. But Aḥad Ha'am accepts as a basic premise the very secular interpretation of Judaism, the loss of belief in the living God. He sees it as a natural sign of the degree to which contemporary Judaism has evolved. He teaches the perplexed of his time to view the way of Israel and the way of Judaism through eyes that have been liberated from the limited view that characterized the stage of naïve belief, which has passed and gone forever.[22]

Aḥad Ha'am tells, in this regard, a simple historical narrative of gradual secularization. This story, like the narrative of secularization more generally, has two main chapters: the traditional past, in which "everyone was religious" and "religion was everything"; and the modern present, in which religion has declined, and is overcome by rational science and nationalist politics. The meaning and essence of the alleged traditional religiosity of the past is quite straightforward: religion means belief and duty (at least in principle) to observe the dictates of Jewish law. As Aḥad Ha'am explains: "In the past, it would seem to everyone among the People of Israel rather obvious that a real Jew [. . .] is exclusively one who believes wholeheartedly in the doctrines of Jewish religion and is careful (or at least tries to be careful) to observe all of its commandments."[23]

Moreover, this "religious" understanding of the meaning of Juda-
ism/Jewishness was also prevalent among the first secularized Jews,
the *maskilim*: "They, too, the '*maskilim*' themselves, had always felt
in their hearts that by distancing themselves from religion they have
also distanced themselves from the people, that they have become
its 'Others,' and that they cannot reunite with [the people] unless it
grows close to them; unless it, too, becomes an 'Other.' "[24]
The second chapter of this Zionist narrative of Jewish secularization is the chapter of (secular) nationalism, tying the two—that is,
secularization and nationalism—together:

> Now things have changed. Thousands of Israelite individu-
> als, some having been educated outside the boundaries of
> Judaism from childhood [. . .] and some having rebelled
> against it as they matured [. . .] have now returned to their
> people and have cogently raised the flag of Jewish national-
> ism, without also returning to the fold of Jewish religion,
> holding its opinions or observing its directives. And these
> new Jews do not at all feel themselves separated from the
> people due to the religious worldview.[25]

Moreover, this also explains why the secularization of the *maskilim*
was lacking, noting their failure to offer a meaningful (nationalist)
alternative to religion.[26]

## Secularization, Ethics, and Myth

Aḥad Ha'am's sense of secularization means, then, the replacement
of religion with national pride (or, in his own terminology, utilizing
contemporaneous European discourse: "the racial sentiment," *regesh
hageza'*[27]) as that which defines the Jewish world. This can be considered a secularizing exercise (and not a substitution of one theological
system, a "religious" one, with another, "national" or "nationalistic"
one) only of we view, following Herbert Spencer's cue (as does Aḥad
Ha'am) national pride or patriotism as a natural fact, and not as a
matter of social construction.
In any event, this notion raises some questions, the answers to
which direct us beyond the realm of rationalist scientism and into the
realm of mythic perception. For even if we do accept this somewhat
murky notion of the national Will, Aḥad Ha'am's notion of secularization is still far from being a coherent idea.[28] Especially apparent

is the fact that Aḥad Ha'am does not forgo the use of metaphysical arguments[29] that could be read as prototypically theological.[30]

This theology centers on the Jewish nation's realization of its ethical or moral calling. In this sense, Aḥad Ha'am's "secularization" defies the traditional theological worldview by substituting its "religious" objects with "national" ones. In Kurzweil's critical reading, this is a doctrine of a "theology-without-a-God, of a belief in the Chosen People without a chooser, of the prophecy of the messenger without a sender."[31] Kurzweil's fury is aimed at what he views as the ideational mediocrity of that "Russian *maskil*,"[32] Aḥad Ha'am. Specifically, he takes issue with the way in which Aḥad Ha'am's secularization distorts the traditional Jewish stance. But Kurzweil, too, clearly sees that Aḥad Ha'am's doctrine amounts to a theology, based on the notion of the people's manifest destiny, of its being "chosen," driven by Aḥad Ha'am's own sense of prophetic mission. The "secularization" he offers seems to focus on the exclusion of the traditional God from the equation, substituting Him with the national "will to life"—an abstract and transcendental concept in for itself.

Aḥad Ha'am did not rely solely on the natural and allegedly universal power of the national "will to life" for the preservation of the collective continuity of the Jewish people. The emphasis he put on the particularistic, moral and ethical mission(s) of the nation clearly shows that he, too, viewed as meaningless the notion of a secularization based on allegedly universal and natural ideas.

Indeed, if the national "will to life" was the whole story, then the reader must wonder: If this is a purely natural matter, an evolutionary fact of the collective organism's life, why must the individuals composing the collective be concerned with its survival? Why, in other words, should individual Jews worry about Jewish continuity if collective existence is a universal matter of the laws of nature, which, by definition, cannot be dependent upon the will of the individuals? What compels us, as individuals, to mobilize for the advancement of "national morality"?

"Reduced to simple terms," Shimoni summarizes, "it may be said that Aḥad Ha'am conveyed a double message to the individual secularized Jew:

> [I]n positivist terms it assured him that Jewish survival was a deterministic function of an instinctive will to life that could find alternatives even for the former indomitable role of religious faith and practice; in idealistic terms, Jews

must actively will their survival as a nation, for, by the prototypically nationalist lights of Aḥad Ha'am, there was no higher form of human association than the nation. Its attributes—such as its language, the territory with which it was associated, its literary heritage—stood at the peak of the scale of values binding upon and endowing meaning and purpose to the lives of human beings.[33]

In other words, Aḥad Ha'am wishes, first, to negate the traditional Jewish theology (what he would name "religion"). And in a complementary move (which, it appears, encapsulates the essence of Zionist secularism) he wishes to replace it with a national theology, one that he would identify as "secular."[34]

This argument is far from being novel. Already in 1913, Yitzḥak El'azari-Volcani (Wilkanski; he also used the pen name A. Tzioni) titled his criticism of what he viewed as Aḥad Ha'am's deficient secularism "The National Theology."[35] El'azari-Volcani was one of the more methodical of the Zionist thinkers to demand a separation between what they viewed as a "Hebrew," essentially secular identity and "Jewish religion."[36] El'azari-Volcani uses the term "theology" to protest against a teleological line of thought that characterizes Aḥad Ha'am's allegedly secular conception of Judaism. This theology-teleology remains loyal to the traditional notion of manifest destiny, of the people having been chosen, since it sees the future of Judaism as ascribed in a higher *telos* or purpose, which is external to the nation itself. (This is the root of Aḥad Ha'am's celebrated notion of "national morality.") El'azari-Volcani's secularism cannot accept this: just as he would not accept "religious" ideas, what he terms "a cosmological theology," which sees the future of the nation as depending upon God, so would he not accept the national theology that remains focused on an element external to itself for realizing the meaning and purpose of its very existence. In El'azari-Volcani's secular framework, this meaning-instilling *telos* must be "internal," that is, to be located within the nation itself: the nation is "a purpose in for itself."[37]

It is important to note that the common identification of Aḥad Ha'am as a primary agent of Jewish secularization tends to withstand (or ignore) this criticism. This, I believe, can be explained by the persistent signification of the concept of "religion"; as long as Aḥad Ha'am is not "religious" he is secular, even if he presents, in a rather straightforward manner, a comprehensive formulation of a "national theology."

*A National Theology*

How, then, does Aḥad Ha'am construct the relationship between the new national theology he is devising and preceding Jewish traditions? As we shall see, this is a highly complicated relationship that combines dependency and loyalty with rebellion and independence.

At the root of his national theology lies the ethnic, or racial constitutive myth (i.e., it has to do with one's biological ancestry, her "blood") as a substitute for the traditional mythology of Jewish collectivity or peoplehood.

This can be better understood if we consider, as Aḥad Ha'am elusively suggests we do, the simple yet profound question: Why would, or should one be Jewish? (or, more simply, "Why be a Jew?") What, in other words, compels the individual to identify with a certain collective, history, identity, etc.? The traditional constitutive myth, speaking of the People of Israel as an extended family of tribes who became a nation through a covenant with God, offers a rather straightforward answer: the covenant demands so. Aḥad Ha'am's national, supposedly secular mythology prefers to speak of ethnicity, or racial genealogy as annulling the very need to reflect upon this profound question, making the answer allegedly self-evident.[38]

Aḥad Ha'am presents himself, and is represented by others, as having brought the "rational," "scientific," "positivist," etc. conceptions of his (modern) times to the world of Judaism; this, in effect, is the meaning of his secularization of Judaism. But when it comes to the fundamental issue (especially for a project of Jewish nationalism) of Jewish identity, he adopts a distinctively mythic tone. For him, the most essential reasoning for one's belonging to one's nation, the root of Jewish collective existence, is beyond what may be put in words. Hence, the "Jewish sentiment"—that which compels one to identify with one's nation and express one's nationalism—is, in the words of a certain "Western rabbi" whom Aḥad Ha'am quotes approvingly,[39] "an instinctive sense that cannot be put in words."[40]

The ultimate answer to the question "Why be a Jew?" then, is beyond reasoning. In this, Aḥad Ha'am seems to be fully in agreement with the "Western rabbi" he is quoting:[41]

> Why are we Jewish? How alien is this very question! Ask
> the fire why does it burn! Ask the sun why does it shine!
> Ask the tree why does it grow! . . . In the same vein, ask

the Jew, why is he a Jew. We cannot but be what we are. It is inside us, without our choosing it, it is one of the laws of our nature [. . .] It emanates and rises from the depths of our soul, it is part of our heart! It cannot be annulled, defeated, denied [. . .].

Just try to uproot if from your heart! You cannot! It is stronger than us. [. . .]

We cannot—even if we wish this a thousand times—detach from the roots of our being. The will to life [*hefetz haqiyum*] rebels against extinction [. . .].

No, it is not the Jewish worldview, not the Jewish teachings [Torah], not the Jewish belief—this are not the original cause, the initial motive; rather, the Jewish sentiment, an instinctive sentiment that cannot be defined in words; call it however you wish to, call it blood kinship [*qirvat hadam*], call it the racial sentiment [*regesh hageza'*], or the spirit of the nation [*ruah haleom*], but better than all would be that you call it: the Hebrew heart![42]

The Jew, then, is a Jew because she is a Jew. Her Jewish identity emanates from the (mythic) essence of her being. Just as the sun shines because it is the sun: they and their essences are the same. This essentialist identification is what stands at the root of the nonlinear, analogical thought, usually contrasted with rational, linear thought.[43] A Jew, according to this mythic conception, cannot avoid-evade her Jewish identity; hence, there is no reason to explain or explicate the *meaning* of this identity. This, clearly, is a tautology. Thus Ahad Ha'am's discussion veers away from the central issue with which, supposedly, he was concerned in the first place.

Yet this contradicts Ahad Ha'am's own assertion that the Jewish identity demands the individual's loyalty and devotion; She is obliged to preserve this identity. Indeed, one of the primary goals of the national theology he outlines is to prevent the assimilation of Jews within the non-Jewish majority. It would do so by encouraging Jews to "compete" with the non-Jews, instead of "imitating" them.[44]

## Ahad Ha'am's Conception of Religion and Tradition

The sources of Ahad Ha'am's conception of religion demand a careful consideration. The way he understands religion plays a major role in his—our—ability to break away from its grip: this understanding allows us to identify religion as relatively insignificant, "only one of the forms constituting culture,"[45] hence a construct we can safely dispose of.

As aforementioned, this understanding of religion nourishes on the positivist ideas of English Empiricism. David Hume's influence on Aḥad Ha'am's thought is especially apparent. Hume has developed and articulated the functionalist (negative) conception of religion. This conception posits that religion—or, to be accurate, religious belief, as the Humean conception of religion already assumes that belief is the essence of religion—may have had a "functional logic" in ancient times. This belief (which modern science knows to be essentially wrong) had functioned, in the past, as an organizing, interpretive agent, instilling reality with meaning. But clearly, modern times, enriched as they are by rational, scientific thought, putting positivist empiricism above all other judgments—an epoch in which science and rationalism triumph over religion (or, again, religious belief)—simply does not have a need anymore for religion. In this sense, Hume brings Thomas Hobbes's atheistic premises into fruition.[46]

Hume can thus be identified as a prominent articulator of the secular, atheist tradition (the irony instilled in this notion is too strong to go uncommented) that has developed in England. In his famous discussion of belief in miracles Hume developed the notion, which has since become an accepted truism, that this belief (which he sees as the essence of religion) is a barbaric idea, with which enlightened civilization has nothing to do. Religion, he states, does not stand up to the test of rationalism; it is a superstitious, irrational belief. Hume has in effect built the line of argument usually associated with Karl Marx, that religion is kind of a brainwash, and that the role of rational science is to expose the lie upon which it is based.[47] And, to return to the subject matter of the current discussion, Aḥad Ha'am seems to adopt this conception of religion wholeheartedly.

But Aḥad Ha'am's understanding of tradition is more nuanced and complex. He acknowledges that one's identity, her consciousness itself, is built by the traditional systems from which she nourishes. Now, the image he uses to explicate this notion, in the context of his discussion of European anti-Semitic tradition, might create the impression that Aḥad Ha'am adopts the antimony, dominant in the rebelling Nietzschean thought (see below), between tradition and liberty; that he views personal autonomy as necessarily demanding breaking away from tradition.[48] His use of the metaphor of hypnosis to describe the way in which tradition constitutes our individual and collective consciousness surely plays into this impression:

> It may, therefore, be said with justice that every individual member of society carries in his own being thousands of hidden hypnotic agents, whose commands are stern and peremptory. "Such and such shall be your opinions; such and such your actions." The individual obeys, unconsciously. His opinions and his actions are framed to order. At the same time, he finds cogent arguments in favor of his opinions, and sound reasons for his actions. He is not conscious that it is the spirit of other men that thinks in his brain and actuates his hand, while his own essential spirit, his Inner Ego, is sometimes utterly at variance with the resulting ideas and actions, but cannot make its voice heard because of the thousand tongues of the external Ego [. . .] in which society enfolds him.[49]

Ahad Ha'am's tone is surely negative. (Again, the context in which he voices these ideas is a discussion on anti-Semitism.) But also apparent is his appreciation of tradition's constitutive role. Moreover, he charts a complex process of a natural change in tradition, of an interaction between competing traditions, and also of a rupture in tradition.[50] In other words, he acknowledges tradition's dynamism. There is no doubt that he views himself as one of those "men of wisdom and foresight [who] observe and proclaim the contradiction between the old and the new before the new has succeeded in secretly undermining the strength of the old."[51]

Being a man of foresight, one who clearly sees the inevitable collision between the traditional, "religious" ways of the past and the modern, rational present, Ahad Ha'am calls for a Jewish reform of a kind. This is to be a reform in the way Judaism is lived and understood. (Needless to say, this should not be identified with Liberal Judaism or the Reform movement, which Ahad Ha'am vehemently rebuts. After all, the reform propagated by Liberal Judaism is "religious," not "national" in nature.) As Berdyczewski, out of explicit disagreement, summarizes it, Ahad Ha'am claims that "there is no way to better the situation unless the heart is cured first, and for this [the nation] must be driven away from the graves of its ancestors and instilled with new life, a humane and national life; for this, fundamental changes in the course of its world and the value of its life are required."[52]

As Berdyczewski critically (if not cynically) argues, this is a reform of a traditional nature. That is, it revolves around a continuous dialogue with tradition, based on a deep knowledge of it. Aḥad Ha'am laments the muting of dialogue and the freezing of dynamism in Jewish tradition. According to his analysis, the disaster that befell the Jewish People is the replacement of such dialogue with blind obedience. He describes it as the difference between a "literary people" and "the people of the book." The latter—that which for generations has been celebrated by Jews—he condemns:

> Our tragedy is that we are not a literary people ['am sifruti] but rather the people of the book ['am hasefer]. The difference between the two is immense. Literature, like the people, is a living force that goes through transformations. You can call a people "literary" only if its life and the life of its literature [. . .] develop together [. . .] But the people of the book is the book's slave, a people whose soul escaped its heart and resides fully within the written. For [this people] the book is aimed not to enrich the heart with new powers, but rather to weaken it and degrade it so it would no longer have the courage to operate "in for itself and according to its needs," but rather all through the text.[53]

"Literature" here is clearly a signifier for "tradition" and "culture." For Aḥad Ha'am, Jewish tradition has fossilized, turning into a heavy burden that smothers the national spirit. In its fossilized state, tradition becomes a menace, and Aḥad Ha'am's position demands that we shake it off our backs. But he also wishes we do so not by foregoing tradition altogether, but rather by preserving its essence. This would be done by rewriting tradition so as to revive and evolve it.

The reform propagated by Aḥad Ha'am thus revolves around what he identifies as the "essence" of Judaism and Jewish identity— on which, by definition, there cannot be room for compromise. This marks him as the "most essentialist" among the Zionist secularizers, that is as speaking for a normative, obliging loyalty to what he identifies as the historical Jewish "culture." Given that the "old" book has fossilized, a (re-)writing a "new" Jewish book is required. Thus he paraphrases Jewish luminaries such as Rabbi Yehuda HaNasi (Judah the Prince, the chief redactor and editor of the Mishnah) and Maimonides, declaring: "We require a new book."[54] Interestingly, this call comes as a prelude to his (ultimately unfinished) project of curating a Jewish encyclopedia.

## The Meaning of Secularity

What, then, does secularity mean for Aḥad Ha'am? He seems to adopt the positivist narrative of secularization as the inevitable process in which religious belief declines and scientific authority replaces religious authority. Secularization for him is first the adoption of a rationalist worldview (in its nationalistic interpretation that views "national vitality" as an empirical phenomenon, fully in tune with rationalism; more on this below). It is the process of "the displacement of rabbinical religious authority over the lives of Jews by advancing scientific knowledge [. . .] in which rabbinical authority and influence was rapidly declining."[55]

Aḥad Ha'am's rationalist-empiricist view is nationalistic at root. It deems the nation's existence as a fact, a fact of nature even, and celebrates it as more inclusive and surely of higher importance than the limited realm of "religious" culture. In this view, Jewish "religion" is an expression of a certain stage in the historical-cultural evolution of the Jewish people; it is far from capturing the essence of the people in its wholeness. This wholeness, in turn, is manifested in Jewish nationalism, which also encompasses religion. As Aḥad Ha'am puts it: "In my view our religion is national, that is to say, it is a product of our national spirit, but the reverse is not true. If it is impossible to be a Jew in the religious sense without acknowledging our nationality, it is possible to be a Jew in the national sense without accepting many things in which religion requires belief."[56] Note that religion is, once again, reduced to belief.

Contrary to his "Nietzschean," "rebelling" counterparts—those Zionist ideologues who (allegedly) wish to cast the yoke of their Jewish traditions off their backs in its whole—Aḥad Ha'am, the father of "*Jewish* secularism" (as opposed, for example, to "universal secularism"), does not see secularism, i.e., the abandonment of religion as a system of belief, as necessitating the rejection of other "religious" dimensions.

One of the more interesting distinctions used by Aḥad Ha'am in this context is that separating religion, (or, to be accurate, religious belief, or religion as belief), which, of course, has lost its raison d'être

(taking with it also the validity of the observance of religious commandments, but not of the essences these practices manifested), from
a Jewish "religious sentiment": "One could be possessed of religious
feeling, although without religious belief . . . beliefs can change completely, yet feeling may remain."[57] To the best of my understanding,
this "religious sentiment" is what Aḥad Ha'am would like to identify
as the essential Jewish substance, upon which the wider historical
construct (now defunct) of belief and commandments is built.

Perhaps most important of all—indeed, "No aspect of Aḥad
Ha'am's nationalist ideology was more significant,"[58]—is his "essentialist" argument, according to which secularization does not free the
Jew from normative duties, that are immanently tied to Jewish tradition. Primary among these is what he calls "the national morals."
These "morals," which are rooted primarily in the "religious" proph-
ecies of the Hebrew Bible, bind even those who do not believe in
scripture. In Berdyczewski's biting formulation, "Aḥad Ha'am wishes
to find some kind of air that surrounds the People of Israel [. . .] and
finds in place of the religion that is given to the heart the Israelite
national morals [. . .] National morals shall save us by giving us a
general basis for our actions."[59]

Indeed, the distinction between "morals" and "religion" is central to Aḥad Ha'am's thought. It would not be an overstatement to call
it the core of his secularization: he approves of "Jewish morals" and
demands that Jews remain loyal to it, a "religious" loyalty even, while
he disapproves of "Jewish religion," and calls for its abandonment.

The reduction of "religion" into mere belief is essential for the
Humean negating explanation of religion. It paves the ground for its
replacement by science. This substitution was not possible prior to
the modern iteration of "religion" (a matter covered in chapter 1).
For the purpose of the current discussion it is important to see how
this idea is translated and adapted as it is imported by Aḥad Ha'am
into a Jewish context. Aḥad Ha'am surely knows that halachic Jewish
tradition does not necessarily sanctify belief as the core, essential matter of Jewish law, and surely halachic Judaism could not be reduced
to matters of belief or "faith." But this reductionism enables Aḥad
Ha'am to draw a distinction between "religion" (that is, irrational
belief) and other, national dimensions (practical, literary, historical,
political, etc.), which he identifies as not religious, that is, as secular.
This enables him to replace the religious, wrong belief with a new
belief, one that focuses on the "culture" or "the will to life" of the

Jewish people—that is, with the belief in the nation. A theology, then, but one that replaces belief in God with belief in the nation. Or, as summarized by Berdyczewski, "the matter of the national morals is just a made up principle, like the other principles, that come and go, come and go. . . ."[60]

## Judaism as Culture

Aḥad Ha'am's proposed substitution for "religious belief" is commonly labeled "Judaism as culture." But what does this term mean? What is "culture"? In effect, Aḥad Ha'am's intellectual project is built on the opposition between two Jewish cultures: One is "old" and religious, the other "new" and not religious. In other words, he does identify religion as a culture, but sees it as outdated, and calls for its substitution by a Jewish culture of another kind, a "secular" one. Needless to say, this distinction assumes the religious-secular binary from the outset. For Aḥad Ha'am, "our national culture," the secular one, which is the root of (secular) Jewish national identity, is composed of science, art, literature, and language; excluding religion, of course.[61]

One of the clearer expressions of the normative aspect of this conception of Judaism as culture—or, in other words, the dialogue of Aḥad Ha'am's proposed cultural project with its Jewish tradition—is its focus on the positive content of the definition of Jewish identity. Aḥad Ha'am does not accept the position, prevalent among secularized European Jews (as among non-Jewish secularizers), that secularization means liberation from a positively normative observance of any (Jewish) kind. He accepts the traditional position that in order for a person to be authentically identified as Jewish this identification must bear some essential, practical (or, in his terminology, "moral") content. The main thrust of the argument Aḥad Ha'am makes in this context is that

> in the Jewish cultural heritage there inhered a distinctive morality, in this case one that differed from the equally distinctive morality of the Christian heritage. There was, in other words, an identifiable essence of Jewishness and the new national Jew remained bound to it no less than he was bound to the Hebrew language and literature, to Eretz Israel, and to identification with Jews as a collective social entity.[62]

This argument is derived from a nuanced understanding of traditions' constitutive role. Aḥad Ha'am sees the ineffectiveness of the Zionist Nietzschean rebellion (see below) that allegedly wishes to erase tradition—indeed, erase history itself—in the name of the individual's and the nation's liberation from the bonds of the past. The group of Zionist Nietzschean ideologues, "which seeks salvation in a Future not connected with our Past, and believes that after a history extending over thousands of years a people can begin all over again, like a newborn child"[63] and create for itself a new national land, a new national life and goals, is "far more dangerous" than Orthodox, rabbinical Judaism, which remains passive in the face of history. This is so since the Nietzschean rebellion is aimed at the liberation of "the particular temporary Ego of each individual Jew," and is willing to sacrifice for this cause "the national Ego."[64]

Jewish tradition's positive content—to which Aḥad Ha'am saw the national project and the secular Jew essentially bound—includes primarily "our homeland and its [Jewish] settlers, the language of our forefathers and its literature, the memory of our ancestors and their history, the fundamental customs of our forefathers and their manner of national life through the generations."[65] Indeed, such a "thick" list makes it quite difficult to understand the meaning of "secularization," for which Aḥad Ha'am speaks (or with which his name is associated). We can grasp the meaning of this secularization only if we bear in mind that hovering above this list—and outside of it—is the spirit of "religion." The latter is unambiguously absent from the set of values Aḥad Ha'am views as enduring and compelling the secular Jew as much as they do the Orthodox. This is what enables him to view himself as "liberated" (*ḥofshi*) or "not-religious" (hence, secular).

In any event, this is where the positive content of the dialogue with tradition propagated by Aḥad Ha'am is clarified. A renewed understanding of the essence of Judaism necessitates a deep knowledge of its tradition. It demands an intimate familiarity with its various layers, its practices, its texts, its history, and its language. Only through such deep knowledge would a reinterpretation—such that would entail an updated realization of Jewish essence—become viable. Aḥad Ha'am personified this in a manner rarely matched by others.[66] Having been an outstanding student at a "traditional" yeshiva during his adolescence, he enjoyed a truly intimate, unmediated familiarity with the traditional "materials," and he has repeatedly made use of them to exemplify his interpretive (allegedly secular) arguments. He repeatedly makes use of his deep knowledge of tradition (textual, or otherwise) for basing arguments regarding the ways in which the essential messages instilled in this tradition should be understood in the present.[67] Not for nothing, Berdyczewski finds foul in the fact that the supposed secular Aḥad Ha'am offers an interpretation of the present through addressing traditional texts, and bases his arguments on "evidence from religious philosophy, from Hassidism, etc."[68]

## Religious and Secular People

Aḥad Ha'am's conception of culture also gives birth to what would become the all too common division of labor between "religious" (or "Orthodox"; modern Hebrew synonymizes the terms) and "secular" Jews in Israel; "religious" culture and "secular" culture give birth to people who are religious or secular, and each group has a sphere of cultural action to which it is responsible. As put by Shimoni, summarizing the cultural program outlined by Aḥad Ha'am:

> [T]he secular national Jews and the orthodox national Jews, each independently and by its own lights, ought to foster Jewish cultural revival. There was a major task to be performed by each section. The orthodox had to reform their traditionalist education so as to imbue it with the national spirit, no less than the secular Zionists had to develop a new enlightened national education.[69]

The national framework requires "unity," or cooperation between these two opposing camps; but the essential distinction between them is a foundational premise of the cultural and social scheme to which Aḥad Ha'am strives. The "Bnei Moshe" society, in whose foundation Aḥad Ha'am played a central role, was supposed to embody the unity produced by such a cooperation, based on what may be described as a dual dialogue with tradition: "that the secularists retain a sense of respect for those religious traditions that had national value while the religious be open-minded about modern knowledge and education."[70]

This notion is premised, then, on the existence of two "types" of Jews.[71] Cooperation and unity between the two sides take for granted and naturally re-present the essential opposition separating them from each other. It also identifies them as the poles defining the field of modern, national Jewish identity and of Jewish traditions in its entirety.[72] Zionist discourse takes this opposition for granted, and it is prevalent among those who identify through it—that is "religious" and "secular" Jews.

Aḥad Ha'am also outlines what would later become a common (secular) Zionist practice among the Zionist settlers in Palestine and in the State of Israel: On the one hand, a negation of Liberal or Reform Judaism (since, given its definition of Judaism as a religion, which also disregards Jewish law, it is viewed as abandoning the Jewish "substance," especially in its national iteration); and on the other hand, a criticism of Jewish Orthodoxy for failing to evolve. In the middle of these two negations lies the principle willingness for what is seen as a "compromise" with those identified as religious, in the name of national unity.[73]

This compromise is supposedly justified by loyalty to the Jewish essence: if a compromise with the religious Jews is to bring about the proper, national consciousness, then the price it embodies (i.e., giving up on certain other principles) is defensible. Aḥad Ha'am writes:

> Do you expect all the Jews to become free-thinkers? I only wish we might have a real people in Eretz Israel, even if it were all orthodox, not in the uncouth fashion [. . .] but decent civilized men like the Christian Englishmen whom I meet here. I should be very happy if I could hope to live to fight against orthodoxy of that type in Eretz Israel.[74]

It is hard to overlook the lack of coherence in Aḥad Ha'am's position. He seems to be tied to a framework that presumes the binary opposition between Jewish tradition and modern national identity, or between religion and secularity/secularism, as he tries to "bridge" the tension between these two poles. This act of bridging forces him to "compromise" in matters pertaining to the definition of the modern present as liberated from commitment to tradition. And indeed, the "more absolutist" among the Zionist secularists—that is, those who adopt the Nietzschean rebelling position and view themselves as supposedly wholly liberated from the bonds of tradition—would argue against Aḥad Ha'am that his interpretation, and the willingness to compromise it carries, is in effect an implied acceptance of the Orthodox claim to Jewish authenticity. These critics have their own inconsistencies, and I shall address those shortly. For now, suffice is to note the dominance of the binary distinction, the constitutive dichotomies of "religion vs. secularity" and "tradition vs. modernity," in the thought of Aḥad Ha'am and his critics alike. Like the Zionist historiographers succeeding them, contemporaneous critics of Aḥad Ha'am, who also built their identity on what they viewed as an essential opposition between Jewish tradition and modern (national) Jewish identity, viewed Aḥad Ha'am as attempting to combine two contradictory poles, that cannot, by definition, cohabitate. This opposition thus became "by far the most significant of the controversies that engaged the secular Zionist intelligentsia."[75]

## Secularism as a Rebellion Against Tradition: Micha Yosef Berdyczewski[76]

*Is a Rebellion Against Nature Possible?*

The main challenge against Aḥad Ha'am came from those who nurtured, inspired by the philosophy of Nietzsche, a defiant stance against Jewish tradition. Defiance, in this context, is rather taken for granted, positioned as it is as a local, Jewish-European expression of a wider phenomenon of revolting against various "old" systems— moral, cultural, religious, etc.—that are deemed corrupt. The motive for rebellion seems to be self-explanatory; it is the *bon ton* of its time. The main challenge facing the Zionist rebellious stance is, accordingly, not to justify defiance or to explain its motives, but rather to explain or justify the lasting commitment to Jewish nationalism. Why, in other words, should one (whose origins, granted, are Jewish) stick to Jewish identity? And what is the essential content of this identity?

The answer offered by these Zionist-Nietzschean thinkers derives greatly from the organic notion of nationalism and ethnicity prevalent in Eastern-Europe. It presents identity (Jewish, in this case), as a quintessentially deterministic matter of one's "blood" or "race." In the terminology common today, these "blood"-focused ideas[77] of origin and identity are usually signified by the term "ethnicity." Shimoni sums it approvingly as "the normal, natural bonds of ethnicity."[78] In any event, to a not-insignificant degree, this stance tends to internalize the anti-Jewish view prevalent in Eastern-Europe of the time: A Jew is a Jew, no matter what she does with her tradition. Jewishness is an organic, immanent fact, and therefore the positive or negative, rebellious or loyal position of the individual Jew toward her tradition is irrelevant to the fundamental fact of her Jewishness.

It is not surprising that the combination of these two elements: an individual's rebellion against what she in actuality cannot shed away (that is, her organic identity) brought to life a high degree of ambivalence, if not an outright contradiction between the various components of these ideologues' identity and ideology. Thus, for example, Shimoni describes Berdyczewski's rebelling position as "the very epitome of the ambivalence toward the Jewish religious heritage and the attraction to secular Western culture that characterized the nationalist Jewish intelligentsia of Eastern-Europe."[79] In the same vein, he identifies "[t]he sheer poignancy and anguish that attended his onslaught on rabbinic traditionalism" as attesting to "his ultimate rootedness in the old values,"[80] against which he allegedly rebels.

Shimoni's description both captures the ambivalence characterizing the defiant stance and testifies to the (secularist) normative premise and epistemology used by Zionist historiography as it attempts to analyze this stance. Note, for example, Shimoni's use of terms such as "Jewish religious heritage" (expressing the notion of the "religious past," that is, the past being defined through religion), and "secular Western culture" (expressing the notion of modern European culture as "secular" and "universal" by definition), as well as his identification of "rabbinic traditionalism" with "the old values." Beyond this, it is also worth noting the way in which Shimoni identifies the existential stance of Berdyczewski's and others as viewing tradition as delimiting and suffocating, while European culture (that is: the European *tradition*) is seen as inherently liberating, holding the promise of redemption: "The dilemma of the uprooted, alienated *maskil* Jew, fettered by the chains of tradition and craving for the freedom of modern European culture."[81]

*Tradition and Liberty*

As aforementioned, the distinction commonly drawn between Aḥad Ha'am and Berdyczewski (and other "rebels") focuses on the object of rebellion. While Aḥad Ha'am defies rabbinical authority, and claims for himself (and for the national "will to life") the authority and the right to dialogue with tradition and to offer a better, modern interpretation for it, Berdyczewski seems (and views himself) to be rebelling against tradition itself, out of a call, at least rhetorically, for a complete liberation from its shackles, achieved from an a priori position of absolute individual sovereignty. As the motto to one of his essays declares (quoting Nietzsche): "If a temple is to be erected a temple must be destroyed."[82]

Since both Aḥad Ha'am and Berdyczewski are positioned firmly inside the context of a "secularization" discourse, they both signify their objects of contention as "religion"; they both self-identify, positively so, as rebelling against religion (usually using the Hebrew "dat"). Zionist historiography follows their cue, viewing both Aḥad Ha'am and Berdyczewski as expressing an essentially identical secular drive. But, as I noted earlier, the framing of the discussion of these ideologues in its entirety as a rebellion against "religion," or simply as "secularization" brings about great confusion. For one thing, it ties together men who viewed each other as ultimate adversaries, and were fiercely critical of the other's ideas.[83]

Shimoni estimates that most of the "secularized" makilim shared Aḥad Ha'am's reinterpretive, dialogical stance.[84] Still, it is hard to overlook the fact that even from Shimoni's historiography itself it is rather clear that the rebelling stance of Berdyczewski's—who "thrust onward uncompromisingly with the haskala revolt"[85]—was the more popular among the "pioneering" Zionist ideologues who settled in Palestine.

Berdyczewski's revolt assumes that tradition means curbing one's liberty. The main dichotomy guiding his thought is the antinomy between tradition and liberty—an especially popular stance among Western intellectuals.[86] Berdyczewski does see the principle value of tradition; there are times, he acknowledges, in which a person remains loyal to his tradition without a trace of criticism and "preserves his heritage and lives in his tradition with a quite heart, carefully observing it, without any questioning of its value and essence." But he sees himself—through the eyes of (his reading of) Nietzschean philosophy, to which he goes back time and again as a source of inspiration—as being "locked in a tight frame of the bonds of tradition, endeavoring to leave it, and to adopt a new life for himself." Thus, there are times in which tradition can play a contributing role, when "the old properties enrich us and fulfill our life." But the final judgment is negative, since such times bear a heavy price: those old properties become a "barrier separating us from nature." His final verdict is decisive: tradition suffocates us and deprives us of our vitality:

"[T]he pain of our ancient heritage burdens us and its weight is heavy. Everything that our heart wants and our brain contemplates is covered by a cloud of traditional and religious concepts, so much so that we cannot breathe."[87]

In short, loyalty to tradition means the surrender of the individual, an "internal submission to the heritage of our ancestry,"[88] that keeps on burdening us even after having lost its vitality. Berdyczewski rejects Aḥad Ha'am's dialogical, dynamic notion of tradition. For Berdyczewski, carrying tradition inevitably means submission, and this submission emaciates the Jew: "We are shadows. And out there the world is big . . . here is life and liberty and we are slaves descending from slaves."[89] Note how he understands the carrying of tradition as a passive act of submission, with no trace of dialogue, reflexivity or criticism: "we are children and grand-children of the preceding generations; but not their closets . . . We must cease to be carriers of books and thoughts that are handed over to us, only handed over."[90] In this picture of one-directional and one-dimensional relation between tradition and its carriers, there is no doubt that the only potential change must be the result of "destruction." This destruction is the basic condition for an "essential and fundamental change in the world of the People of Israel and its spirit."[91]

*Past and Present*

Following Nietzsche—on which Berdyczewski constantly relies, like some sort of an intellectual anchor—and like Descartes and Pascal, Berdyczewski, too, sees tradition as a heavy burden of notions, ideas, ways-of-life, values and rules that originate in the past and are carried by the individual without being questioned. This would almost necessarily make the individual and her nation alienated from their essence:

> We are not ours, our dreams are not ours, our thoughts are not ours, and our will is not the one planted in us. Everything was taught to us in the past, everything passed over to us. Every use of our senses, each one of our observations and thoughts, our imaginings and our heart's wishes, our inclinations and preferences, our desires and yearnings already have names and concepts, expressions and explications, directives and orders, advices and hints—

all prepared and ready in advance. For every relation to
the world outside us, and our inner world, for all of our
wonderings and questions there are already plentiful of
answers. Everything is specific and marked in its borders
and confines, everything is carefully measured and weighted,
in rules and directives, so much so that human beings who
wish to know themselves are helpless, and are unable to
find their "self."[92]

In this vein, Berdyczewski and the members of the "Tze'irim"
(youth) circle claimed that Aḥad Ha'am's propagated notion of an
obliging loyalty to national morals (that is, his loyalty to certain
aspects of Jewish tradition) amounts to a regression "from his original
advocacy of the new national Jew's unlimited free thought."[93] Berdyczewski viewed Aḥad Ha'am as preaching for "our total surrender
and submission to the weaklings of our heritage [*nemushot yerusha-
tenu*]"[94]; or, as his quote from Nietzsche puts it, the Jews are required
to overcome the "rumination, of the historical sense, which is harmful
and ultimately fatal to the living thing."[95] The past, then, asphyxiates
the present: "The past has rejected the present; it took from us the
treasures of the present, and made us carriers, mere carriers."[96]

In Berdyczewski's Nietzschean conception there can be no value
in the past. The rupture with—or release from—the past means that
the latter has lost its meaning for us, in the modern present. This
forfeiture of meaning is what enables the assimilation of Western-
European Jews, a phenomenon Berdyczewski describes as the "step
from East to West"[97] (that is, leaving the religious, "Eastern" Jewish
past, in favor of the "secular" West; The traces of colonial thought are
easily discernable here). Hence, while in the case of other nations the
past may have value (it is apparent from his writings that the Hellenistic tradition has a valuable place in the formation of the modern
Western culture, for example), the Jewish case is different. For the
Jews, the past is dead—or the Jews' tie with it has withered—since
it smothers the present. There is no place, then, for dialoguing with
tradition or reinterpreting it. A complete release is of the essence.

This antinomy between tradition and liberty is tied to another
antinomy prevalent in Zionist thought, namely the one identifying an
abyss separating the traditional past from the modern present, or, in
a terminology more in tune with the Zionist discourse, between the
"old" and the "new" (Jew, in this case). Being a new and liberated Jew,

one who feels himself (in part thanks to his defiance against tradition) to be a "new person who has a new soul," the rebelling intellectual expects to see himself as fully liberated from the "burden" of tradition. He "wakes up" from the sleep forced upon him by tradition, "finds the courage to undermine the foundations of his tradition" and to build a "new" value system, and draws the decisive conclusion: "he must negate the things he used to carefully observe."[98]

We must bear in mind that the name commonly in use among the Zionist ideologues to signify their "non-religious" stance is "*ḥofshi*," i.e., "liberated." This name, in itself, betrays the dominant presence of the first dichotomy mentioned above, pitting tradition as the opposite of liberty. This seems to be especially relevant for Jewish tradition: Berdyczewski's musings give the clear sense that the particular character of Jewish tradition brings about a disjuncture between the Jewish national essence and (traditional) Jewish life. Because of this tradition, "when we come to treat our life-hope we find that we do not have a life at all. . . ."[99] In this vein, he is highly critical of Jewish monotheism, accusing it of having constricted Jewish life to the point of suffocation. Jewish tradition prevents the expansion of the Jewish person's horizons:

> Will the dwellings of Shem [i.e., Jewish life] be forever closed to the beauty of Japheth [i.e., European culture]?
>
> How narrow are thy tents, O Jacob, thy dwellings, O Israel![100]
>
> Thy dwellings, O Israel, have become ruins, your tents are sealed and closed, and outside life goes on, flowing and washing—and it so happens sometimes that a passerby would turn towards the dark alleyways and see the images of those people whose stature has become bent down in front of God [. . .]—and he would become depressed. . . .[101]

In the same vein he concludes that the Greek, pagan, polytheistic heritage—or, indeed: tradition—is far preferable to the monotheistic Jewish tradition, since the former, unlike Judaism, induces a fuller, wider human experience:

> Such is the difference between the People of Israel and the Greeks. The latter had explored the whole land and life in its fullest, they paid attention to what is in the sea and on the land, to the skies above and the earth and all

the host of them; and the former [i.e., the People of Israel] only knew how to build one tower, and everything else but this tower is nothing [. . .] And the People of Israel did not limit themselves to a narrow corner only in regards to their relation to the world, but also in regards to themselves, to their essence and the foundations of their life, they based their being on matters that hang up in the air. . . .[102]

Jewish tradition, then, inhibits; while the Greek tradition expands one's horizons. There can be little doubt which of the two should be chosen—or, indeed, adhered to—by an individual or a nation that wishes to live.

## Body and Spirit

So far, I have focused on two antinomies prevalent in the "rebellious" thought: tradition vs. liberty and new vs. old. These are accompanied in the rebellious Zionist ideology by the opposition between "spirituality" (ruḥaniyut) and "worldliness" (gashmiyut; also translatable as corporality and materialism). Jewish "religion" and tradition are identified as having brought about a deformity of Judaism, rendering it wholly immersed in the spiritual and devoid of any substantive relations with real, "material" or "bodily" reality. Jewish tradition has directed Jews toward the Torah (which is, in this critical reading, spiritual by the very apolitical definition of religion, which Berdyczewski wholeheartedly adopts):

Without paying attention to the rest of the natural conditions that are required for every nation, without which life is impossible; the heavenly air above us, while there is no ground below our feet and a national body for our soul; the excessive focus on the "life in the hereafter" while neglecting the daily life that are needed for inhabiting the world—these have clearly shown what becomes of the life of a people in such extreme spiritual levels . . . They have shown the great damage that we suffered because of it as a nation and as human beings.[103]

The natural "secularist" conclusion, according to Berdyczewski, is that a continuation of a dialogue with tradition, as proposed by Aḥad Ha'am, is but a prolongation of the submission to that external force, that deprives the nation and its individual members of their vitality. It should be noted that the rebelling stance does not view this rupture as happening naturally, but rather as a duty demanded of each individual being liberated. And so, while Aḥad Ha'am remains committed to the idea of dialoguing with tradition, in an attempt to "assemble the new upon the old," Berdyczewski argues that "in actuality, it is the other way around: negation precedes sanction [. . .] there is no building without a preceding destruction, and there is no existence without cessation."[104] There is no room for dialoguing with tradition. Before anything else, it must be shattered, bringing about the complete release of the individual from its bonds. Only then will the stage of building a new tradition take place upon its ruins; "destruction and building;"[105] "The new imperatives will materialize after the old one are annulled."[106]

Against Aḥad Ha'am's suggested "amendments" to Jewish tradition, Berdyczewski, who is situated in this tradition in an unmediated manner, demands "changes": "We require changes, fundamental changes in all of our way of life, thoughts and souls."[107]

This rebellion in enabled by the taken-for-granted presence of the secularization narrative. Thus, in reply to Aḥad Ha'am's argument against the group of Nietzschean Zionist ideologues who wish to bring about "a future without a past,"[108] Berdyczewski argues that European secularization proves that it is possible to begin everything anew: "The assumption that a people cannot, after a long history, begin everything anew does not correspond with the reality of the capitulation of religions in the world."[109]

The secularization narrative enables Berdyczewski to justify his rebellion against tradition with the claim that the national body is larger than mere (religious) tradition; that the national vitality does not depend on tradition. "The wisdom of Israel, [and] the religion of Israel are but various elements, given to each individual according to his wishes and inclinations; but the People of Israel precedes them."[110]

*Between Rebellion and National Duty*

It will not be out of place to remind the reader that we are dealing here with *Zionist* ideologues—that is, people who call for the understanding of Jewish identity in terms of modern European nationalism, and take it for granted that one's identification and belonging as Jewish is of positive value. I mention this obvious piece of context here since Berdyczewski's defiant energy (as is the case with other ideologues, who will be also discussed in chapter 6) may encourage one to wonder whether their defiance against Jewish tradition does not amount to a renunciation of their Jewish identity? In other words, how do they understand the very notion of Jewish belonging, if their energy is focused in its fullest on a negation of what they themselves describe as the infrastructure of the "old Jew," that is, of their history? What, then, defines them as Jewish?

Needless to say, this question occupied these ideologues constantly. Yet as I noted above it seems that the general consensus, shared by both rebels and reinterpreters, is that this question is in actuality irrelevant—or, to be more accurate, it is beyond the limits of discussion: Jewish belonging is assumed to be a fact of nature, a natural given of organic nationalism (having to do with "blood"). This fact is beyond our reach: we cannot change it, hence we are also not required to proactively defend it.

Jewish national ideology—or the forcing of Jewish traditions into the ideological discourse that has been developed in Europe around the nation-state—is supposed to solve the tension that lies at the very foundation of a Nietzschean Zionist rebellion against Jewish tradition; it is this ideology that enables Berdyczewski, contrary to the "compromising" Aḥad Ha'am, to be (viewed as) a Jew who nevertheless "thrust onward uncompromisingly with the *haskala* revolt."[111] To repeat the Nietzschean motto mentioned above, it is the building of a new temple, the national one, that justifies the destruction of the old ("religious") one. And this new temple is clearly built upon nationalist ideology, which is taken to be the ultimate remedy for the illness that allegedly befell the Jewish People. The Jewish "heart" demands therapy, and this shall happen only if the Jew leaves "his ancestors' graves" and his heart is instilled with "a new spirit of life, human and national life."[112]

Berdyczewski sees the rebelling effort as a movement from "Judaism to Jews, from abstract Jews to Hebrew Jews."[113] This movement, a "change of foundation and content," means leaving "our narrow world toward both a personal and national liberty. The two are interdependent."[114] In this vein he draws the distinction separating the "Jewish" Aḥad Ha'am from the "Hebrew," rebelling, Nietzschean, ideologues: "Aḥad Ha'am has a kind of an abstract Judaism [. . .] And we are simply Hebrew, Hebrew in all ideas we adopt, in all thoughts we think."[115] Berdyczewski does not hesitate to draw this distinction, which may be read as suggesting that the rupture at hand does not pertain only to Jewish tradition or "religion"; it is also about breaking away from Jewish identity itself.[116] To those who "intimidate us by saying: our worldview will never unite with Judaism" he replies that he does not wish to identify with Judaism, but with Jews:

> They tell us: protect Judaism; and we say: we are Jews and nothing else. You have chosen for yourself a nice and righteous Judaism, that is the only reason we exist and exclusively for which we are permitted to be; And we have no use of such a being, in which the right to exist was given to us only to find a higher method in Torah and life. The People of Israel is an actual event, and not a set and limited account of the world. We are a people, and we also thought so and so; but not for thinking so and so.
>
> It is not some abstract Judaism, Judaism of this or that kind, that will be our guiding light. We are Hebrews, and we shall revere our heart.[117]

Being a nationalist Jew, Berdyczewski, of course, opposes the assimilation of Jews among the non-Jewish nations. Or might this not be so apparent? If a destruction of the "old," "Jewish" values is of necessity, and the culture offered by the Hellenistic West is rich and fertile, why would it be wrong to adopt the European tradition in place of a Jewish or "Hebrew" one? Why would it be wrong for one to become "a German national of the Mosaic faith"? Berdyczewski's nationalist, almost generic answer is that the assimilated individuals do not contribute to the national, collective wellbeing and vitality:

> In spite of the personalities from among the People of Israel who were fruitful and created viable creations in life and literature, in poetry and singing, in industry and thought, in nature and science, we as a people have no impression of this. That is, all of the work of these private individuals does not add up to the general account of Hebrew intellectuality. They are swallowed one by one in that same place where they work, without giving us a thing as a people.[118]

While the case in other societies is that the work of individuals accumulate and become a collective contribution to the nation's life, the (nationally) "non-normal" situation of the Jews[119] does not permit for the creations and accomplishments by assimilated Jews to accumulate into a Jewish national project: "Our best sons work in a field of foreign intellectuality, and we do not have intellectual life at all . . . We position spiritual soldiers outside, and we do not have intellectuality and culture."[120]

Nationalism, in other words, is what enables Berdyczewski to adopt a quintessentially Cartesian position of undermining that which has been passed over to him from his ancestors; And, much like Descartes,[121] he, too, fails to appreciate the role of tradition in constituting his own personal identity. Thus he is able to both proclaim a wholly independent stance vis-à-vis tradition, and to come out in declarations of the wholly nationalistic mythical manner (these appear just a few sentences apart):

> If I can judge as I wish the beliefs and ideas handed to me by my predecessors, then I also have the right to judge these values or to totally invalidate them, without breaking the connection between me and my people [. . .]
>
> We are standing on the main road, our hands are clean. Whoso is on the side of the uplifting of the people's spirit, let him come onto us.[122]

The form—theological[123]; the content—national (and supposedly secular); the call—identical. Should not this alleged secularism, too, be judged as a national theology?

*A Rebellion Born from Intimate Familiarity*

It should be noted that Berdyczewski personifies the revolting exercise of secular, Nietzschean Zionism: He was born into and had grown in the moral and traditional system against which he rebels in adulthood. The "sheer poignancy and anguish"[124] that accompany his rebellion are also an acknowledgment of the object of rebellion, tradition's authority. In this regard, Berdyczewski's intellectual biography presumes the unmediated knowledge of tradition: he was born into it before he was able to "invalidate" it. Berdyczewski's remade individuality invalidates that which he himself used to "carefully observe."[125] He does not celebrate indifference and ignorance of that which he views as outdated; rather, he manifests throughout his writing a deep knowledge of this object of derision.

Berdyczewski's intellectual character is fascinating since he, who grew inside tradition and calls for its destruction in the name of liberty, understood, one way or another, that this call for destruction touches upon the foundation from which the individual—in the name of which this destruction takes place—is supposed to grow. This is the background to Shimoni's identification of Berdyczewski as being "plagued by ambivalence and doubts.

> His writing is consequently shot through with contradictions. Whereas at one moment Berdyczewski speaks as if the heritage of the past is wholly dispensable, at another he recognizes, with Aḥad Ha'am that there can be no cultural creativity without building upon the heritage of the past.[126]

And so, as opposed to his description of tradition as a heavy, frozen load passively carried by the numbed Jews, Berdyczewski also appreciates tradition's constitutive role. Note, for example, the dynamic and dialogical conception of tradition appearing as if from nowhere in his essay *Ratzon ve-Dat* ("Will and Religion"):

> The people, the public, is the immortality of the individual's soul. The prosperity of the individual is dependent upon the public. What he cannot achieve by himself [. . .] he will achieve by his belonging to others, who give him from theirs and endow him with theirs.
>
> Those same properties given from one generation to the other, from family to family and from house to house, they are the endowment of the individual, who originate prior to his coming to the world. He does not need to begin the work from the beginning, if he had the energy to go forward and enhance that which was given to him . . . Culture is an inherited spiritual property, that incorporates all of the human spiritual life and puts it into a set and inherited-popular spiritual form, particular to a certain collective. And if we wish to put it in an abstract language we shall say: Culture is the eternal remnant of the life of their time and the needs of their time. A remnant endowed from father to son and from generation to generation. Each son begins where his father ended, and each generation inherits from its predecessor, and finds work ahead of him according to his evolution and progression.[127]

Berdyczewski solves the tension between his call for the destruction of the old before building the new and his understanding that it is the old that builds the new by arguing: "we do not have an existing culture." He further builds another antinomy, one contrasting "a living culture" with "an ancient culture, that is not an endowment, only a heavy burden."[128] Nevertheless, the bottom line emerging from the tension between, on the one hand, the revolting drive, on the dichotomies that give birth to it in the first place, and, on the other hand, the dynamic, dialogical understanding of tradition as constitutive is an existential, personal distress: "When we triumph over the past, we are in actuality the losers.—On the other hand, if the past triumphs, we and our successors are the losers. The potion of life and the poison of death in the same thing."[129]

# 6

# Main Zionist Streams and Jewish Traditions

This chapter shall study the stances taken by the three main Zionist streams—Socialist, Revisionist, and Religious—toward Jewish traditions that preceded them and have continued to live alongside the Zionist project as a whole. The chapter is concerned primarily with Socialist-Zionism (discussed in the first parts of the chapter), which has been the dominant and most influential stream in the formative stages of the Zionist project and the State of Israel. As such, it played an unmatched role in shaping the overall Zionist/Israeli stance toward Jewish traditions. To a large extent, both Religious and Revisionist Zionism (which are discussed in the latter parts of the chapter) were reacting to, or against this dominance, and the stances they formed should be understood in the context of the Socialist-Zionist dominance.

## Socialist-Zionism: "Crypto-Religious," "Crypto-Secular," or Otherwise?[1]

A study of Socialist-Zionism's stance toward preceding Jewish traditions gives a rather immediate impression of the distortion caused by the secular conceptual framework. This framework, which assumes an essential—epistemological as well as ontological—distinction between Socialist-Zionist ideology and Jewish "religion," viewing them as occupying separate spheres of human reality (the secular and the religious), struggles to find the proper way in which to understand the clearly "religious" aspects of Socialist-Zionist ideology and practice. Some, endeavoring to preserve the dichotomy, prefer to view Socialist-Zionism, as in the case Socialism in general, as "religion-like."

Nevertheless, the distinction remains blurry. What exactly distinguishes the alleged imitation from authentic religion?

Gideon Shimoni, who, as mentioned earlier exhibits complete loyalty to the secularization narrative as he tells the story of "Zionism as a Secular Jewish identity,"[2] offers a fascinating expression of the attempt to bypass this conceptual distress while at the same time preserving the essentialist distinction it entails. He explains that the combination of two contradictory, mutually repelling ideological organs—i.e., radical Socialism (which is universal by its own self-understanding) and Zionist nationalism (which is particularistic by its own self-understanding)—gave birth to "a comprehensive belief system" which was "a functional equivalent of religion."[3] Shimoni seems to be adopting a functionalist definition of religion while at the same time insisting to distinguish "real religion," which fulfills certain functions, from "religion-like," which fulfills the same functions, but is still "not really religion" since it is, supposedly by its very definition, secular.[4] Thus he retains the distinction, while constantly refuting it. Moreover, he seems to appreciate the "religion-like" construct as preferable to its alternatives, since it "relieve[s] Socialist Zionists of some of the ambivalence toward their traditionalist roots that so tortured the souls of liberal literary intellectuals like Berdyczewski."[5]

As I shall argue herein, the use of rhetoric and terminology pertaining to the "similar-to-religion-yet-essentially-different" nature of Socialist-Zionism does not promote our understanding of it. Furthermore, it also tends to blur some of the central tenets of Socialist-Zionism's confrontation with preceding Jewish traditions. If we focus instead on matters of tradition and free ourselves from the shackles of the distorting secularist conceptual scheme, we are confronted with a rather clear picture that does not require such rhetorical acrobatics. Having been committed to two parallel, often contradictory, totalistic ideologies,[6] Socialist-Zionism strove to promote a political agenda that is based on the invention of a new tradition. It often viewed preceding Jewish traditions as adversaries and judged itself to be equal in status and preferable in value to them.[7]

The nationalistic component in the (new) traditional system propagated by Socialist-Zionism—a component it identified as Jewish—gives the picture its complex texture. This is so since, as I have discussed earlier, the Zionist invention of national tradition (of a Socialist hue, in the case at hand) did not wish to, nor could it, fully disengage itself from certain fundamental components of the

Jewish past. As we shall see later on, this was a major motive for Socialist-Zionism's confrontational interpretation of preceding Jewish traditions.

The totalistic commitment to an alternative traditional system, competing against preceding Jewish traditions, is what explains, at least in part, the lack of ambivalence mentioned by Shimoni. The ambiguity characterizing non-Socialist discussions of Jewish history and tradition dissolved into an absolute negation of (the "old," "Jewish") "religion."

## Naḥman Syrkin: A New Religion

It is not hard to see that this competing system of meaning and interpretation, which seeks to overtake the place of an existing system, professes a total negation of its predecessor-competitor. In Naḥman Syrkin, for example, the picture is colored with a striking opposition of light and darkness, as he portrays rabbis who "hold the masses in their benighted state," while "Zionist Socialism declares war on these forces of darkness in the name of the light." This image puts the "friend vs. enemy" relationship into sharp focus.[8] Thus Syrkin states in his "proclamation to the Jewish youth," published in 1901: "Socialist Zionism sees practical Jewish religion,[9] which is, in [Heinrich] Heine's masterful saying, not a religion but a disaster, as the main obstacle obstructing the Jewish People's path towards culture, science, freedom, [and] liberty. Practical Jewish religion corrupts the Jewish mind and the Jewish soul, hinders any independent action, [and] chains the people in bondage."[10] Moreover, he celebrates the desecration of the "old" Jewish sacred.[11]

For Syrkin, reality is about two competing, totalistic paradigms:

> Since the people is resurrecting to life and to national existence, Judaism, too, is resurrecting from its Talmudic degradation, and arises as a creative spiritual and moral force of the movement of national revival. But this Judaism stands as a total opposition to medieval Judaism, to religious Judaism, to the Judaism of the exile. Zionism does indeed uproot religious Judaism in a more forceful and deeper manner than Reform and assimilation. This is so since while Reform and assimilation uprooted ['aqrou] Judaism

from the outside in an artificial way, and their result was
either absorption [among the non-Jewish communities] or a
revival of Talmudism, of traditional Judaism, [. . .] Zionism
uproots [*me'aqeret*] traditional Judaism from the inside, as it
creates new contents of Judaism, as it changes the people's
spiritual values of life,—uproots and eradicates [*meshareshet*]
it for once and for all.

The Judaism that is reviving on the occasion of Zionism, at a time in which Hebrew religion, Talmud, [and] the
rabbinate have lost their value among [the People of] Israel
because of the internal and external cultural currents, is a
new ideology in Israel. As it develops, and as Zionism is
realized, this ideology can rise to the level of a new worldview and a new view of life, [to become] a new religion
[*relegia ḥadasha*] that will hover over all aspects of life.[12]

Syrkin, then, does not hesitate to identify Socialist-Zionism as a new
religion. His use of the non-Hebrew term here is important: It allows
him to identify Socialist-Zionist ideology as a new "*relegia*" without
associating it with the disease that has plagued the "old" Jewish religiosity, the "medieval" and "exilic" Judaism. But this wordplay does
not blur the wider picture drawn here. The Socialist-Zionist project
explicitly self-identifies as offering an all-encompassing, alternative
traditional system, out of direct confrontation with the Jewish traditions from which the carriers of this new tradition emerge.

This confrontational model was prevalent among those associated with the "second '*aliyah*," ideological Zionist immigrants from
Eastern-Europe who arrived at Palestine in the beginning of the twentieth century. These immigrants, who would later become the political and cultural elite of the Zionist project and of the State of Israel,
developed, maintained, and propagated the dominant Zionist ethos
of the Labor Movement. "In respect of their Jewish identity profile,
they were a remarkably homogeneous group. Most had emerged
out of a traditionalist religious background but had abandoned it in
their youth."[13] This biographical-historical characteristic is of special
importance: the rebellious, confrontational act is based on an intimate,
unmediated knowledge of the object of revolt (i.e., Eastern-European
Jewish traditions).

As Shimoni concludes, these ideologues-immigrants preferred
Syrkin's and Berdyczewski's confrontational approach to Aḥad

Ha'am's dialogical approach. Their rhetoric was "antirabbinical, contemptuous of *halakhic* minutiae, and disdainful of the *galut*, past and contemporary. [. . .] [T]he main ideological thrust was toward the divorce of the new Hebrew identity from all religious authority and influence and the normalization of the Jewish national culture on a secular basis."[14] Again, the dominance of the secularization narrative forces a perception of this confrontation with tradition—as well as the building of a new tradition and a new *"relegia"*—as "secularization." But this clearly misses the deeper meaning of the project at hand.

## Yitzḥak El'azari-Volcani: Anti-Theology?

As aforementioned, Yitzḥak El'azari-Volcani is considered one of the more methodical and articulate ideologues to have formulated this "secular" stance. El'azari-Volcani rejects Aḥad Ha'am's interpretive dialogue with tradition, arguing that this dialogue substitutes one theology—the "religious" or "universal"—with another, which he terms "national theology." This theology is not satisfied with the alleged natural fact of the very existence of the nation, and demands that national life remains committed to a certain *telos*, such as being a moral exemplar to the nations of the world.

According to El'azari-Volcani's self-image (which Shimoni seems to accept uncritically) he himself—an ideologue of Socialist-Zionist nationalism—in effect develops the "Jewish self-understanding of the thoroughly secular national Jew."[15]

There is no doubt that El'azari-Volcani's stance is "atheist"—or, to be precise, Nietzschean.[16] He writes on "the illusion of God," clarifying that "each nation created its God in its own image." In the same vein, he also employs the "religious wars" narrative, reminding his readers that nations have needlessly spilled each other's blood in the name of religion.[17] Against the religious world of lies and illusions El'azari-Volcani charts "another path," one in which "the selfhood [or essence] of the free Jew gushes."[18]

Who is this free Jew? Firstly, it is a man without a God: "God has left him, and belief has been totally wiped out of his heart." This Jew—and this should not go unnoticed: El'azari-Volcani takes an active part in a *Jewish* identity discourse—sees clearly the state of "hypnotization" in which God holds his worshipers. And he surely "does not need this illusion for sensual mesmerization." He is a

Nietzschean super-man, who encounters nature with a clear vision, ready to concur it:

> He faces the sights of nature in awesome respect [*herdat qodesh*], but not in self-annulment; He is not startled by the fear of thunder, nor is he broken by the great waves of the sea [. . .] He rules over the world of spheres [i.e., heavens above] [. . .] and tomorrow he will conquer what is impossible for him to achieve today. The empty space forming around him cannot be filled with ghosts of desolation and in false imaginings: He fills it with his actions, his deeds, [and] his creations [. . .] He cannot be attracted by the lure of illusions of worlds he has not seen. His creative powers, the manifestation of his selfhood, they, they are his God![19]

El'azari-Volcani gives ample expression to a confrontational stance vis-à-vis Jewish tradition. He portrays the image of the "free Jew" as a sovereign agent who can (and must) judge tradition unreservedly. This Jew can be "indifferent" to "what his successors considered to be sacred;" El'azari-Volcani does not hesitate to say that tradition in its whole can be considered dead to this free Jew: "He can view all of the estate that was passed over to us in inheritance as dead property that belongs to archives of antiquities." The liberated Jew is not bound by any particular creed, moral system, or doctrine; he can adopt other cultures/traditions (foremost among them is, of course, "the substance and wisdom of Greece," in which the liberated Jew can find "the crowning glory of all generations"). In short, "everything, everything that was for our forefathers a source of life during their years of wonderings, does not have to be exalted and sublime in his eyes."[20]

At the same time and in the same breath, El'azari-Volcani does acknowledge the past's constitutive function: "We are a ring in the chain of generations. We cannot uproot everything and be released from all influences of our ancestors' inheritance [. . .] It is not for man to choose the different elements from which his soul is composed, and he does not rule over it."[21]

## Blood, Identity, and Tradition

This necessarily addresses the reader's attention to the "Jewish question," namely, why should this liberated super-man not be free to also release himself from his Jewish identity? Alternatively, what makes him a Jew? In answering this, El'azari-Volcani oscillates between the traditional notion of Jewish identity and the biological, or racial, "blood"-centered one, saying that "what entered our ancestors' blood is endowed to us in spite of our opposition." We may, of course, be self-reflexive and, using our "reason," "criticize severely" the characteristics passed over to us as inheritance; but this may prove to be a lost cause: "The psyche subjugates reason, too."[22] However, since this is a biological matter of "blood," it does not merit discussion: One cannot truly reflect upon the natural fact of one's "origin" or "race," nor can she change it.

But a committed ideologue and sophisticated thinker such as El'azari-Volcani cannot accept the passivity this understanding implies. And so, in spite of all the Nietzschean fervor, he fashions a rather practical stance, which does indeed understand tradition as constitutive, yet insists on preserving the reflexive subjectivity of its carrier. For this, he transforms tradition into a matter of biological inheritance:

> We can carve new tablets, but they will always carry over glimmers from the old ones, always, even if we try to extinguish them with all our might. We can create a new morality, to create another content of life, but we cannot escape the mode of creation, the form of expression, the mold into which the matter is cast. The "what" can be different than our forefathers', but with the "how" we follow in their footsteps, driven by a hidden propelling force. [This is so] since if the axe cuts the tree trunk, another shoot will branch out, nourishing on the same roots hidden in the ground where it grows, upon which the "axe of generations" does not have any control.[23]

El'azari-Volcani thusly exempts himself (or the liberated Jew) from the duty of loyalty to tradition. What sounds at the beginning like a grievance against tradition's enforcing power turns out to be a license to be released from it. Since it is in our blood, we should not worry about ceasing to be Jewish. We are a priori Jewish—indeed, this fact shall hunt us—and this in effect also releases us from the necessity to dialogue with the meaning of our Jewishness.

El'azari-Volcani's Hebrew is loaded with imageries pertaining to this deterministic understanding: from Kabbalistic mythology of "glimmers" (*nitzotzot*), through the notion of "blood," to botanical imagery of "tree trunk" and "branches." The phenomenology at hand is not human: it is not a matter of choice. A matter of biology, "some special essence [*'etzem meyuḥad*] in us, remnants of generations that have been absorbed in our blood and milk,"[24] our (ethno-)nationality is not subject to our personal preferences. Similarly, blood/biology is also what explains anti-Semitism.[25] The agency of the individual is thus also rendered irrelevant: El'azari-Volcani clarifies that one cannot rid oneself of the national, racial (or "ethnic") essence, even through (religious) conversion: "The sin of race [*ḥaṭat hageza'*] is engraved in all of our thoughts and actions, and it shall by all means transfer also to the assimilated Jews [*meshumadim*]. Holly water cannot erase it."[26]

The next step is the argument that "Judaism" is whatever "Jews" do: "Living Jews will create this or that kind of Judaism. Whether it is in the spirit of the prophets or not, it shall still be a bifurcation of their selfhood [*hista'afut 'atzmiyutam*]."[27] This, then, is the national-traditional "bottom line" of a biological, racial notion of identity: Blood/race/ethnicity defines culture. Everything done or created by persons of this alleged Jewish "blood" is considered "Jewish" and even "Jewish tradition."

*Nationalist Theology*

The national "selfhood," or "essence" (*'atzmiyut*) is, then, the term that requires explication. For El'azari-Volcani, this national selfhood amounts to a fact of nature, which is by definition not mythical or irrational. It is this notion that enables an enthusiastic ideologue of Zionist nationalism to view his doctrine as "secular" and not "theological."

National selfhood/essence is viewed in this scheme as a purpose in for itself, and not as aimed at achieving some higher "good." For El'azari-Volcani, the position that does promote such a virtue is mere "theology" or "religion"; On the other hand, nationalist ideology which is committed to the collective's (being a natural organism) life, he considers "scientific," "factual" and "secular."

And so, El'azari-Volcani, the supposedly vigorously secularist, rationalist Zionist, does not find any difficulty in speaking about the (collective) "Hebrew soul," which is restrained by chains in any place other than the land/state of the Jews (that is, of the "Hebrews"; the tension between these terms will haunt Zionist identity). In the same vein, El'azari-Volcani calls for Zionism to be committed only to the "practical" (*ma'asi*) and "material" (*gashmi*) aspects of the national project. These include "settlement, the Hebrew language, and Jewish labor. The spiritual dimensions would follow naturally and spontaneously."[28] Note this: language and the political struggle for land and labor become "natural," material issues, and not cultural or traditional (in the case of language) or theopolitical (in the case of the struggle over land and labor).

To make sense, this argument must presume the (taken-for-granted, hence also repressed, or even denied) nationalist metaphysics, or theology. Only upon the basis of this metaphysics can secularism be constituted.

The ethno-nationalist logic is, then, the basis upon which alienation from tradition takes place. It is this logic that permits this alienation, since it offers a readymade alternative: No matter what we do, our actions shall be considered Jewish, nationally if not religiously, since Jewish ethno-nationalism is in our "blood." It is, in other words, secularist ideology's "taken-for-granted," the assumption that the existence of the nation is a biological fact that enables El'azari-Volcani to self-identify as "liberated," and allows Zionist historiography to identify him as "secular," explicitly disregarding the mythical, indeed (to borrow his own criticism of Aḥad Ha'am), the nationalist-theological, elements of his worldview.

## Brenner and "Radical Secularism"

Yosef Ḥaim Bernner[29] is commonly referred to as having represented the "extremist" or "radical" variety of Socialist-Zionist secularism. His position, identified by Shimoni as a "radical" and "open-ended secular understanding of the new Hebrew identity,"[30] has been the focus of a heated controversy among the Zionist ideologues of his time. Brenner seems to have been able to put into sharp focus (and clear formulations) some of the otherwise blurred arguments of his contemporaries. His controversial positions on a series of issues pertaining to Jewish tradition and "religion," and his categorical challenge against the authority of rabbinic Judaism mark his secularism as "radical."

Brenner's biography is not dissimilar to that of most Zionist immigrants of the "second *'aliyah*": he, too, had been educated in traditional Jewish institution, which endowed him with an unmediated familiarity with East-European Jewish tradition, before adopting

Socialist ideology.[31] For him, too, this change was associated with a "rupture" and rebellion against the tradition from which he emerged as an individual. As Brenner himself reminds his readers, one of his critics threw at him the cussing "A yeshiva student who converted" [*baḥur yeshivah she-nitpaqer*]. And Brenner's reply: "Very well: I accept this 'cussing' not without pleasure: Smolenskin and Gordon, Lilienblum and Berdyczewski, are also yeshiva students who converted, and their 'sound of song and joy' [*qol 'anot*] has yet to expire."[32]

## Tradition, the Sovereignty of the Individual, and "National Consciousness"

One of the central foundations of Brenner's stance is his view of himself as sovereign in his relations with Jewish tradition: "All that I think, and especially all that I do, I do not think or do exactly because Talmudist Judaism, in which I was educated, had taught me to think or do so, but rather because I want it or am compelled to."[33] Brenner describes his "contemporary national consciousness" as "wholly secular, atheist, atheological," but clarifies that this does not mean that his identity is based solely on negation. Rather, it also involves independent, totally free choice of whatever he deems fit, while being completely liberated from the authority and dominance of tradition, Jewish or otherwise: "I can be religious-vulgar [*dati-hamoni*], can be religious [*religiozi*] in the exalted meaning of the word, and can also be not only a- [i.e., non-], but even antitheist, antitheological [. . .] As I wish, according to my mood."[34]

This principle allows Brenner to do with tradition whatever he sees fit. In one famous instance, he declared that this sovereignty allows him to disregard the sanctity of traditional texts and to celebrate texts that are traditionally seen as heretic.[35]

Brenner is willing to see a limited use of tradition/past as valuable: The past can offer a non-binding perspective on the present and on the future. Tradition for him is but a general orientation, an advice, and not a binding law or decree; We can address it "a little bit," as it is humanly apt, but "not in order to give directions [. . .] not to outline by it a path, not in order to make the deeds of wretched ancestors a sign for wretched successors."[36]

Nevertheless, the individual-sovereign stance, in the context of a "rebelling" generation, remains focused mainly on the emancipation from tradition, and not on seeking its advice. See, for example, how

Brenner describes, in apparent approval, the attitude of "liberated" (or "secular") ideologues like himself toward the tradition from which they have risen and against which they rebel. He speaks for "the liberated Hebrews [ha'ivrim hahofshiim]" of his generation, saying: "The human feeling in us can relate in utter hatred to our whole past, all of our 'history,' in disrespect to our forefathers who had a 'messianic idea,' they themselves, who did not bequeath a thing to their succeeding generations but many books of nonsense [sifrei hevel]."[37] This, then, is the ultimate expression of the liberated position, the clear expression of the individual's sovereignty in relation to the past and tradition: the ability to relate to them in utter hatred, to boast about disrespecting the ancestors, to break free from the burden of these "books of nonsense."

But even Brenner himself acknowledges that this relation to the past does not solve the present's question, i.e., the issue of the contemporary meaning of (national) Jewish identity. Contemporary reality confronts these liberated Hebrews with the clear danger of detachment, which may result exactly from that sovereign emancipation from the past and the "religion" it has forced upon us (see below). "The question of the present" is clear, and difficult: what would give meaning to their (national) identity as Jews?

> After all, we are alive, and it is not our religion that ties us to our people, nor would another religion take us from it, and we do not want to, nor can we, go to another society [. . .] Not only is "the religion and belief of our [non-Jewish] friends' ancestors" foreign and unneeded for our free soul, for our true essence ['atzmiyut], but also is the cultural society of our friends, of their sons, from which we wish to learn and which we want to imitate [. . .] foreign to us [and does not enable us] to enter it or assimilate in it. We want their culture on our very streets, on our very land, in our people, and we are willing to do what we would have done were we to assimilate among them, among ourselves, our way.[38]

## "Jews" and "Jewishness"

What, then, defines the Jew? What is it that which makes this group of liberated, sovereign individuals, who do not hesitate to cast off

their backs the burden and traditions of the past, and their predecessors' authority (i.e., those agents and institutions who have "traditionally" put meaning in the notion of Jewish identity)—a group of *Jews*?
Brenner's writings make it rather clear that his basic answer nourishes
on those same ethno-national, racial, "blood"-oriented notions that
were prevalent in Eastern-Europe of the time. As with other ideologues discussed above, for Brenner, too, this question is not really
valid, since Judaism/Jewishness is a natural fact, a given, a matter
of "ethnic kinship,"[39] that is not chosen nor can it be erased. Being a
matter of such "organic ethnicity," one's Jewishness leaves her with a
limited choice, or concern, namely whether to be loyal to this ethnicity (that is, to its national, political expression), or to betray it (either
through pointless religious rituality or through assimilation).

This means that ethnicity/race/blood defines what counts as
Jewish; or, to be accurate, it is the individual Jewish agent—i.e., the
person of Jewish origin—who defines her creation as Jewish. In short,
anything Brenner and his fellow liberated Hebrews do is Jewish:

> "What makes you Jewish, if you do not observe the Jewish
> religion?" We are Jewish in the real life, in our hearts and
> our feelings, with no intellectual definitions, no absolute
> truths, and no written commitments. All that is dear to us
> nowadays, all that we see as having value, all that emanates
> from our free essence—with no enforcement and coercion,
> of any kind—is our Jewishness [*yahadutenu*], if you insist
> on this word.
>
> Moreover: Love for our people and for its positive
> aspects.[40]

Accordingly, all concerns for tradition are misplaced; the criticism
pitted against Brenner and his colleagues, blaming them for being dis-
loyal to their Jewish identity or tradition (i.e., to their Jewishness and
to Judaism), is misguided. As Brenner slams at his critics: "Hypocrites!
We are telling you once again: There is no Judaism outside of our
lives and us. There are no stable, eternal beliefs, which bound us."[41]

This, then, is another instance of a material and biological-racial
understanding of Jewish identity. Judaism/Jewishness is what those
Jews do. As for themselves, they are considered Jews because they
were born this way. This is a given datum of their existence, and this
biological fact dictates their personal psychology, which they cannot

change. And—unlike the assimilated Jews of the West and the "totally savage or semi-savage Jews of the Eastern exile"[42]—they choose not to alienate themselves from it.

Such understanding is the necessary condition for identifying the creators at hand as Jews, hence also their creations as Jewish. This is the pre-discursive background of the whole discussion: their identity as Jews is not a matter of choice, and it is this determinis- tic fact that also defines their actions/creations as Jewish, as Juda- ism proper. Avi Sagi, who views Brenner as a "Jewish existentialist," describes this idea as the shifting of focus from "Judaism" to "Jews": "Brenner's significant innovation, which reflects his existential stance, is that Judaism, in any meaning ascribed to the term, depends on the existence of Jews as real people. Indeed, only because there are Jews do they generate a culture that we call Judaism."[43]

Brenner rejects Aḥad Ha'am's "essentialist" conception of Juda- ism, which identifies a concrete, essential content of Jewish tradition: "Judaism was created for the Jews, and not the Jews for Judaism,— that is, Jews create Judaism and not the other way around [. . .] And so, wherever Jews live real life, [they will] produce something, that we shall call 'Judaism.' "[44]

Instead of worrying pointlessly about the existence of "Juda- ism" (or Jewish traditions), the focus should be on the existence of Jews—that is, descendants of the Jewish ethnos/nation:

> The Jewish question of our life is not the question of Jew- ish religion, the issue of "the existence of Judaism." This crossbreed idea should be deracinated. Aḥad Ha'am did it once and regretted it. But we, his liberated Jewish friends, we have nothing to do with Judaism, and nevertheless we are among the collective by any means no less so than [observant Jews].[45]

Brenner understands Aḥad Ha'am as arguing that "Judaism comes first, and whoever does not accept it, is not Jewish!"[46] In his view, this argument is absurd. Sagi sums this up clearly:

> Brenner's basic claim is that cultural creativity is second- ary and contingent on the existence of actual people who create it. The existence of these people is not contingent on their creativity, just as the creator is not dependent on

the creature. Brenner drew the conclusion warranted by
this stance: if Judaism is not an autonomous entity, but
contingent on the activity of Jews [. . .] Judaism has no
essentialist features of its own. Judaism is Judaism because
it is the Jews' cultural creation, and only its being such a
product determines its being Judaism.[47]

But, as Sagi himself is quick to note, this is far from being an accurate description of Brenner's stance, for he adds a condition: For an
act done by Jews to be considered Jewish, it must be aimed at the
*telos*, or purpose of "the continued existence of the Jewish collective
[. . .] Only those practices unique to the Jewish environment, that
is, practices that create a network of meaning and communication
between Jews, are Judaism."[48] In other words: the national conceptual
framework replaces preceding conceptions of the essence of Judaism;
"religious" essentialism is substituted by a nationalist essentialism.
After all, Brenner does not accept assimilation as a Jewish creation.

The same ethnic-organic, or racial conception that lies at the root
of Brenner's nationalism, enabling him to view everything done by
(Zionist) "Jews" as "Jewish," is also that which enables him to present his controversial (at least at the time), positive appreciation of the
New Testament and Christian theology. "The 'New-Testament' is, too,
our book, our own flesh and blood," he writes:

We, the living Jews, whether we atone on Yom Kippur or
eat during this day meat mixed with milk, whether we
uphold the ethics of the Old Testament or are loyal students of Epicurus in our worldview—we do not cease to
feel ourselves as Jews, to live our Jewish lives, to work and
create labor-forms of Jews, to speak our Jewish language,
to nourish spiritually from our literature, to labor for our
free national culture, to protect our national honor and to
fight our war of existence in any manifestation of this war.[49]

The issue at hand, then, is not culture, history, practice, and tradition—all that is commonly labeled as "Judaism"—but what may be
identified as the "national biology," that is, the material existence of
people of Jewish blood/origin, who also have a national consciousness—what modern Zionist discourse, following Brenner's cue (see
chapter 8) shall enthusiastically call "whole Jews":[50]

> We are nationalists, zealous nationalists (*leumiim qanai*m)
> [. . .] Our nationalism is—the betterment of our life and
> the enrichment of our life-forms, which are pleasant to us.
> Therefore, do not attempt to subjugate us in its name to
> some tradition, because we will reject such nationalism.
> We are living Jewish persons—not more—and for us Jew-
> ish labor is important [. . .] and our language is dear to
> us [. . .] and our honor is sacred to us, the honor of our
> people, and this is our nationalism![51]

The decisive measure, then, is the Jew's "national consciousness."
Brenner's writings show that even though he identifies himself as
"atheological," he, too, shows the same symptoms of being blind
to his own national theology. He puts nationalism as the ultimate,
exalted measuring rod, higher even than his sovereign, individual
consciousness. It is nationalism that dictates, at the end, his relation
to the past, to religion, to tradition, to Jewish texts, to the danger/
possibility of assimilation, and so on. Needless to say, nationalism,
or the political, comes before "religion," and is independent from it:
"The major life-forms of the individual and the nation do not nourish
on religion, nor do they live by it."[52] Supposedly, this is what makes
him "secular."

In this vein, it is Brenner's "national consciousness" that decides
the whole controversy surrounding his positive appreciation of Christian values and morals, as well as the general matter of his attitudes
toward "religion":

> My national consciousness does not have anything to do
> with this [religion], has nothing to do with what is beyond
> and what is below the tangible visions, has nothing to do
> with heavens, with the creator of the world, and with what
> comes after death. My national consciousness does not
> prevent me from thinking about the value of our religion
> and the religions of the nations of the world, the belief of
> our masses and the belief of their masses. Our thoughts
> and their thoughts, our books and their books—as I wish.[53]

That is to say: Brenner's national consciousness as a Jew (and not, to
give but two obvious possibilities, his individual consciousness as a
human being or his class consciousness), is what enables him to freely

pick and choose from any tradition he wishes to draw upon—Jewish,
Christian or otherwise—and (this is the decisive point here:) to still
be Jewish.

National theology also dictates that the individual remains committed to this ethno-national consciousness. There seems to be little
doubt that the individual's sovereignty is pushed back stage, if not
denied outright, when the discussion shifts focus from "religion"
and "tradition" to "nationalism." Brenner and his co-ideologues,
those "liberated Hebrews of the generation"[54] pride themselves in
making this essential distinction: They are loyal to their nationalism,
and despise their predecessors' religion. They have "an instinctive
national sentiment [. . .] that makes them love their people, that is:
themselves, and compels them to instill meaning in their life, a vital
meaning to their present, and they see a danger in a life of peddling
and not-working, but not in the negation of Judaism, which other
than themselves is not real for them."[55]

*Secularist Radicalism and Jewish "Ambivalence"*

In spite of Brenner's purported secularist radicalism he, too, is judged
as having ultimately been chained by "ambivalence" toward his Jewish, "religious" heritage. This, for example, is how Shimoni summarizes what appears to be the other side of Brenner's "greater extremism":

> [N]ot only the rebellious negations that characterized
> Berdyczewski are to be found in Brenner but also the coun-
> tervailing ambivalences. His writings too are punctuated
> with contradictions and doubts. The pathos of personal
> crisis pervades the whole, and Brenner vacillates. At one
> moment there is the almost nihilistic assertion of individual-
> ity and total freedom of thought; at another, cognizance of
> the Jew's deterministic bond with the national collectivity,
> the inescapability of Jewish national fate.[56]

What is the meaning of this "ambivalence"? Or, more accurately, what
is the meaning of identifying the multifaceted, complex attitude of the
ideologue, who rebels against his tradition, as a matter of "ambivalence"? It is apparent that those who judge this complex stance as
ambiguous tend to assume that someone who is "truly secular," who
"truly" rebels against his tradition, should be defining herself wholly

independently of this tradition. The fact that Brenner continues to correspond and dialogue (confrontationally or otherwise) with the tradition against which he rebels, that he nevertheless sees his Jewish tradition as heaving in his reality, even when he seeks total liberation from it, is read as a testimony of "ambivalence," that is, the incomplete nature of his rebellious stance. Brenner himself seems to have shared this assumption. It is not difficult to see that he struggles to find his sought-after Jewish self-definition or identity, which is indifferent to tradition.

In this sense, Brenner, like many of his readers and commentators, fails to appreciate the constitutive nature of tradition. He misrecognizes tradition's role in constituting his private identity, also as a rebel against it. In other words, I propose that we understand the notion of "ambivalence" in a "traditionist" context, i.e., in the context of tradition. Ambivalence is the outcome of the tension between a self-perception of individual sovereignty, prevalent among Brenner and his peers, who view themselves as capable of building or reinventing themselves "from scratch," nourishing on "whatever" they wish to (in actuality, this "whatever" is often limited to Western, Christian culture, combined with varying aspects of Jewish traditions), and their determination to nevertheless define themselves as Jewish—while denying the role of tradition in constructing their identity. These are Jews—by their origins as well as by their personal and collective self-identification—who seek to rebuild themselves as Jews that are indifferent to the tradition from which they have emerged as Jews, as having uprooted themselves from their own traditional background. Ambivalence is the result of the tension between the imagining of absolute individual sovereignty and the existential reality of the constitution of the individual (also) through her dialogue with her traditions.

My argument can, then, be framed in terms of the failure of "radical" *Jewish* (as opposed to universal) secularism: The "ambivalence" at hand is a testimony to the failure of the attempted radical-secularist formulation of a nationalist Jewish identity, that rejects Judaism. It is the outcome of a failed attempt at erasing tradition, while still self-defining as a derivative of it. In this, these ideologues boast a self-contradictory stance. They believe themselves to be anti-tradition, "total seculars," who supposedly have nothing to do with Jewish tradition, but nevertheless rely on a certain interpretation of this tradition for their self-constitution as Jewish nationals.

Brenner's own formulation of the tension at hand became, in itself, constitutive: "How can we be become not-us?"[57] he asks. This question already testifies to the alleged "catch" of the Zionist project, which self-identifies as secular (in its mainstream manifestations, of course), as rebelling against its past, seeking to constitute a "new" Jewish identity, that appears to be nevertheless bound, nevertheless not-free, since it is a *Jewish* identity. Is a building of totally new, a wholly novel creation-invention of personal and collective, political identity feasible?

> We nowadays live in a non-environment [*ee-seviva*] [. . .] and we must begin everything anew, to lay the first stone. Who would do this? Us? In our [current] character? This is the question. For our character to change as much as possible, we need our own environment. And in order for us to create this environment by ourselves, it is required that our characters will fundamentally change.[58]

Brenner's answer to this potentially devastating riddle is to simply forego the analytical, supposedly theoretical trap (which has to do with his Zionist ideology and Jewish identity), and to devote his attention to the Socialist cause instead:

> Reason can present whatever questions it wishes to. The yearning for life [*kosef haḥayim*] in us, which is above reason, says differently. The yearning for life in us says: Everything is possible. The yearning of life in us whispers to us a hope: laborers' settlements, laborers' settlements.
>
>     Laborers' settlements, this is our revolution. The one and only.[59]

In other words, Brenner's focus on Socialist ideology, which functions as at least a surrogate tradition, a system of meaning aimed at taking the place of the Jewish tradition he is rebelling against, is what enables him to be "less anguished"[60] regarding his ambiguous Jewish identity. Socialist ideology enables Brenner, as the quote above suggests, to put aside the essential tension that lies at the basis of his stance toward his Jewish tradition, and to stick to the horizon offered by the new (Zionist, Socialist) tradition he adopts and in whose construction he takes part.[61]

In a wider historical frame, as we shall see in the succeeding chapters, the agent that "saves" this secularist-Jewish stance from the imminent logical collapse and allows it to nevertheless endure is not Socialism, but the state. The sovereign nation-state that identifies as the (nonreligious) state of the Jews, if not even as a Jewish state, dictates (or enforces, "coerces") Jewish "religion" and tradition upon the public sphere, and into certain aspects of the personal lives of its citizens. The state upholds the coercive aspect of an evidently non-nihilist, sovereign theopolitics. Doing so, it enables Israeli Jews who identify as secular to be both and the same time "sovereign" in relation to their tradition and even ignorant of it (as an expression of their healthy independence from it), and still uphold, mainly through practice, a certain interpretation of this tradition. I shall elaborate on this later on.

## Assimilation and "Religion"

The concept "religion" also plays a central part in solving Brenner's "ambivalence." The set of meanings he constructs as an alternative to "Judaism" (or Jewish tradition) is also built on a narrow definition of this Judaism as "religion." The role this construction plays can be grasped through Brenner's oppositional stance regarding the general outcry concerning the growing assimilation among European Jews at the turn of the twentieth century. Brenner has nothing but scorn for the assimilated Jews, as he clarifies: "The thousands, maybe tens-of-thousands among us who have already assimilated beyond repair, who already became ready to Christianize—we do not even spit on them."[62] But, he also makes it very clear that he is not at all agitated by the "spectacle of religious conversion,"[63] which seems to be capturing the attention of his misguided, concerned contemporaries. He views the matter as having to do with "religion and belief,"[64] i.e., as pertaining to religious conversion (and not cultural or national assimilation). The cause for his scorn toward the assimilated is national-theological, not religious-theological:

> Say what you want, I am not at all shocked to see in the Zionist German Viennese newspaper, time after time, the names of the converted, who are denunciated publicly. Moreover: I do not understand, whom those wretched Adolfs and Bernards, who have been alienated from Jewish

society and religion from childhood, and for the purpose of
entering Christian society also accepted its "faith," harm?
What did we have of them before, when they went to the
Jewish temple, and what did we lose from them having
pleasurably sprayed themselves with the holy water?[65]

Unlike his concerned contemporaries, whom he views as hysterical,
Brenner is stoic. For him, the spectacle of religious conversion is mar-
ginal. This is so since it is limited from the outset by a conceptual
framework that assumes a narrow meaning of "religion," which is
irrelevant to the essential matters of Jewish nationalism. The authentic
yardstick for raising concern, Brenner clarifies, is the national one—
i.e., the concern for the construction of a Zionist political community
in Palestine. Brenner is not unconcerned for the existence of the "Jewish People"; but he defines this concern in a context of a Zionist,
nationalist discourse.

Moreover, a close reading reveals Brenner's cynicism against the
fears of assimilation as based on a Christian understanding of the
meaning of religion, which enables him to reject it as a worthless
remnant of a benighted past. Thus he can present a comparative view
of world religions,[66] and identify "religiosity" (using, in his Hebrew,
the term *religioziyut*) throughout history. Moreover, Brenner does not
hesitate to praise religiosity "in the exalted sense of the word." In any
event, "Religion itself, with all of it ceremonies and nonsense, is but
part of the forms of life, which humans have created [. . .] Religion
takes form, changes form, it is born, [and] it dies."[67]

Religion, in other words, has—or rather had—a functional value; the various instances of "deceit [*tarmit*]" and "exploitations" that
characterize the "history of belief and religions" fulfill "very deep
needs."[68] But once modern, liberated consciousness enables us to overcome this deceit, we are surely released from its hold. There is no
reason to fear the phenomenon of individuals leaving Jewish religion,
since this religion is just a deceitful construct. Brenner thusly uses
an overtly cynical and critical tone when he writes that reading the
warning calls regarding the growing phenomenon of assimilation one
may conclude that "religion in general, and the study of religion in
particular, is the essence, the essence of life."[69] If this were true, reality would have been truly menacing; Yet Jewish leaders' alarming
cries, and the general sense of agitation, are misguided: "Please, do
not mislead us to believe that the existence of the Jewish collectivity

is in danger because of this [religious conversion], and do not make this an issue."[70] Religion is redundant. Religious conversion does not pose a threat to the Jewish people.

Once he has framed the problem of assimilation as an issue of religious conversion he can dismiss it, focusing instead on national theology to which, no doubt, he is fully committed and for which he is deeply concerned. The young European Jews who are bothered by questions of identity "know and feel that they are not whole persons, that as Hebrew youth with no whole Hebrew language, with no Hebrew homeland and with no Hebrew culture, not all is well with them."[71] But issues of Jewish morals vs. Christian morals, the "nonsense of theology,"[72] are obviously negligible, since they deal, by definition, with the apolitical.

## Secularism, Hebrewism, Exile, and the Negation of the Other

What becomes of the identity of the Jew (or "Hebrew") when she accepts her self-identity as a given? How does she understand herself? Reading Brenner it becomes rather apparent that the negation of this new Hebrew's "Others" play an important part in this self-understanding.

Ammiel Alcalay is one of the perceptive readers to have identified the revolutionary, deconstructive Zionist exercise—articulated, among others, by Brenner—as a transition from the understanding of Jewish identity through diverse traditions to a racial, biological definition of this identity, i.e., "the exchange of the legal, covenantal, and communal basis of Jewish existence for the racial, the ethnic, and the national, a rupture whose further implications and deeper marks are only beginning to surface."[73]

Alcalay finds the "archeological" evidence to this Zionist rupture in "the initial collapse of terminology used by European settlers"[74] in Palestine for describing both Jews and non-Jews. He notes specifically one of the constitutive moments of this stance, in Brenner's encounter with the Promised Land. Alcalay addresses us to the first impressions of Brenner's protagonist, the storyteller in one of his novels (which, as Ehud Ben-Ezer clarifies,[75] are based on Brenner's own impressions): Having just arrived in Haifa, he encounters "a band of Arab urchins," who insult him and his comrades. On which he notes, "Well . . . yet again . . . there is yet another species of Gentiles in the world we must suffer . . . We also have to suffer this filth."[76]

Brenner's protagonist tries to see the other, or at least says he tries to do so, but the only option he has is the Orientalist one: "And still, I made an effort to see mystery in the bloated bellies of the wretched sons of Hagar." But his failure seems to be preordained, and his negation of the other peaks when it addresses other Jews:

> But oh, oh . . . the French colony[77]—what repugnance! [. . .]
> This colony in its entirety gives the impression of a fat and contemptible beggar, who was seated at a master's table, and is drawing from the bowl with his dirty, leprous, thick hands . . .
> The colony's clerks and officers—fattened pigs, whose feet are too weak to walk, from fat, to make even one step; But once they are no longer fattened, they are not capable of even lying like so, with no movement, alive. . .
> The natives of the land, the naked and corrupted, the indolent and despicable, the majority in this place, sell all needs of food. One of them jumps suddenly and tells me in a Jewish-Romanian accent about a beast they have stolen and had sex with, and his eyes, filled with pannus and trachoma, wink and smile. . . .[78]

Brenner's Socialist-Zionism embodies the negation of the Oriental, or Arab-Jewish option. It exposes the great debt Eastern-European, secular Jewish (or "Hebrew") identity owes a quintessentially European tradition, in which hatred to Jews and the East coalesce. As put by Ben-Ezer: "Everything [in the stories of Brenner's *Mikan Umikan*] teems with a certain fear of assimilation in the East, and Brenner says—what did we leave Europe for, we would be better off among the Poles and Russians—and not to come here and assimilate among the Arabs."[79]

Ben-Ezer, and Alcalay following him[80] suggest that Brenner's last novel, *Breakdown and Bereavement*,[81] sheds a special light on the issue at hand. The main protagonist of the novel is plagued by paranoia, whose main object is "the image of the Arab [. . .] who threatens the existence of the Israeli man."[82] An encounter with an Arab family, who is searching for its disappeared young son, arouses in the protagonist blood-libel anxieties. Ben-Ezer summarizes the gist of the matter: "This scene illustrates how, in Brenner's protagonist, [. . .] the ring of hatred from which the Jew seeks refuge, that is, the East-European anti-Semitism—repeats itself in the surrounding of a Jewish minority by a hostile Arab majority in Palestine."[83]

The protagonist's refuge from the "accusation" (which is, of course, a figment of his paranoia) returns to "blood": his alibi is the claim that the blood flowing in his veins is not really Jewish, but rather Slav. "He knew that he will prove—his blood is gentile blood [. . .] He was born exactly nine months after the first pogroms, and he is not Jewish at all, he is gentile, eighty-percent Slavic race. How would the Arab girl not understand that her little one is not with him?"[84] As Ben-Ezer notes: "Brenner's tormented protagonist was born in 1881, the year of pogroms in Russia [. . .] and this is also Brenner's own year of birth; he saw himself as of the same age as his protagonist [. . .] who, facing the absurd accusation, of a blood-libel [. . .] tells himself that he is not really a Jew, because his mother was raped, he is mostly gentile, hence her accusation does not hold."[85]

Alcalay and Ben-Ezer bring additional testimonies, attesting to Brenner's alienation from his non-Zionist surroundings. This amounts to a severe negation of the Other, that also broadcasts a negation of the self. It is quite striking in its inability to see the "East" not through the eyes of a tormented Eastern-European Jewish eyes.[86]

The racial, biological, blood-oriented definition of Jewishness finds its meaning, then, through the opposition to and negation of the Other. In this vein, Brenner describes the larger group of people who share his opinions, the "liberated Hebrews," through their opposition to the "old Jew": positively speaking, these are "[t]he best of the People of Israel, in Palestine and abroad, who do not believe in the messiah and have nothing to do with traditional, theological Judaism."[87] In contrast to them, the Other, "religious" and "exilic" Jew receives Brenner's fierce, hateful negation. As Shimoni identifies, "Brenner's harangues against *galut* and the Jewish past were sometimes so harsh that he came close to justifying gentile hatred of the Jews."[88] Brenner does indeed present a severe articulation of the negation of exile, holding Judaism itself as responsible for the sickness of exile; "There could be no liberation from the *galut* condition without prior liberation from that [i.e., normative, rabbinical] Judaism."[89]

## Jacob Klatzkin:
## Secularist Radicalism and Statist Sovereignty

Jacob Klatzkin's "radical" or "extreme" secularism (which won him the title of "the most devastating antitraditionalist, of all the rebels within Zionsim"[90]) can shed further light on the subject matter of the current discussion. Especially important is the connection between Klatzkin's negation of Aḥad Ha'am's dialogical stance toward tradition, and his commitment to the nation-statist ideology, culminating in his "favoring a maximalist political program aimed at sovereign statehood."[91] As Hertzberg notes, Klatzkin's ideology, and especially his vehement negation of exile (see below), should be understood through his singular emphasis on the state. Klatzkin "is the most important Zionist thinker to affirm that a third-rate, normal, national state and culture would be enough."[92] These seem to be complimentary aspects of the same picture: the deified state takes over the authority of tradition.

Arguing against Aḥad Ha'am, Klatzkin claims that national identity—Jewish or otherwise—is not based on tradition, or "putative fixed values and ideas—a so-called 'spirit of Judaism.' "[93] Rather, it is based on material and political foundations. Adhering to Nietzschean vitalism, Klatzkin propagated a materialist conception of nationalism, which highlights the importance of material or "formative" and "objective" conditions (namely ethnic kinship, language, and territory) in defining the nation.

The interesting paradox lies in Klatzkin's understanding of the collective for which he speaks (i.e., the Jewish People) as based primarily on history—together along with ethnic kinship or race/blood, of course. His initial point is the negation of a "religious" definition of this collective:

> [T]he Hebrew experience means neither religious precepts nor philosophical principles. It has transcended its former religious and abstract meaning and assumed a purely national meaning. We are neither a religious denomination nor the embodiment of a philosophical system; neither the bearers of a single belief nor of a single world-outlook, but rather we are the sons of one family, bearers of a common history. That which unites us and distinguishes us from others is not an objective covenant of ideas but a subjective covenant born of a common history and future. Hence, the holding of heretical beliefs does not disqualify anyone from belonging to the nation any more than holding supposedly correct beliefs includes one. A Gentile does not become a Jew by virtue of belief in the religion of Israel or a Jewish spiritual outlook, and a Jew does not cease being one if

he balks at religious precepts or at that supposed spiritual
outlook. In short, national consciousness neither demands
nor negates any specific views and ideas.[94]

It is not systems of thought and ideas that define the Jew, but rather
kinship/origin and common history; history defines the Jews but does
not shape them, and does not burden them with duty. Or does Klatzkin only refer to political history?

Note that his argument could be interpreted as fatalistic, as
positing that joining the Jewish people or leaving it is simply impossible: that Jewish nationalism is a closed, pre-defined group. Klatzkin
realized this, and strove to argue that his view is not deterministic.
He thus clarifies that "whoever evades the common war, the war of
redemption,"[95] is to be considered as having left the Jewish nation,
even if she is of Jewish ancestry. On the other hand, a gentile in ancestry and history, who wishes "to take part in the life of the Hebrew
nation" acquires "future Judaism."[96] The yardstick for inclusion or
exclusion, then, is the active participation in "the war of redemption,"
i.e., the political project of the creation of a nation-state. It is the politics of the nation-state that sets the coordinates for judging reality.

As in Brenner's case, so it is with Klatzkin: the new tradition
he has adopted (in this case, Socialism seems to be overshadowed by
the theology of the sovereign nation-state) allegedly solves all tensions
and paradoxes. This, in Shimoni's reading, is what explains Klatzkin's
"insistence upon the attainment of a Jewish territorial state."[97]

The reorientation toward the sovereign state as defining Juda-
ism/Jewishness gives birth to the following prediction regarding
the future of the Jews: "Our people shall then [after the establishment of a sovereign nation-state of Jews] be parted into two collectives. A Hebrew collective in [Palestine] and a Jewish collective in
exile . . . Two nations with different faces."[98] As we shall see later on,
this possibility, which Klatzkin seems to celebrate, of distinguishing
the "Hebrew" (or, post-1948, "Israeli") people from the Jewish one,
and the conception of the nation-state as belonging to and representing only the former, has come to be seen as an almost existential
threat to mainstream Zionism.

In any event, according to Klatzkin, this distinction between the
("Hebrew") people or collective that is defined by the nation-state
and the Jewish people that does not partake in the state naturally
brings about the total negation of exile: "Exilic Judaism is not worthy

of survival. Exile [*galut*] distorts our national character [. . .] Exile corrupts the human in us [. . .] Exilic existence cannot be called life, neither from a national perspective nor from a human one."[99] He thus arrives at the conclusion that the Jews are destined to immigrate to Palestine, whether willingly so or not; otherwise they will be wholly assimilated and eventually cease to be Jews.

## Socialist-Zionism in Palestine and Jewish Traditions

The "theoretical" ideas propagated by Aḥad Ha'am, Berdyczewski, Brenner, and other ideologues took a concrete, practical shape in the wide-ranging project of the invention of Social-Zionist tradition in Palestine. This project has, of course, won a great deal of academic attention. The academic field offers a comprehensive examination of the relation between "religion and nationalism" in the Zionist movement in Eastern-Europe,[100] and in Palestine;[101] a study of the "civil religion" built by the Zionist Labor movement;[102] an examination of central elements of this "civil religion," such as the rewriting of the Passover rituals and texts;[103] and an analysis of the narrative-mythical system lying at the base of the Zionist "invention of tradition."[104] Needless to say, this list is far from exhaustive.

These analyses (which I do not intend to repeat here) offer a rich picture of the wide-ranging historical, political, and cultural project of the invention, or rewriting, of national tradition, whose inventors/ creators identified as Jewish. This extensive project is based on the notion of a reinterpretation and rewriting of preceding traditions, which the Zionist ideologues knew as Jewish, as they were determined to rewrite the meaning of their Jewish identity.

### Radically Secularist, Yet Not Absolutely Secular

Taken together, the abovementioned studies all tend to accept the secularist framework as the primary analytical tool through which to view reality and interpret the Socialist-Zionist (re)invention of tradition. Needless to say, all writers also note the inefficiency of a simplistic application of this framework. For one thing, the allegedly "secularist" ideological project at hand has noticeably relied on "religious" elements, and was even focused on the invention of a new, national, "religious surrogate,"[105] or even "secular religion."[106]

Now, this religious surrogate is seen as "extremely secular," since it vehemently rejects "religious" tradition. Thus, while "the phenomenon of secularization has been prevalent in secular Zionism throughout its diverse manifestations," it was "specifically, explicitly expressed in Socialist-Zionism."[107] Yet this same "very secular" system "was ostensibly grounded in values that were present in Judaism itself, and many of the symbols which conveyed these values were derived from the Jewish tradition."[108]

In short, the study of (Socialist-) Zionist "civil religion," as opposed to "traditional" (or "real") religion, begins with the assumption that Zionism should be viewed primarily as a secular and secularizing phenomenon. But as soon as this assumption has been laid, this secularization is revealed to be impure, since it relies on Jewish (religious) tradition in an essential manner. See, for example, Don-Yehiya's concise summation:

> The process of secularization was strikingly expressed in Zionism's, and especially Socialist-Zionism's secular attitude toward traditional Judaism [. . .] This emanated from, on the one hand, the adverse stance, prevalent among wide circles in the Labor Movement, towards many of traditional Judaism's values and symbols [. . .] and, on the other hand, [these circles'] wish to instill their ideas and project with "Jewish legitimacy." Hence the phenomenon of relying on concepts, phrases, and ritualistic patterns that are derived from the sources of traditional Judaism, while introducing far-reaching changes in their form and content, aiming at adapting them to Socialist-Zionism's set of values and concepts.[109]

One may wonder: how did it come to be that ideologues who were driven by such "militant secularism" repeatedly and continuously relied upon the system of symbols, values, and identities which they themselves identified as "religious"? If we accept the distinction pitting the secular and the religious as mutual opposites, and adopt the narrative according to which Socialist-Zionism is a secular, secularist and secularizing phenomenon, the political reality that begins with the Socialist-Zionist project in Palestine may indeed be confusing. Or, if we adopt a secularist-ideological stance,[110] we might argue that Zionism deceives itself; that it has not really released itself from the suffocating hold of rabbinical, "religious" Judaism.

*Not a Paradox, but a Misguided Conceptual Framework*

A careful reading of the literature encourages one to view this paradox as undermining not Socialist-Zionism, but rather the conceptual toolkit guiding the mainstream analytical discussion of it. Thus,
for example, an attentive reading of the insightful phenomenology
offered by Liebman and Don-Yehiya in their groundbreaking work
on what they conceptualize as Zionist "civil religion"[111] (i.e., national
ideology as a "secular surrogate" to "real religion") forces one to
wonder: why should we identify all those reinterpretations of Jewish
tradition, the instilling of new, alternative ideological content in old,
traditional symbols and ritualistic forms, and even the full-fledged
adoption of traditional symbols and rituals into the Socialist-Zionist
ideological system as "secularization"?

A common solution to this tension between the secular conceptual scheme and the sociopolitical reality it aims to explain is the
expansion of the meaning of the concepts involved. Don-Yehiya, for
example, explains that the "secularization" he is writing about can
oscillate along a wide range of attitudes toward religious tradition—
from "total and explicit negation"; through reinterpretation, in which
secularization is manifested not in the abandonment or negation of
the religious, but in "the very phenomenon of emptying concepts of
their original religious content and filling them with secular content,
while copying from the traditional system in which these concepts
have been created and developed, and integrating them in a new
normative system, which has a quintessentially secular character"; to,
paradoxically enough (keep in mind that this is Don-Yehiya's description of secularization), "the integration of traditional elements, 'as
is,' with no explicit change of content and form, into the system of
values and symbols prevalent in Jewish society."[112] Thus, the scholar's insightful, deep-penetrating understanding of the ways in which
Socialist-Zionism has shaped its relation to Jewish traditions that preceded it compels him, even if he does not explicitly acknowledge it,
to abandon the common, accepted meaning of "secularization"; yet
he hangs on to the very term.

The reader attentive to the epistemological argument with which
I opened this discussion can now more easily appreciate the distorting
effects of the introduction and application of the "secular vs. religious" conceptual framework into/on the Jewish and Zionist contexts. It is this conceptual scheme that encourages the expectation that

Socialist-Zionism, (marked as "secular") shall reject Jewish "religion"; and it is the discrepancy between this expectation and—well: reality—that necessitates the convoluted "secular-in-principle-but . . ." type of argument. Needless to say, the problem is not with politico-historical reality that does not give in to the conceptual dichotomy; neither is it with the individuals whose practice does not fully correspond with this dichotomy. The problem is with the conceptual dichotomy itself.

It should also be noted that the Socialist-Zionist ideologues encourage this confusion, as they self-identify through that same narrative of secularization. They view their actions through the (distorting) conceptual lens of religion, secularism, nationalism, modernity, etc., and take upon themselves the label "secular"; they thus often believe themselves to be wholly indifferent to "traditional Judaism."

This ideological identification demands interpretive sensitivity. It would be patronizing and foolish to dismiss the dominance of the secularization narrative, of the individuals' and the collectives' self-identification through it, as a conceptual error, and to ignore the ways in which these concepts—wrongheaded as they may be—function in the construction of Socialist-Zionist identity, as well as other Jewish identities in pre-statehood Palestine and then in the State of Israel. (This shall become further explicated when we take into consideration Religious-Zionism. See below). The important sociohistorical fact is that the dichotomy has functioned as an influential anchor, which plays a crucial role in the shaping of political, private and social identities in the Zionist society before and after the establishment of the state. Zionist settlers—Socialist or otherwise—followed by Israeli Jews, have identified, and still do, primarily as secular or religious, later complemented by *masorti*.[113] And they have been building their self-understanding, their being in the world, through this conceptual framework. We can, of course, trace apparent "blind spots" in the identities and worldviews built along these interpretive schemes. But it would be critically wrong to ignore these social-historical-political facts.

## *"Confrontation" with Tradition, Form, and Content*

The important question at hand has to do, then, with the ways in which those Socialist-Zionist ideologues, the revolutionaries who have propelled the Zionist project in Palestine during the first half of the twentieth century and have outlined the main coordinates of the

Israeli nation-state, have related to preceding Jewish traditions. The comments above, following the works of Liebman, Don-Yehiya, and others have already touched upon a primary notion in this regard: the Zionist project, under a Socialist dominance, has involved a wide-ranging dialogue with tradition. This has been a confrontational dialogue, full of resentment.[114]

This stance may be more accurately described as a rebellion against an acknowledged authority. Individuals who had been educated in traditional Jewish institutions and were raised upon traditional Jewish values reinvented themselves as secular Socialist-Zionists and sought to cast away the authority of their Jewish traditions, or the ways of life into which they were born. They, who have had an intimate, unmediated knowledge of these traditions and ways of lives, sought to reinterpret, rewrite and recreate parts of these traditions, values, and practices. In this sense, whether explicitly and ideologically or implicitly and through self-denial, the Socialist-Zionist project in Palestine accepted, as a matter of practice, Ahad Ha'am's argument regarding the need to identify an "essence" of Jewish identity and to reinterpret it so as to render it applicable to what its practitioners have identified as a radically new, modern, national context.

They have done so through a confrontational, resentful stance. Thus, to give but one of the most familiar examples, they have rewritten the Passover *seder* ritual and the text of the *haggadah* it revolves around, so as to adapt them to their ideology and worldview: They have thus taken God out of the text, and replaced Him, as savior, with Labor, Land, or even Vladimir Ilyich Lenin. Other Jewish holidays (such as Shavo'ot and Hanukkah) have also been rewritten, while others were abandoned and forgotten. Others still have been reinvented.[115]

One of the striking characteristics of the project of the invention of Zionist tradition, or the reinterpretation of Jewish traditions so as to render them applicable to the Zionist ideological agenda, is the basic distinction between form (which has been largely preserved) and content (which has been confrontationally rewritten). The rituals of the *seder* and of the presentation of *bikurim* (new produce) during Shavo'ot exemplify this clearly: Central *religious* elements of the rituals' *form* have been rather zealously maintained; a ritualistic dinner, focused on the reading of a sacred text (moreover, the text, which has been subject to ideological rewriting, is still identified as a Passover *haggadah*), held on the "Hebrew" (Jewish) date of the "traditional" holiday of Passover; the collection of *bikurim*, (interpreted liberally, so as to included not only farm produce, but also machines and humans) and their presentation to a figure of authority, also held on the Hebrew date of Shavo'ot. But the *content* of these rituals, their messages and their normative-ideational objects, have been radically rewritten: the redeemer at the center of the *seder's haggadah* is not God but Labor, "the National Spirit," or other God-surrogates; the *bikurim* are presented not to a *cohen* (priest), but to the collective, or commune. And so on. The form—preserved. The content—radically, ideologically rewritten.

How are we to understand the exercise of a punctilious, zealous, formal observance of these Jewish, religious rituals, and the accompanying confrontational, rebellious rewriting of their content so as to render them consistent with the allegedly secular Socialist-Zionist ideology? Specifically, which of the three central ideological stances reviewed above—Aḥad Ha'am's interpretive dialogue, Berdyczewski's individual ambivalence or Brenner "secular-Jewish existentialism"—does this Socialist-Zionist project correspond to? In other words: which secularist ideology, or "theory" guides this project?

As I noted above, it seems to me that Aḥad Ha'am's essentialist notion of Jewish identity won the upper hand. The *Jewish* practices developed by Socialist-Zionist settlers are so—i.e., Jewish—since they uphold to the idea of dialoguing with tradition, resentful and confrontational as this dialogue may have been. The Socialist-Zionists did not completely abandon this tradition, but sought to rewrite it. They, too, ultimately viewed Judaism/Jewishness as expressed (also) in "traditional" rituals held by Jews on certain Jewish dates, dictating certain practices, etc. Socialist-Zionists, in other words, held on to the idea that to be authentic, Jewish identity demands a certain "essence." They did not simply settle for their Jewish blood; the wide-ranging political project they conducted has been a national Jewish one, and was compelled to positively understand its Jewishness. It could not be justified only by its agents' origins, especially when its violent, conflictual nature (as a struggle over land, labor and overall dominance against the native inhabitants of the land) came to the fore.

However, a careful examination of this dialogue reveals it to be also loyal to the existentialist idea propagated by Brenner, even if only implicitly so. As we saw, Brenner tended to view the Jewish body (or, in the current terminology: form), that is, the ethnic/racial origin of the agent as a Jew, as guaranteeing that the "content" of this agent's acts, whatever it may be, is also Jewish. If the (Zionist) Jew makes it his, it is Jewish: The (Jewish) body, the form, guarantees that the content/identity shall also be Jewish.

If we compare the Socialist-Zionist rite to Brenner's Jewish identity, we will be able to understand the essence of the Socialist-Zionist project of a confrontational dialogue with tradition. The aforementioned "new" rituals, who substitute ideological, radical content for traditional values, are deemed Jewish because their "bodies," their "origin" (i.e., their historical form) is taken to be Jewish; the Socialist-Zionist ideologues can thus explicitly negate the traditional meaning or message of the holiday,[116] and still view this new celebration as a quintessentially Jewish (national) act.

It should be noted that this aggressive confrontation with tradition, crude as it may be (as demanded by the heavy ideological hand guiding it), is still an expression of a dialogue with tradition, based on an intimate familiarity with it. But once the ideological fervor has subsided, and the unmediated familiarity with tradition was no longer, the sons and daughters of the ideological pioneers were left with a mixture of a bitter resentment toward tradition and religion and a general ignorance of the content of these. They remain Jewish in their self-identity, of course. But the positive meaning of this identity, beyond their commitment to the project of building a nation-state for Jews, has diminished. The dialogue between them and their tradition has gone silent.

## Religious-Zionism: A National Movement[117]

The fallacy of the religion vs. the secular/politics/nationalism is thrown into sharp relief in the case of Religious-Zionism, both in terms of the academic study of the movement, and in terms of its self-understanding. This, to a certain extent, is a reflection—a mirroring indeed—of the presupposition that the modern politics of nationalism and the sovereign nation-state is essentially secular, while religion is (or should be) apolitical. Thus, if the case of mainstream, "secular" Zionism presented its students with the task of accounting for the "impurity" of its secularity, the study of Religious-Zionism deals mainly with the "infusion" of the religious element into the allegedly secular-in-essence Zionist project. Trapped in this epistemology, the academic field (on the adjoining political discourse) has failed to see Religious-Zionism as the nationalist movement dedicated to the theopolitics of the sovereign nation-state that it is.

The dominance of the secular epistemology in the study of Religious-Zionism cannot be overlooked. While there are varying, sometimes contradicting readings of the movement in light of this epistemology, these are nevertheless all variations on the notion that religion and nationalism are two distinct realms of human activity, categorically separate, who come into mutual play in the case of Religious-Zionism. The main issue to be debated among students of the movement is thus the nature of this interaction.

*Religion, Fundamentalism, and Nationalism: A Delicate Balance?*

The mainstream study of Religious-Zionism has taken the aforementioned infusion of religion into nationalist politics as a perversion of sorts, a carrying over of an element of the past—i.e., religion, or theology—into (secular) modernity. This anachronism renders Religious-Zionism missing at best (dangerous at worst), as not fully accounting for the revolutionary sense of Zionist secularism. As I mentioned earlier, Yosef Salmon, who rejects this distinction, notes critically that certain historiographers and sociologists have been so entrapped in the secular presupposition that they view the very notion of a religious Zionism as incoherent, a logical inconsistency if not an outright oxymoron.[118]

This approach highlights the "religious" element as the key to understanding Religious-Zionism. It views the movement as an essentially theological, religious, phenomenon that takes over elements of nationalist ideology in order to promote its theologically messianic, theocratic aspirations. In this context, the historical-political movement of Religious-Zionism has been placed in the framework of the distorting discussion on "fundamentalism," culminating in the "Fundamentalism Project."[119] A basic premise of this project is that fundamentalist movements are, by definition, found in a conflictual relationship with the modern, secular nation-state. Accordingly, Religious-Zionism is to be understood as a sociohistorical (inherently failed?) attempt to bridge the apparent tension that the very hyphenated term entails.[120]

A predominant approach to this issue focuses on "messianic fundamentalism," or simply "extremism" as the "religious norm."[121]

Echoing the "myth of religious violence," this conception views religious claims for authority and legitimacy (and the ensuing uses of violence) as illegitimate, while those of the sovereign state, being "secular," are taken to be legitimate by definition.[122] The scholars are thus required to explain the largely "moderate" stance (in terms of its presumed religious extremism) taken by the Religious-Zionist movement throughout Zionist and Israeli history, especially prior to 1967. This rather unnatural moderation is commonly explained by the cultural, social and political ties between the Religious-Zionists and their secular counterparts. The secular-political is assumed to have kept the fundamentalist, messianic DNA of the Religious-Zionists at bay.[123]

The political developments since the 1967 Six Days War are understood, in this framework, as a gradual release and realization of the always present fundamentalist potential of Religious-Zionism. It is, in other words, a narrative of the release of the "religious" element from the moderating "national" hold. This, it has been assumed, amounts to an undermining of the state's sovereignty; once the Israeli, Zionist nation-state diverged from a messianic path charted for it by religious fundamentalism, so the argument goes, Religious-Zionism sacrifices the most cherished meaning and institutions of Zionist sovereignty in order to achieve its messianic, theocratic goals.[124]

Thus, if the hyphenated term entails two competing sanctities: that of the Land (seen as the expression of a religious belief; a questionable issue in for itself) and that of the State, then the history of Religious-Zionism is read as the gradual breaking up of the delicate balance in favor of the religious sanctity of the Land; once the sovereign state no longer adheres to this sanctity, its politics are rendered heretical.

This, in short, is an evolutionary narrative built upon the secularist epistemology. It views the phenomenon at hand as essentially unstable, as it mixes theology with politics, and assume the former to have gradually overtaken the latter. Nationalism, in this reading, only serves theology/religion, an instrument designed to facilitate the messianic end of times.

"Revisionist" scholars who have rejected the view of Religious-Zionism as a fundamentalist movement nevertheless hold on to the epistemological dichotomy it nourishes on. They thus claim that a study of the history of Religious-Zionism shows that patriotism, or the sanctity of the state, or simply "politics" is the stronger party in the duality of the phenomenon at hand. Religious-Zionists, so this revisionist argument goes, are indeed found in an everlasting tension between their religious commitments and their political affiliation with the Zionist state; but they have time and again solved the tension by adhering to the sanctity of the state's sovereignty.[125]

This, again, is a story of an immanent collision between the essentially secular-political and the theological-religious engagements characterizing Religious-Zionists. But in this view, statism is a central, organic part of Religious-Zionist ideology. The sociopolitics of the movement are thus read as a continuous attempt at negotiating the tensions posed to this commitment by a religious creed—to the point where Religious-Zionists give up on their historical attempt at redefining the meaning of genuine orthodoxy. This latter task is left for the Ultra-Orthodox who, lacking the political-Zionist organ, are in effect granted a monopoly over the definition of this theological commitment. Put differently, this "revisionist" stance, which strives to show that (Jewish) Religious-Zionism does not threaten the sovereignty of the nation-state of the Jews, adheres to the same epistemological and conceptual frame of the discourse on fundamentalism. It only argues that the category should not be applied to Religious-Zionism, since it has, consistently so, preferred the political, the state, over the theological.

*Religious-Zionism Beyond the Secularist Dichotomies*

This, I would argue, is yet another instance of the distorting influence of the secularist epistemology. A wide field of competing interpretations is nevertheless based on a single, coherent (and misleading) duality of politics and religion. It assumes the term "religious" in Religious-Zionism to be a manifestation of the universal category carrying the same name. This modern, Protestant notion is hardly challenged. Indeed, one would be hard pressed to find scholarship dealing with the phenomenon of Religious-Zionism that puts into question the "Religious" in this title; it is taken to be clearly known (and given to a comparative view, as in the Fundamentalism Project), its meaning taken-for-granted. Correspondingly, these varying interpretations assume the essentially secular nature of the second part of this hyphenated duality, Zionist nationalism, to be also "a given."

As I noted above, what seems to evade this epistemologically secular gaze at the phenomenon at hand is the substantial degree to which this is yet another iteration of the theopolitics of the sovereign

nation-state. Religious-Zionism is, at root, a political-national(ist) ideology. Needless to say, its adherents view their relations with their
tradition in a different light than that of other, self-styled "secular"
Zionists; theirs is an Orthodox notion of preserving the "religious
past" in a rather conservative manner. But it is nevertheless based
from the outset on the notion that this religion is categorically separate from their political engagement as committed Zionists. The main
issue becomes, then, the manner in which they propose to "bridge"
the alleged conceptual abyss stretched between the two elements
composing their identity: religious conservatism and secular nationalism. They may, following the spiritual forefather of the movement,
Rabbi A. Y. Hacohen Kook,[126] view it as their mission to "synthesize"
the two categories, or elements, rendering the formerly separate theology and nationalism a monolithic whole; or they may wish to preserve each in its "pure" meaning, so as not to disturb the categorical
distinction between the two (as did, for example, Rabbi Isaac Reines,
who in 1902 founded the Religious-Zionist party, Mizraḥi).[127] Either
way, Religious-Zionism is, as the name suggests, based on the notion
that there is "Jewish religion" and there is "Jewish nationalism,"
particular manifestations of the alleged universal categories or
concepts.

In this sense, Religious-Zionism provides us with yet another
manifestation of the effects of the imposition of the modern, Protestant category of "religion" on the histories and traditions of Jews.
Viewed from this point of view, Religious-Zionism, too, testifies to the
degree to which the invention of Jewish religion drives and solidifies the Zionist idea: a negation, as a theopolitics of the nation-state's
sovereignty, of the idea that Judaism is a religion, which is (the said
negation) primed on the very epistemology that gives birth to this
idea (i.e., that Judaism *is* a religion) in the first place.

Overcoming the secularist epistemology, we may easily see
the degree to which Religious-Zionism should be understood as a
national(ist), *Zionist*, phenomenon, which adheres to the dictates of
the theopolitics of the (allegedly secular) sovereign state, reading,
as it does, Jewish traditions so as to serve this same theopolitics.
As Yeshayahu Leibowitz noted,[128] this amounts to a corruption of
these traditions, that is, the "religion" which Religious-Zionists
wish to preserve. The *politically* messianic tendencies adopted by
the movement (especially following the leadership of Rabbi Zvi
Yehuda Kook) are an instance of this nationalist theopolitics. This

theopolitics is centered around the sovereign state, and it follows corresponding commitments, such as militarism and statism. As a comprehensive interpretative analysis of Religious-Zionist discourse clearly shows,[129] these are *not*, as some observers focused on the "fundamentalist religious" element of the movement have argued, instances of crypto-theological-messianism of the movement. Rather, this is a political-theology, in which the state, it sovereignty, its military power, its control over territory, and the aspired absolute correspondence between its citizenry and its national identity take center stage. In other words, it is a rather generic instance of national(ist) ideology, in tune with European, Western, modern notions of the politics of the nation-state.

What distinguishes the Religious-Zionists from their nonreligious counterparts is their competing understandings of the proscribed role of Jewish "religion" in this political theology. While the "secular" Zionist engage mostly (as we have seen in the case of the dominant Socialist-Zionists) in an adversarial dialogue with these traditions, the Religious-Zionist see their conservative preservation as serving the theopolitics of the state. As put concisely by Noam Hadad: "Religious Zionism is not a harmonious mixture of mutually corresponding nationalism and theology; rather, these manifest an ontological unity; patriotism does not contradict theology; rather it is in itself the essence of this theology."[130]

Take, for example, two of the central issues advocated by Religious-Zionists in contemporary Israeli political culture: militarism and territorialism—or the sanctification of both the Land and military. Far from being unique to the Religious-Zionist camp (historically, in both instances, Religious-Zionism in effect follows the cue of Socialist-Zionism), these are the most explicit manifestations of the sovereignty of the nation-state. They are about the state's monopoly of power and the nationalist aspiration for a complete homogeneity of identity in the nation-state. The use of Jewish traditions so as to serve these political aspirations is problematic at best. In any event, it does not testify to the "taking over" of the nationalist cause by a religious commitment; rather it tells of the ways in which Religious-Zionism reinvents the meaning of the Jewish traditions it allegedly preserves for the sake of serving the sovereign state. The modern state being "religiously" sanctified is a matter of the theopolitics of sovereignty; as the committed Zionist Leibowitz himself noted, it has very little to do, if anything, with Jewish "religion."

## Revisionist-Zionism:
## The Nationalization of Jewish Traditions

If the Zionist division of labor with regards to the nature of the uses (and abuses) of Jewish traditions positions Socialist-Zionism and Religious-Zionism as two opposing "poles," then Revisionist-Zionism is tasked with the role of occupying much of the space spanned between the two poles. As such, it represents a continuous, nonconfrontational appropriation of Jewish traditions so as to serve the theopolitics of the sovereign nation-state. Tellingly, this evolution-of-sorts—starting from a prototypical "secularist" negation of Jewish "religion" and ending with a rather "organic" adoption of certain elements of this religion/tradition so as to serve the Zionist project of Jewish sovereignty—is to be found in the political-intellectual evolution of Vladimir (Zeev) Jabotinsky, the founder of Revisionist-Zionism himself. But what seems to be more important than this gradual change is the contested manner in which it is debated and explained in Zionist historiography.[131]

Giving birth to what might be termed a "sub-genre" of attempts at accounting for it,[132] Jabotinsky's developing assessment of the role of Jewish traditions in the Zionist cause is clearly taken to be more important than the personal intellectual history at hand. It is seen as symbolic of the larger scheme of historical-political development, especially with regard to Jabotinsky's political successors' rule of the Israeli state. Indeed, reading the various, competing exegeses of a rather uniform corpus of Jabotinsky's writings, one is struck by the intensity characterizing the discourse on the matter of "Jabotinsky and religion." Whether seen as an alarming betrayal of the exulted values of secularism or as a blessed realization of the value of Jewish "religion," Jabotinsky's evolving stance is clearly seen as projecting (positively or negatively—depending on the observer's own stance) on the ultimate authenticity of Jabotinsky's *Zionist* commitment.

That is to say: the competing interpretations all nourish on those same notions of the essentially secularist nature of the historical Zionist project. Jabotinsky's apparent evolving realization that a simple secularist rejection of "Jewish religion" might not be the correct ideological and practical stance to be taken is thus understood as directly implicating his ideological commitments. Probably most indicative of this is the attempt by Jabotinsky's son, Eri, who approaches the matter with the zeal of fighting against defamation, to set the historical record straight. For Eri Jabotinsky, himself deeply committed to a secularist understanding of the very meaning of the Zionist revolution, the claim that his father has, indeed, gradually adopted—both in his personal life and in his ideological worldview—a "more religious" stance amounts to slander. As he puts it, a paper purporting to retrace this evolutionary course of Jabotinsky's is not simply "riddled with distortions [. . .] It is one long distortion, from beginning to end."[133]

Eri Jabotinsky leaves no room for doubt: the argument at hand carries serious implications to the very reputation of his father. He is thus denouncing "a glorious list" of historians who "wish to Judaize the founders and leader of the Zionist movement,"[134] motivated as they are by "the Religious-Socialist coalition ruling our state."[135] In other words, it is the Socialist-Zionists, the bitter political and ideological nemesis of Revisionist-Zionism, accompanied by the Religious-Zionists, their minor coalitional partner, who are attempting to delegitimize Zeev Jabotinsky by "*Judaizing*" him. This, indeed, makes no sense outside of a Zionist ideological framework that takes vehement, anti-religious secularism to be an integral part of the Zionist project. It assumes the essential, central value of the secularist negation of "religion" as standing at the core of the Zionist stance towards Jewish "religious" traditions. Eri Jabotinsky thus complains against tactics of "censorship and distortion" taken by these interested parties, which are to blame for the mistaken sense that Zeev Jabotinsky was not truly, wholeheartedly and absolutely *not*-"religious."

Eri Jabotinsky's accusations against censorship and intentional distortions notwithstanding, there seems to be little, if any, disagreement among the scholars on the very textual evidence of the evolution of Jabotinsky's stance. (The arguments are reserved for the competing understandings of the motives behind the text, and there meaning.)

This evolution can be summarized as consisting of three main phases. Initially, Jabotinsky had advocated a rather straightforward secularist nationalist negation of "religion." He approached religion "instrumentally and apprehensively."[136] Espousing primarily to nationalist ideologies of the time, he viewed religion in a rather generic Secularist-Zionist manner—a matter of the exilic, passive past, that is bound to be rejected in order for Jewish (secular) nationalism to gain hold. As he put it in 1905, "not religion, but the national exceptionality"[137] is what have preserved the Jewish People throughout history. Religion, in this historical scheme of the negation of exile, has functioned as a preserving agent, a "sealed wall" separating Jews from Gentiles, while at the same time preserving the nation's unity. This, in other words, is a rather straightforward Enlightened, liberalist view of tradition: its ability to function as a preserving agents is derived from its lack of dynamism, of it being a sealed package of directives. Exile has resulted in the freezing of tradition, which is rendered, ultimately, redundant. In exile, "the internal development of Judaism as a religion has ceased [. . .] Once the People of Israel has lost its land [i.e., sovereignty] Judaism stopped changing and evolving."[138] Religion, in other words, is seen here as an obstacle to the modern form of sovereign national life.

The second, intermediary phase in Jabotinsky's thought is characterized by a gradual "moderation" of his stance on the role of Jewish religion—or rather, at this less-negative context: heritage and tradition—in the wider Zionist project. Taken against the background of negotiations between Jabotinsky's newly founded Revisionist movement in 1925 and the Religious-Zionist movement, this moderation carries a rather easily discernable air of political pragmatism: It allows Jabotinsky to court the Religious-Zionist faction more easily, highlighting the difference between his stance and that of the now dominant Socialist-Zionists. At this stage, Jabotinsky is far from positively exulting Jewish tradition. He famously even vetoed an attempt by members of his movement to officially note the positive role of religion in the Jewish national revival. His stance at this point "can be defined as a 'neutral' stance, mixed with expressions of, on the one hand, reservation, and on the other hand appreciation of certain aspects of religious tradition."[139]

This evolution has culminated in the third phase, during which "Jabotinsky did not become a religious person, but his attitude toward religion has become very positive. He assigned great importance to religion as a central element in the national life of the Jewish people."[140] Taken against the context of the Revisionists withdrawing from the Zionist establishment and instituting the New Zionist Organization (in 1935), this stage also charts the outlines of the political practice that would later characterize the Herut party, and the Israeli (non-"religious") Right more generally.[141] This "positive" stance consists of an explicit attempt at "nationalizing" certain elements of Jewish tradition so as to buttress the Zionist project. Unlike the confrontational position taken by the Socialist-Zionists, Jabotinsky does not attempt to rewrite or reinvent parts of this tradition(s). Rather, he selectively highlights certain elements of these traditions as conducive to the larger nationalist project.

Now, as aforementioned, a review of the literature dealing with this evolutionary history of an ideologue and his ideology highlights the degree to which the competing assessments of this evolution are driven by a sense of the purity (and the danger of contamination it entails) of the secular(ist) nature of the Zionist idea. In other words, what emerges as an advocacy of the purity of Jabotinsky's ideology betrays the degree to which the "secular" nature of the Zionist/ nationalist ideology he espoused is taken to be essential to the very notion of modern Jewish sovereignty.

What may be called apologetic interpretations claim, one way or another, that Jabotinsky's apparent moderation toward Jewish tradition or religion was motivated primarily, even exclusively, by political considerations, and does not betray such a potential "contamination" of his secularist nationalism by a religious sentiment of sorts. As one typical rendition of this puts it, Jabotinsky has been "a total agnostic," who did not believe in God, and even when he did refer to God this was not accompanied by an "acknowledgment of the reality of God, nor did he have a need to refer to Divinity for establishing his political doctrine." Indeed, Jabotinsky did use "terms that are derived from the world of religious tradition," but this does not mean he genuinely believed in their referents: "Judaism for him was a heritage of a national culture [. . .] [for Jabotinsky] Religion is an instrument used by the nation." Similarly, "his relation to the [Hebrew] Bible was [only] instrumental." The bottom line, then, is clear: "Jabotinsky derived inspiration from religious tradition being a universal cultural heritage and a particular national heritage. Inspiration—yes, authority—not!"[142]

Tellingly, a central rhetorical maneuver in establishing this claim is to present Jabotinsky negatively vis-à-vis "religion." His cherished secularity is constructed by negation, as the rejection of or indifference towards what the authors take to be signs of Jewish religion (these include primarily belief in God and certain well-known Jewish practices). Thus, for example, Eri Jabotinsky stresses that "My father has never taken me to synagogue, and when I turned 13 he did not bother to organize for me a traditional 'Bar-Mitzva' [. . .] [H]e did not observe kashrut, did not pray, did not fast on Yom Kippur, and did not observe the Shabbat."[143]

An account of Jabotinsky's somewhat contradictory ideological commitments shows these—or rather the contradiction they entail—to be the prime determinants of his developing stance towards Jewish tradition. In this account, Jabotinsky's secularism, driven by his liberalist inclinations of nineteenth-century Europe clashed with his advocacy of organic nationalism, which stresses race, or blood, as the primary determinant of national identity.[144]

Jabotinsky, in other words, shared the "blood-centered" notion of Jewish identity, which, as I have discussed earlier, shaped much of what is taken to be the "secular" Zionist stance. He, too, viewed the nation's cultural heritage as derived from the biological "fact" of national, biological kinship. But unlike the secularist Zionist rebels, he did not—at least at last count—view this biological fact as sufficient for preserving an authentic sense of Jewishness. His, no doubt, is a theopolitics of sovereignty through and through. And in this ideological scheme, tradition is appropriated instrumentally so as to serve the larger project of nationalism. His is "an agnostic political theology, that wishes to erase the dichotomy between the theological and the political by including the theology in the realm of the political as one component of its essence."[145]

Moving along this (limited) spectrum of stances toward tradition, Jabotinsky had forecast the way in which David Ben-Gurion's statism would incorporate certain elements of Jewish tradition into the political theology of the State of Israel, replacing Socialist-Zionism's confrontational stance.[146] The latter seemed, at last count, to be incompatible with the maturing Zionist sense of *Jewish* sovereignty. This trajectory was further emphasized by the rule of Jabotinsky's political successors from 1977 onward. An appreciation of the ways in which the State of Israel has constructed and handled the meaning of Jewish sovereignty is now in place. This would be the focus of the rest of the book.

# Part III

# The Israeli Nation-State and Jewish Traditions

The current part of the book shifts its focus from pre-statehood Zionism to the Israeli nation-state. Were this book to follow the cue of the academic mainstream, this part of the book might have been titled "Religion and Politics in Israel." Instead, remaining loyal to the epistemological discussion I opened with, I shall offer here a reconsideration of the matters usually discussed under this label as issues pertaining to the relationship between the theopolitics of the state and Jewish traditions that preceded it and continue to live alongside it. This section thus aims to study the ways in which the sovereign nation-state, which identifies as the state of the Jews, or even a Jewish state, has negotiated some of the apparent tensions in the Zionist stance toward preceding Jewish traditions. The state has taken a central, dominant role in the construction of Israeli national identity, which involves an active maintenance of Israeli-Jews' Jewishness. This necessarily reflects upon the state's self-identification as a democratic state of the Jews.

Chapter 7 studies some of the intersubjective meanings that are commonly associated with Israeli national identity. More specifically, the chapter focuses on the tension between Israeli statehood and Jewish nationhood. It arrives at this through a consideration of rulings by the Israeli Supreme Court, which held that there is no such thing as an Israeli nation. Chapters 8 and 9 are devoted to a study of the Jewish identity maintained by the nation-state.

I begin, then, with the rather curious case of the Israeli court denying Israeli nationalism. As we shall see, this sheds some illuminating light on the matters at hand.

# 7

# Israeliness vs. Jewishness

## National Identity in Israel and Jewish Traditions

### Israeliness, Jewishness, and the Court

Is there such a thing as an Israeli nation, or Israeli *national* identity? Does Israeliness constitute a nationality, in the "thicker" meaning of the term, as it is commonly used in public and academic discourse?

This, indeed, may sound like an absurd question. Moreover, examined more closely, it may seem "doubly absurd": a simple answer to the question may be both and at the same time self-evident and logically impossible; looked at from different points of view, the answer is both obviously "yes" and surely "no." On the one hand, can we assume that a rather viable nation-state of some seventy years (the State of Israel, of course), based in turn on a politically triumphant nationalist ideology more than 100 years old (i.e., Zionism) will *not* bring to life an equally viable national identity? On the other hand, if we do accept that Israeli national identity is a viable, distinct identity, what are we to make of the state's self-identification as the Jews'—not the Israelis'—state? Or, even more problematically, how are we to square an Israeli national identity with the state's now-constitutional self-identification as a *Jewish* (and democratic) state?[1]

Let me explicate just two of the problematic—indeed, politically and ideologically caustic—implications of these binary answers. The possibility that the Israeli nation-state has indeed brought to life a "native" national identity may shed a negative light on a fundamental tenet of the state's own guiding ideology, according to which all Jews compose a distinct—and unified—nation. It may amount (and, as we shall see shortly, has indeed amounted) to a claim that Israelis are a distinct national group, separate from Jews; that the two terms are,

163

from a nationalist point of view, mutually exclusive—one's identification as belonging to the Israeli nation would mean she does not
belong to the Jewish nation.[2]

On the other hand, an explicit identification of Israeliness as
equal to Jewishness would mean that Israeli national identity is
reserved exclusively for Jews, or at least that non-Jews cannot partake
equally in it. It would amount to an assertion that Palestinian-Arab
citizens of Israel cannot, by definition, take a viable, genuine, and
equal part in the identity sponsored and upheld by their state. To put
it even more bluntly, it would amount to an assertion that Israel is
not *their* state, even though it proclaims them its citizens. This must
shed a negative light on Israel's alleged democratic character.[3]

But do we truly have the ability to decide one way or another, in a binary manner, whether a national identity of some kind is
"real" or not, exists or not? Social scientists (or, better put, students
of the human sciences/studies), who accept as a matter of an obvious (social, human) fact that these matters are not naturally given but
rather sociopolitically constructed, would understandably be critical
of the absurdity of this question. Surly we would be better advised
not to mess with such absolutist, quasi-empirical riddles, and focus
instead on an analysis and interpretation of the intersubjective meaning[4] people, cultures, individuals etc., carry or manifest regarding the
wider symbolic, material, social and political reality that is what we
would usually term "national identity."

Nevertheless, the Israeli Supreme Court has taken upon itself
more than once to do exactly this: to decide one way or another—a
yes or no answer—whether the existence of an Israeli nation has been
positively proven. And it so happened that the Supreme Court of the
(nation-) State of Israel, time and again, decided the answer to be in
the negative. In doing so, the court highlighted the complicated nature
of the State of Israel's self-identification as a democratic nation-state
of the Jews. It exposed some of the more sensitive, explosive threads
of Zionism's unresolved, complicated relationship with the Jewish
traditions that preceded it. As such, this ruling provides us with a
rather straightforward articulation of what is at stake here, namely,
Israel's inability to fully decipher the very meaning of it being a Jewish state, following Zionism's claim to be a political movement of the
Jewish nation.

After exploring the way in which the Israeli court tackled the
issue, as well as explicating the historical context in which it should

be studied, I shall offer what I take to be a more sensible way of approaching the matter of Israeli identity, namely an examination of the construction, development, and practice of the meaning this notion carries. This will involve primarily a consideration of this identity-construct's ability to accommodate or pronounce Israel's identification as a democratic sovereign state of Jews. I shall argue that while it would be quite difficult to deny the viability of Israeli national identity, this identity is not independent from a certain understanding of a Jewish identity and Jewish traditions that is, at root, a product of the nation-state that self-identifies as the state of *Jews*, not of Israelis. This brings to life a de facto identification between Israeliness and Jewishness, which renders any discussion on Israeli national identity a "complicated" matter.

## Jews, (New) Hebrews, and Israelis: A Historical-Ideological Context for the Case at Hand

As we shall see, the judicial case at hand is rooted directly in the afore-discussed tension between Zionist ideology's sense of a modern, "secular" national revival and the movement's ethnoreligious, Jewish history or tradition. Both the appeal and the court's response cannot be fully assessed without taking into consideration this historical-ideological background.

One obvious conclusion of the study of Zionism's stance vis-à-vis preceding Jewish traditions (presented in the preceding section of this book) is that this stance has been "ambiguous." This ambivalence was not just a matter of personal or collective biography of the Zionist ideologues, but also a rather central characteristic of mainstream Zionist ideology itself. Harsh as its criticism against Jewish tradition/"religion" may be, Zionism has been nevertheless claiming a *Jewish* national identity that simply could not give up on either Jewish ("religious") history or Jewish peoplehood. In this context, we should keep in mind that Zionism sought to position itself as a *universally Jewish* movement—one that includes, at least in principle, by the sheer logic of national cohesion—all Jews: whether religious or not, exilic or not, even Zionist or not.

As critics have long pointed out, this ambivalence put mainstream Zionism in a jeopardized position vis-à-vis competing narratives of Hebrew nationalism, which sought to wholly and explicitly negate any relation between those ("new") Hebrews and their Jewish ancestry.⁵ Taken to its logical conclusion, the "negation of (Jewish) exile" pitted Hebrews (the name preferred by Zionist ideologues)⁶ *against* Jews. It had become quite difficult, if not outright inconsistent, to defend the "Jewish" element in this image of national revival. It is not difficult to see why mainstream Zionism's "insistence" on a Jewish self-identification, combined with its severe negation of that same traditional Jewishness, would eventually become somewhat hard to defend, especially when considering second- and third-generation Zionists, young women and men who were born into the ideological hotbed of mostly Socialist-Zionism, fed as they were by a resentment toward Jewish "religion" and "tradition," but lacking their parents' unmediated knowledge of this tradition.

"Young Hebrews" was indeed the original name of a politically weak yet intellectually and culturally influential group of formerly Zionist intellectuals, who had articulated and further developed this logical conclusion of the negation of exile and traditional Jewishness. Without dwelling too deeply into an exposition of this rather fascinating group, it would suffice to describe the Young Hebrews as having constructed a historical, cultural and political narrative/identity, which presented Hebrew nationalism as originating in pre- (or, better put, non-) Jewish history. They further presented themselves as wholly unrelated to exilic Jews, and severely criticized the supposedly secular Zionist establishment for being trapped in the hands of rabbinic Jewish authority. For them, Hebrew national identity was primarily a matter of territory and language, the exclusive identity of those who live on the land of the ancient Hebrews and speak their language. Hebrew national identity, they argued, has nothing to do with Jewish religion. Moreover, they viewed this religion as a historical shackle put on the legs of the Hebrew nation in exile. Culturally, the Young Hebrews sought to reappropriate pre-Jewish cultural assets—namely, Canaanite (pagan) myths, symbols, heroes and heroines, narratives and the like—as the building blocks of a reviving Hebrew identity. Hence, the name "Canaanites" that originated as a Zionist pejorative pitted against the Young Hebrews and was later reclaimed by them.⁷

The Young Hebrews' "Othering" of Jews was not as simple as their professed ideology might suggest. For one—critical—thing, they could not deny or escape the sense of identification, empathy, and ultimately brotherhood Hebrews like them felt toward Jewish victims of European anti-Semitism. In this regard, the Holocaust marked the limited nature of such a territorial-lingual national identification of what we might call "formerly Jewish" nationalists.[8]

This might be the main reason why the Young Hebrews never managed to pose a real political challenge to the Zionist establishment. Nevertheless, they were quite successful in articulating and professing a sense of distinct national—territorial, lingual, and historical—identity that is separate from Jewish identity.

This piece of cultural history is of relevance for the purpose of assessing the judicial case at hand, as the case replays Zionism's ambivalence regarding its own Jewishness. As I alluded to above, following Kurzweil, the Young Hebrews present a Hebrew-national "purist" position that exposes the unresolved nature of Zionism's relation with its own Jewish heritage—a point that would be replayed in the court case discussed. This short historical note can also be used as a biographical prelude to this judicial case, as several of the plaintiffs in this case were personally involved with the historical (now defunct) movement of the Young Hebrews. I will now go on to present the case in more detail.

## On the (Legalist) Viability of an Israeli Nation

So, how did it come to be that the Supreme Court of the State of Israel reached the decisive conclusion—and officially declared to this effect, as a matter of legal fact, as courts do—that there is no such thing as an Israeli nation?

### Israel's Population Registry—Nation, Religion, and Citizenship

It has to do with the fact that the State of Israel, through its Interior Ministry, holds a population registry, which includes, in addition to names, gender, personal status, addresses, etc., also the categories of Religion and Nationality (*leom* in Hebrew). These terms can be confusing, as in English-speaking countries "nationality" may be read as equal to citizenship; in the Israeli registry, Citizenship is a separate category. Nationality has to do with one's belonging to a certain nation, in the rather ideological notion of the term.

Given that the State of Israel grants almost immediate citizenship to those it identifies as Jews—probably the most important aspect

of the state's self-identification as the state of the Jews—most political and legal challenges involving this registry and its formal inter-
pretations/practices have revolved around what eventually became
a supposedly religious matter of "who is a Jew?" namely, matters
of inclusion or exclusion of individuals as members of the Jewish
people through the categories Religion and, by implication, Nationality. Some well-discussed historical legislative decisions and legal
precedents made it a matter of legal and procedural practice that in
the case of Jews the two categories (Religion and Nationality) are
taken to be essentially identical.[9]

The state thus "forces" a Jewish ethno-national identity on those
it deems (regardless of their own subjective views on the matter)
members of the Jewish majority. To give but one example: if a non-
Jew with French citizenship/passport were to become an Israeli citizen, she would be registered as French under Nationality (that is, in
this instance the registry will identify nationality with citizenship). If,
however, she happens to be a Jew, who is acquiring Israeli citizenship
based on her Jewish origin, she would be "nationally converted"—her
nationality will be marked as "Jewish." This logic also works negatively: the state does not accept, for example, formerly Jewish persons
who have converted to Christianity as members of the Jewish nation
(i.e., if they are registered as "Christian" under Religion, they cannot
register as "Jews" under Nationality, even if they were born Jewish).

### "I Am Israeli" Against the State of Israel

This is the procedural and ideological background against which a
group of Israeli citizens, who are registered by the state either (in
most cases) as Jews or as members of other nationalities (Arab, Druze,
Buddhist, Georgian, Burmese) appealed to the court in 2003 with a
request that the state registers them as "Israeli" under Nationality.[10]
This was an admittedly declarative appeal, as the appellants requested the court to pronounce Israeli nationality a viable category. Most
importantly, the appellants explained that their positive request to be
registered as "Israeli" also has a negative aspect. As the court put it:
"they do not feel themselves to be members of the Jewish nation."[11]

The main appellant in the case—and its instigator—was Uzi
Ornan, a former member of the original Young Hebrews (his brother,
Uriel Shelaḥ, was the leader of the group), and a longtime activist
dedicated to the cause of separating the "religious" Jewish element

from Hebrew/Israeli nationalism. Often campaigning under the banner of secularism or secularity, Ornan's activism also focused on the formalities of the State's Population Registry. In previous administrative and judicial appeals he managed to have the Interior Ministry change his registration from "Jewish" under both Religion and Nationality to "Hebrew" under Nationality, and as "Of No Religion" under Religion. His rhetoric seems to have shifted along the years from a national discourse of distinct Hebrew identity (in line with the ideology of the Young Hebrews) to a civil rights discourse that protests against the prevalent preference of Jews over non-Jews in Israel. As one of his incarnations as a political activist, the "I am Israeli" civil association, explains:

> A regime of discriminations prevails in the State of Israel. Citizens are granted or denied rights based on their being Jews or non-Jews [. . .] The Interior Ministry works diligently to classify each citizen as belonging to one of the religious groups [. . .] If you are classified with the Jewish group, for example, then rabbis (who live on our expanse) will tell you what to eat, will halt public transportation on Saturdays, and will disallow or "permit" you to marry [. . .]
> The [State of Israel's] Population Registry and Identification Card are the main tools of "classification." You pull out your card—and based on it or based on the registry kept with the Interior Ministry—the clerk knows which sector you "belong" to [. . .] and what you are not entitled to, because you do not "belong."[12]

This is the general context against which Ornan and his fellow appellants requested that the court grants a declarative decision that would compel the state to register them as "Israeli" under the category of Nationality. As Ornan explained, by virtue of the very existence of the state, its citizens should all be considered members of the "nationality of the state" (or, the state's nation—*leom medina* in Hebrew; supposedly the flip-side of the notion of a nation-state):

> Even by Israel's constitutive document, the Declaration of Independence, all citizens of Israel are considered members of the common nationality of the state, that is the Israeli nation. [. . . Nevertheless], there is just one nationality of

state [*leom medina* in the Hebrew original] not recognized by the State of Israel [. . .] This is the Israeli nation! [. . .]

In order to enable a citizen who views himself as just Israeli, and does not want to be forcibly ascribed as belonging to a certain, separate religious-ethnic group, the 'I am Israeli' association [. . .] appealed to the court with a request to order the Interior Ministry to register the appellants as 'Israeli Nationality' in all formal documents of the state.[13]

## *The* Tamarin *Precedent*

As it were, Ornan and Others are not the first to have petitioned to be registered as members of the Israeli nation. All instances of the court discussing their appeal relied on a precedent ruling from 1972, the *Tamarin v. The State of Israel* appeal to the Supreme Court,[14] in which Georg Refael Tamarin, an Israeli citizen of Croat origins, who was at the time registered as Jewish under Nationality and "Of No Religion" under Religion, requested that the court orders the state to change his registration to "Israeli" under Nationality.

Tamarin was critical of recent legislation on matters of "who is a Jew?" (a legislation that in essence identified Jewish nationality with Jewish religion, and assigned Orthodox interpreters of Jewish law with the task of determining who can gain almost immediate citizenship by virtue of their Jewish origins). He was appalled by what he viewed as the "racial-religious" measure set by the new legislation for determining one's belonging to the Jewish nation. This "changed his feeling regarding his own belonging to this nation."[15] He had thus requested that the court orders the state to erase his registration as Jewish, and instead register him as Israeli under Nationality.

Tamarin's appeal to the court was thus an early instance of a declarative request that would, as all sides involved understood, separate Israeli identity from Jewish identity. The court's reasoning for denying his request tended to be fully in the framework of mainstream Zionist ideology. What is quite remarkable about it is the court's very blunt denial of the viability or existence of an Israeli national identity; and this precedent denial, as we shall see, has proven to be enduring.

Tamarin himself seems to have exhibited a more nuanced, sociohistorically sensitive view. His 1972 appeal acknowledged that back in 1949, when he was first registered with the Interior Ministry, he was hesitant regarding the viability of the notion of an Israeli nation. He concluded then that the process of the coming-to-being of an Israeli nation is still in its infancy. Hence, he decided back then to be registered as Jewish under Nationality (a more accurate formulation, he argued, would have him registered as Jewish and Croatian). After more than two decades of—well, Israeli—statehood, he argued, "to the best of my understanding, today, a consolidated Israeli nation already exists, [and] I belong to it by all subjective criteria (identification, the feeling of belonging, loyalty, and a declaration reaffirming this)."[16]

A lower instance of the court, whose decision the Supreme Court eventually upheld, determined that Tamarin's abovementioned subjective measures are irrelevant. "A person cannot create a new nation" by simply saying it exists and by feeling affinity to it. Rather, according to the court, the question at hand is of an objective—one is tempted to say: scientific—measurement, determining the very existence of a certain object or being, in this case: an Israeli nation. Nevertheless, the lower instance did not feel obligated to deal with such objective measures, since "by my own feeling as a judge who lives within his people, and possibly out of my judicial knowledge, I can say unhesitatingly that an Israeli nation does not exist separately from a Jewish nation."[17]

The ideological implications seem to have dominated much of the court's attention. Thus, for example, after noting that the Declaration of Independence explicitly designates the established state a *Jewish* nation-state, the Supreme Court, considering Tamarin's appeal, warned against the potential outcome of an explicit recognition of an Israeli national identity:

> The renewal of the political life of the Jewish People in its homeland did not come to us in order to create a schism inside the people settled in Zion, so as to divide and break it up into two nations—a Jewish one and an "Israeli" one. Such a division, if happened, may it never happen [*ḥalila* in the Hebrew original], would have been contradictory to the national goals, for which the state was established. [18]

Indeed, inside the ideological framework that dominated the establishment of the State of Israel (i.e., what is usually termed Political

Zionism) the potential outcome of such national separation is devastating. It would mean "hindering those [national] goals, and undermining the unity of the whole Jewish People."[19] The court viewed the appeal as manifesting a "separatist course of action," and decided that it is illegitimate, since it entails "the political and social disintegration of the whole people."[20] It thus concluded: "It has not been proven that [. . .] an 'Israeli nation' exits, and it is not proper to encourage the creation of new 'slivers' of nations."[21]

*Forty Years On, and Still No Proof*

Ornan and his fellow appellants argued that the forty odd years that have passed since this precedent was established had rendered it irrelevant. The District Court, the first instance to discuss their appeal, disagreed. The court concluded that while it cannot deny Ornan's subjective feeling that he belongs to an Israeli nation, from a legalist point of view, "there is no Israeli nation, and the court should not create such a creation out of nothing."[22] In other words, the District Court simply did not accept the "naturalist" claim of the appellants, according to which a group of people living together, for several decades, cherishing their common territory and sharing in the same political system (i.e., the nation-state of Israel), naturally compose a nation. The court thus viewed the appellants' request a matter of a "new creation," of "creating a new status."[23]

Nevertheless, the District Court was reluctant to go into the obviously ideological, sociopolitical argument at hand. Instead, it denied the appellants the declarative decision they were seeking by interpreting the matter at hand as located essentially outside the framework of legal-institutional decision making; "*Normatively*, the matter can be examined by judicial tools, but *institutionally* it is not a matter for judicial decision."[24]

The appellants appealed the District Court's decision, and the Supreme Court accepted that this is, after all, a matter for judicial decision. Nevertheless, it denied their request, this time on the basis of their failure to objectively prove the existence of an Israeli nation. The court concluded that the *Tamarin* precedent still holds: there is no Israeli nation.

Like in the *Tamarin* precedent, the Supreme Court's decision was explicitly attentive to Zionist ideology. In this respect, the legalistic debate between the appellants and the court reads like a repetition of the ideological/political debate between the Young Hebrews and the Zionist mainstream. Thus, for example, the appellants denied the foundational Zionist notion that Judaism *is* a nationality, i.e., that there is a Jewish nation: "One cannot define all Jews in the world as belonging to 'the Jewish nation,' since all Jews [. . .] belong to the nation of the state of which they are citizens."[25] This, the court insisted, is a "delicate, controversial issue, that has accompanied the Jewish people for many years and the Zionist movement from its inception. The notion that Judaism is not just a matter of religiosity but rather of national belonging is a cornerstone of Zionism."[26] A concurring judge was more determined:

> Regarding the Jewish nation—it has been proven that the Visionary of the State, Dr. Binyamin Zeev Herzl, was right when he determined in his book, *The Jewish State* (1896): "I think the Jewish question is no more a social than a religious one, notwithstanding that it sometimes takes these and other forms. It is a national question . . . We are a nation—one nation!"[27]

Moreover, the court also adopted an explicitly Zionist, rather polemic position, formulated by two scholars who set out to defend some of Zionism's basic premises against contemporary criticism.[28] One of the intriguing aspects of this position is the way in which it redirects a central argument of the appellants against them: while the appellants argued that Israel's insistence on a *Jewish* national identity excludes non-Jews by definition, and that an Israeli national identity will be, again by definition, inclusionary by virtue of applying equally to the whole population regardless of ethnoreligious differences, the argument referenced by the court claims the opposite. It claims that the adoption of an Israeli nationhood might, instead of including the Palestinian[29] minority as part of the nation, exclude it civilly; that it would deny their equal status as citizens of the State of Israel. As the court quotes Yakobson and Rubinstein: "In the Arab sector, many avoid or even expressly refuse to define themselves as Israelis, either because of the term's lack of national neutrality or simply for political reasons."[30] A reaffirmation of (a not-necessarily Jewish) Israeli national identity would then mean, according to this logic, an exclusion of the Palestinian citizens of Israel. Needless to say, for this logic to hold we must assume as given the practical identification between Israeliness and Jewishness, as well as the opposition between Jew and Arab as mutually exclusive categories (matters to which I shall turn shortly). It ignores, in other words, the appellants' non-Jewish (or even anti-Jewish) redefinition of Israeliness, as well as the various alternatives to the construction of "Jew" and "Arab" as mutually exclusive opposites

The Supreme Court's decision goes on to note the academic controversy surrounding the very concept of "nation." It references the major works by Gellenr, Hobsbaum, and Anderson,[31] but seems to completely ignore their critical view of nationalism. Following Yakobson and Rubinstein, the court identifies the State of Israel as based on "'Ethno-Cultural Nationalism,' in which the individual's association with the national group is mainly the outcome of common objective characteristics (language, religion, culture and common history)."[32] The court hence deemed it essential that the appellants "prove in objective criteria"[33] the existence of an Israeli nation. This would entail an objective proof that the 1972 decision (the *Tamarin* case), in which it was ordained that "the existence of an Israeli nation has not been proven in objective criteria,"[34] should be reversed. The court ruled that the appellants failed to do so, hence its reiteration that there is no objective proof of the existence of an Israeli nation.

*The State's Position*

One of the more remarkable aspects of this case is encapsulated in the State of Israel's arguments in the court. The State demanded that the court denies the appellants' request. It insisted that there is no Israeli national identity, or rather no Israeli nationality/nation, in the "thick," ideologically meaningful sense of the term. The state argued that what unites its own constituency—i.e., the various ethnic and national groups it rules over—is Israeli *citizenship*, not nationality. It further argued that the ethno-national division inside the society in Israel (given the State's own position, one must be weary of using such non-citizenship-based unifying terms as "Israeli society") is a given that cannot—and apparently should not—be denied.[35] Furthermore, this was preceded by a procedural clarification by the state's representative (a state whose founders tended to prefer to view themselves as Hebrews rather than Jews) in the District Court that Ornan's registration as "Hebrew" under Nationality is "a historical mistake," and that there is no real basis for such a registration.[36]

## The Liberal-Zionist Stake in Israeli Nationalism

The court's decision did not fail to raise the ire of certain parties who do not necessarily identify with the implicit non-Zionist stance of Ornan and Others but still have an obviously high stake in the very viability of a "secular" (as in independent of a "religious" reading of Jewishness), liberal-democratic—indeed, Zionist—Israeli identity. These parties viewed the court's denial of the existence of an Israeli national identity not only as offensive (since they, at root, do identify as belonging to an Israeli nation; their national identity *is* Israeli), but also as regressive. For them, the court's decision amounts to a declaration that religiously based, non-liberal-democratic Judaism is and should be dominant over competing, secularist readings of Israeli identity. The fact that this comes from the Supreme Court, probably the most venerated symbol/institution of Liberal-Zionists in Israel only further heightened their sense of being wronged. Probably the most coherent among these was the voice of the newspaper *Haaretz*, who dedicated its celebratory 2014 Independence Day editorial to a renunciation of the Supreme Court's verdict. The argument presented by the paper is captured quite clearly in the editorial's title: "There is Such a Thing as 'Israeli.'" The editorial board viewed the matter as closely related to the controversial legislative measure that would constitutionally enshrine Israel's self-identification as the nation-state of the Jewish people:[37]

> Both the court ruling and the ceaseless parliamentary efforts to legislate such a law [i.e., the Basic Law: Israel—the Nation State of the Jewish People] put forth a very narrow portrait of "Israeliness." For 66 years now "Israeliness" has attempted to gain recognition and win independence, and has been rejected repeatedly by the establishment. It has been described as the "slivers of peoplehood" whose existence has not been proven, while at the same time, no one seeks to legislate a law that will define and protect it. Again and again it is forced to bow before its "big sister," the Jewish state.
>
> But while [Binyamin] Netanyahu's motivation [in promoting the aforementioned Basic Law] can be explained by his obsessive desire to Judaize Israel and not to allow

its minorities to "feel at home," it is hard not to wonder
what exactly the basis was for the court's determination
that there is no such thing as an Israeli nationality [. . .]
Does it not suffice that a group of people lives together
for decades in a country called Israel, to call this people
"Israeli"? The creation of Israeli literature, Israeli art, Israeli
music, Israeli theater, Israeli humor, Israeli politics, Israeli
sports, an Israeli accent, Israeli grief—are all of these not
enough to speak of an "Israeli people"?[38]

## A Sociopolitical Approach to Israeliness:
## On the Development and Viability of Jewish-Israeli Identity

As attested to by both the court's explicitly ideological comments and
*Haaretz'* equally ideological criticism of the court's ruling, the supposedly judicial matter at hand touches upon two critical sociopolitical dimensions. On a most immediate sense, these have to do with
the very core of the Zionist project of establishing a nation-state of
Jews: (1) The relationship between Israeli Jews and "diaspora" Jewry;
namely the question of the proper relation between "the State of the
Jews" (and its Jewish citizens) and the Jews of the world; and (2) the
relationship between the majority of Jews and the minority of non-
Jews, specifically Muslim and Christian Palestinian citizens of Israel;
namely, whose state is it? Does it "belong" to—or rather cater to the
interests of—the "Jews" (as defined, of course, by the state), or rather
of those of (all) its citizens?

Put more broadly, the judicial-procedural case at hand brought
to life a rather crippled discussion (crippled, since it was bound by
the judicial rules of the game) on the very meaning of being Israeli
or of Israeliness. In addition to the two matters mentioned above, this
also touches upon Zionism's unresolved and conflicted relationship
with its own Jewish identity; the failed attempt to force Jewish traditions, histories, and identities into conceptual frameworks that would
categorize them as either religion or nationality; and the sense and
meaning of Israeli Judaism.

As in most cases of such clear-cut opposing arguments—arguments posed by two mainstays of Liberal-Zionism in the case discussed here (the court and *Haaretz'* editorial)—sociopolitical reality
seems to defy either argument. In a sense, both are correct to a certain
degree, and both are wrong in ignoring forceful arguments to the

contrary. Each of them assumes a given, ideologically driven answer to the fundamental question: "What does it mean to be Israeli?" and ignores the very contested nature of their answers.

A sociopolitical consideration of the matter at hand would have to begin, then, with an attempt at understanding how the meaning of Israeliness is constructed and interpreted by it "practitioners," or carriers. In other words, we are dealing here with the fundamental (human) question of how collective and private identities are constructed, understood, negotiated, and developed. Needless to say, these questions are central to understanding politics. If we are successful in beginning to understand the meaning associated with Israeli identity by it carriers, that is, the meaning Israelis associate with being Israeli, we may also be able to begin to understand the political world they maintain, and its relation to other political worlds, both near and distanced.

*The Israeli State and Israeli Identity*

The Israeli case presents an even more pressing need to offer such an analysis, as the project of building and maintaining a collective national identity (the name of which—Israeli? Jewish? Zionist?—can be left unresolved at this point.)[39] has been one of the central endeavors of the nation-state of Israel. The conflict-ridden history of the state and the controversial nature of this identity construction only further highlight the importance—and sensitivity—of such a study.

Indeed, the state's role in the construction of what amounts, at the end, to a personal identity (one's identification as Israeli, or as Jew, or otherwise), cannot be exaggerated. This can be explicated if, for example, we consider the very political-administrative practice that the court took as a given: the state's holding of a registry, which marks every individual's "religion" and "nationality." The history of the application and shaping of this registry is beyond the scope of this book. Nevertheless, we may wonder what this registry is aimed at achieving and expressing. After all, not all modern nation-states make an effort to so categorically classify their population along religious and national criteria; others may not demand, as is the case with the Israeli registry, to have "objective" proof of one's belonging (or not-belonging, as the case at hand suggests) to a certain category.[40]

Taken on its face value, the registry immediately brings to the forefront several critical points: (a) the ideological notion (rooted in the very core of the Zionist idea) that Judaism is not, or not just, a religion, but primarily a nationality, which in turn is, essentially, separate from and superior to "religious" Jewish belonging; (b) the practical sense in which the registry enables the state to distinguish Jews from non-Jews, specifically Palestinian Muslims and Christians, and to put in practice a preference of the former over the latter (either as a matter of explicit ideology or as a measure of "security"); and (c) the ways in which the registry is used to accomplish explicitly political aims of achieving dominance through the manipulation of identities (as in the practice of separating Palestinian Druze citizens of Israel from other Palestinians by identifying Druze as a nationality).[41] It should also be explicated that the court never questioned the practice of holding this registry in its current form.

The statist practice of maintaining this registry should be taken into consideration inside a larger framework that deals with the (nation-) State of Israel's ongoing project or process of self-creation and self-definition. The fact that Israel is a rather young nation-state, the establishment of which has been a culmination of an ideological project, highlights a characteristic that is sometimes left hidden in plain sight: Israeli nationalism—or, to put it differently, the national identity that is maintained by the State of Israel—lacks a long running tradition. Even by the measures of other invented (or, better put, sociopolitically constructed) national traditions, this one has a fairly short history. Of course, part of this invented tradition is an attempt at reappropriating certain chapters of Jewish history, but this should not be confused with the deeper sense of tradition. In other words, when considering the matters at hand we would be better advised to remember the rather simple fact that Israel is a state that was built upon an ideological bed, and, to a very large degree, *preceded* its own population; it is a state that came to life before its society did. And the state has taken a formidable role in the very "creation" and shaping of this society. Indeed, one of the bigger projects undertaken by the State of Israel is the one dealing with the very creation of what it (in line with Zionist ideology) viewed as Jewish national identity.

The reverse side of this last fact is often neglected by observers of Israeli politics: the State of Israel has not put much, if any, efforts in the construction of an *Israeli* identity. Indeed, as argued by the state's representatives in court, and echoed by the court itself in the cases discussed above, the State of Israel views Israeliness as a procedural matter of one's citizenship. In the most fundamental of senses, it views itself as a state of the Jewish nation—that is of Jews, not of

Israelis. Thus, the formidable project of creating a Jewish national identity in Israel—which has involved the government's ruling-over or heavy intervention in the educational system, the cultural field, the media, the army as a socialization agent, etc.—has been dedicated to the creation of Zionist-Jewish nationals, not of Israeli ones. Given some heated debates over the Civic Education curricula,[42] one may even argue that the State tends to prefer the creation of Zionist nationals over Israeli *citizens*. In any event, the point to keep in mind when considering the viability of an Israeli identity is that the nation-state in which this identity is said to be forged is not invested in fostering Israeliness; indeed, as the court made clear, the state (as well as the court itself) tends to view Israeli identity as threatening the state's founding, Zionist self-identification as a state of Jews.

Israeliness, then, might be viewed not as an identity of the nation-state (this, I should mention, was the core argument by Ornan and Others appealing to the court; what Ornan termed "a state's nation," *leom medina*), but rather as an identity forged, negotiated, and maintained in other spheres, namely the market, civil society, and, of course, the private sphere. Given the "less formally-institutionalized" nature of these spheres, the discussion at hand cannot, as the court assumed, provide "objective" proofs and disproofs.

Instead, we would be better advised to discuss, through interpretation, the viability and nature of Israeli traditions. namely: (a) the degree to which Israeli traditions have indeed been forged and maintained in these spheres; (b) the agents who play a central role in the shaping and maintenance of these traditions; (c) the sources upon which these tradition nourish; (d) the symbolic vocabulary and grammar of these traditions; most critically: (e) the worlds of meaning they carry, or associated with; and lastly, (f) the viability of these, especially when confronted with competing traditions (mainly, in this case, the Zionist-Jewish tradition propagated by the state).

*Israelis, Jews, Zionists—and Palestinians*

The above are, indeed, general criteria that are not unique to Zionist or Israeli history. The particular characteristics of the case at hand necessitate a consideration of two crucial points. In a very crude formulation these include the complementary matters of the "Jewishness" of this Israeliness, and its "civilness"; In other words, the relationship between Israeliness and the state-sponsored Zionist-Jewishness on the one hand, and Israeliness's inclusion or exclusion of non-Jews on the other. Indeed, this may sound like a cumbersome formulation of the oft-discussed alleged contradiction between Israel's Jewish identity and its democratic regime. But, as I hope my discussion until now has clarified, such a one-dimensional framework—i.e., a rather naïve identification of the Israeli nation-state as an "essentially secular" political entity whose commitment to democratic principles is curtailed by a "Jewish" yoke imposed on it by virtue of it being a state of Jews—is more misleading than clarifying. For one thing, it completely ignores Zionism's complicated, unresolved relationship with Jewish traditions that preceded it. Moreover, this is done via the imposition of wholly foreign conceptual framework and binaries (i.e., the secular vs. the religious, modernity vs. tradition, politics vs. religion, etc.) on Jewish histories, identities, cultures, and systems of intersubjective meanings.

We must remember that the relationship between Israeliness, Jewishness, and Israeli citizenship is to be taken into consideration in the wider framework of the dominance of Zionist ideology and its application in the nation-state of Israel. As Gershon Shafir and Yoav Peled put it,[43] a consideration of "who is Israeli" must take into account *three* critical dimensions of Zionism and the Israeli nation-state: these include not only Jewish-Israeli ethno-nationalism and democracy, but also colonialism. Given that the main, fundamental— indeed, constitutive—trait of the political Zionist/Israeli project is the conflict over land, against its inhabitants (namely non-Jewish Palestinians), the project of establishing a state of Jews—or a Jewish state—is mainly interpreted and applied as a ceaseless drive to secure a "Jewish majority" (a project put under the banner of a "demographic threat"), and securing the sovereignty of Jews.[44]

A full analysis of the meaning of Israeliness would demand a much larger consideration than is allowed here.[45] In order to explicate the complex nature of the matter at hand, namely what the judicial discussion of the matter failed to capture, I will limit myself in the remainder of this chapter to the critical issue of the ways in which Jewish identity is negotiated as an Israeli trait.

*Israeliness = Israeli-Jewishness*

Considered sociopolitically, the relationship between Israeliness and Jewishness sheds a rather critical light on both the court and the appellants in the cases mentioned above. The different parties seem to have completely ignored a rather straightforward, de facto identification between Israeliness and Jewishness in the dominant Israeli mindset. Viewed from the point of view of Israeli political culture, the very distinction between Jewish nationalism and Israeli identity seems to be a wholly artificial one. The two terms are often used as synonyms, and common discourse in Israel clearly tends to see "authentic" Israeliness as manifesting a distinctly Jewish character. This identification is, of course, mutually applicable: what might be viewed by outsiders as "Jewish" acts are often taken by Israeli Jews to be manifestations of their Israeliness—of their national (supposedly "secular") identity, that has little if anything to do with Jewish "religion."

This sociopolitical fact has to do with how the state constructs its identity as a Jewish nation-state: The identification between Israeliness and Jewishness is largely dependent upon the rather elaborate system of symbols, rituals, and ideology that the state promotes as national and political (hence as allegedly secular), which derives quite heavily from a specific interpretation of Jewish ("religious") traditions.[46] This "mix-up" between Israeliness and Jewishness can thus be attributed to the state-sponsored culture, popular practices, collective memory (specifically, the trauma of the Holocaust), and of course the educational system, which upholds a rather "thin" Jewish content, but nevertheless broadcasts a clear message that one should respect and observe certain elements of Jewish tradition as expressions of one's authentic nationalism, that is, her Israeliness.

The Israeli public sphere, and especially the popular media, where Israeliness is constantly constituted and maintained, service this identification between a certain meaning of Jewishness and Israeli identity, reaffirm it and market it (indeed, usually for servicing the interest of the market itself) as a matter of taken-for-granted daily practice. A recent explicit exposition of this cultural/political reality simply argues that the best, if not only, way to understand Israeli (note: not just Jewish-Israeli) culture is to view it as a *Jewish* culture: Given that it is "a culture that is (1) carried by Jews, (2) relates directly to their Jewishness, and (3) pertains to other Jewish cultures," we must conclude that Israeli culture should be analyzed as "an independent Jewish culture." Moreover, "[t]here are Jewish cultures that are not Israeli, but there is no mainstream Israeli culture that is not Jewish."[47] The author reaches the manifestly positive conclusion that given the above, "there is little sense, if any at all, to the supposed contradiction between 'Jewish' and 'Israeli.'"[48]

As aforementioned, the de facto identification between Israeliness and Jewishness is bidirectional: not only does it render Israeli

identity "essentially" Jewish, but it also renders certain Jewish (religious or quasi-religious) practices a political matter of manifesting
one's (supposedly secular) Israeli, national identity. The state's reliance on a rather narrow interpretation/appropriation of certain traditional Jewish practices and institutions (such as the Jewish or Hebrew
calendar, the Shabbat, and Jewish holidays) creates an historical novelty: the state of Israel is the only place (and historical period) where
an individual's Jewish identity can be meaningfully maintained and
upheld without her taking an active part in a communal or practical
observance/upholding of her Jewishness.

The state, in other words, maintains Israelis' Jewish identity for
them. It enables them to partake passively in an ongoing project of
affirming their Jewish identity, and to enjoy the political fruits of their
identification with the majority group, without explicitly or actively
maintaining their Jewishness. Israeli Jews can avoid taking an active
part, for example, in the marking of Jewish holidays and still experience or even celebrate them, by being transferred—by virtue of acts
taken by the state's agents, by the media, etc.—into a framework of
time and space that are detached from the routine flow of the daily
construction of time and public space. Needless to say, non-Jews cannot enjoy this privilege.

Echoing the doubly absurd nature of the discussion mentioned
above, this de facto identification between Israeliness and Jewishness
sheds a critical light on both the notion of a viable, independent-from-
Judaism Israeli national identity and on the denial of the existence of
an Israeli, *national* identity. To put it bluntly, there seems to be little
doubt that there is an Israeli identity, but this identity if fundamentally dependent on the state that denies the viability of Israeliness.
There obviously is what an honest observer may identify as an Israeli,
national identity, but it is not independent from a certain understanding of a Jewish identity/tradition that is, at root, a product of the
nation-state that self-identifies as the state of *Jews*.[49]

*Diaspora Israeliness?*

Israeli identity is fundamentally dependent on a statist interpretation
and maintenance of a politically Jewish tradition and identity. Con-
versely, this Jewishness is distinctly Israeli—it is viable only in the
framework of the nation-state of Israel. It is difficult, if not outright
impossible, to see Israeliness, in its thicker meaning, perpetuate itself

outside the confines, patronage, and authority of the state, such as in cross-generational continuation in diaspora communities of Israelis.

For one thing, these diaspora Israelis can no longer enjoy the privilege of being identified as Jewish while totally indifferent to practicing or institutionally marking their Jewishness. Hence the rather curious phenomenon of "totally secular" Israeli-Jews joining Jewish denominations and synagogues once they have emigrated to the United States—something they would not even bother to contemplate doing while in Israel. Lacking the backing of their (Jewish) state, their very Israeliness (which is, again, identified with Jewishness) is threatened. They thus perform a rather straightforward act of what Herbert Gans[50] termed "symbolic religiosity," i.e., "the consumption of religious symbols apart from regular participation in a religious culture or in religious organizations." But unlike what Gans identified as the motive driving this symbolic religiosity, the diasporic Jewish-Israeli case is driven—from the point of view of the practicing agents themselves—not by "the purpose of expressing feelings of religiosity and religious identification,"[51] but rather by feelings of (ethno-)national identification (which are, indeed, quite indistinguishable from what might be viewed as religious; nevertheless, they are viewed as "basically secular").[52] Indeed, the identification between Israeliness and Jewishness renders this attempt at disentangling the two categories quite meaningless, and surely confusing.

## Israeliness and Non-Jews

This, then, also sheds a critical light on the ways in which Israeliness, by sociocultural definition, tends to exclude non-Jews. The state propagates and maintains a collective identity construct that puts non-Jews in a jeopardized position: if they accept the "national" symbol system, they must also buy into an identity construct that self-identifies as Jewish.

Sociopolitical history delineates two primary options, or rather paths (for the involved parties seem to have very limited choice here) into which the state directs its non-Jewish population. One path is a direct derivative of the abovementioned fundamental fact of the Zionist-Palestinian conflict over land, namely the ongoing construction of Israeliness/Jewishness as the opposite of "Arab" or "Palestinian." Symbolically speaking, there can be little doubt that the "significant Other"[53] in the Israeli national narrative is "the Arab."

Indeed, Zionism has introduced into Jewish discourse a rather novel opposition, in which Arab and Jew are taken to be total opposites, the two poles of a dichotomy that supposedly defines the history of modern Israel.

This leaves Palestinian Israelis in a peculiar position: were they to adopt *Israeli* national identity, they would, in essence, signal themselves (being non-Jewish Arabs) as their own worst enemies. This, of course, is nothing more than a theoretical conundrum. In practical senses, the option discussed here in null. Palestinian Israelis have no viable path in which to join, if they wanted to, in Israeli nationalism or national identity. All they are left with is a distinct status of a minority that cannot share in the majority's identity. They are marked as the Israeli ultimate, significant Other. Palestinians, in other words, can never really be "Israelis."

But Israeliness also proves that it can, and does, open up to include non-Jews (as long as they are not Arab/Palestinian, of course), and to assimilate them into a *Jewishness* of sort. The main case in point here is that of non-Jewish immigrants from the former Soviet Union, who are offered not only almost immediate citizenship (by virtue of their remote familial relationship to Jews), but also a clear path to inclusion inside the framework of Israeliness/Jewishness. This has led students of Israeli society to coin such terms as "social conversion" and "non-Jewish Jews"[54] to capture the inclusion of these non-Jews as members of the Jewish-Zionist ethno-national collective. This attests to the fact that by becoming "authentic Israelis" these non-Jews (who, it must be stressed, choose not to convert into Jewish "religion," nor would they self-identify as Jewish, regardless of religion), also become *Jewish*. Other, more critical students of Israeli society see this fact as necessitating the identification of Israel as a "non-Arab state."[55]

*Jewish-Israeli* ḥiloniyut *and the Meaning of Israeliness*

The de facto identification between Israeliness and Jewishness also sheds light on the dominant (Jewish) identity among Israelis, namely Israeli *ḥiloniyut*, or secularism. One of the most intriguing facts about Israeli society, a fact that tends to confuse outsiders and is ignored by many insiders, is that while many, even most (surveys usually put the number around 50 percent of the total Jewish-Israeli population) Israeli Jews self-identify as "secular," secularity, as a social phenomenon (as the term is commonly understood in non-Israeli, Western contexts), is extremely rare, if not outright practically absent from the Israeli context. Indeed, the lamentation over the unviability of the group/category of Israeli seculars has been a recurring trope in such Liberal-Zionist (and proudly secular by self-definition) circles as *Haaretz*.[56] This puzzle can be at least partially solved if we take into consideration the peculiar nature of Israeli national identity.

As I have argued elsewhere,[57] a key to understanding Israeli *ḥiloniyut* is exactly the afore-discussed "mix-up" between Israeliness and Jewishness, or the (Jewish, in a Zionist rendering of the term) ethno-national nature of Israeli identity. Viewed from a traditionist point of view, one that focuses on Jewish-Israelis' attitudes toward their Jewish histories and traditions, Jewish-Israeli *ḥilonim* (seculars) do indeed seem to have little, if any, pronounced *personal* loyalty or commitment to their Jewish traditions. But this is far from saying that these traditions, or some crude, "nationalized" (i.e., dominated by a Political-Zionist interpretation) version of them do not play a critical role in their life. These Jewish-Israelis are able to view themselves as secular and still rely rather heavily on what they themselves may view as Jewish "religion," since their attitude toward their Jewish tradition is constituted primarily through their ethno-national identity, i.e. their *political* (not necessarily civic) identity. They are, in other words, politically Jewish. Indeed, given the Israeli nation-state's dominance over this political definition, it may be more correct to call them "statist Jews." I shall elaborate on this in the next chapter.

Those "non-religious"[58] Jews' Jewish identity is primarily a political matter, as it marks them clearly as members of the majority group, the group whose state Israel is. What might be considered, in a "religious," "Orthodox," or even "traditionist" context as primarily *Jewish* practice (that is, a practice that is not necessarily tied to Israeliness as a political identity), is commonly understood in a *ḥiloni* context as an expression of one's or one's group's political, (ethno-)national identity. In other words, these supposedly "Jewish" practices manifest the *ḥilonim*'s Israeliness. The cumbersome nature of my formulation here may be attributed not just to my ineloquence, but also to the very peculiar nature of the very attempt to disentangle "Israeliness" from "Jewishness." The two are, indeed, undistinguishable. In the context of a nation-state that favors—both in a symbolic/ideological manner and a material/political-practical sense—Jews over non-Jews, one's identification with the state-maintained Jewishness caries obvious implications.

The "Jewish" practices observed or maintained by those "non-religious" Israelis (usually following a rather narrowly interested Zionist interpretation of these practices) mark their practitioners as members of the (Jewish) majority, and distance them from weakened minorities. "Religion" or "Jewishness" is used, in this context, as a political "Israeli" tool in a context of an ethno-national conflict. Thus, one can observe what to the outsider may seem a wholly Jewish, even "religious" practice and still view oneself as a secular who has nothing to do with Judaism as a religion. For her, this identification is a matter of her Israeliness, i.e., of her political identification.

We should note that this political-national dimension of Israeliness also plays a major part in the identity constructs of nonsecular groups of Israeli Jews (such as Orthodox and traditionist Jews). The heavy hand of the "nationalization" of Jewish identity by Zionism and the State of Israel are quite apparent among these groups, too. The difference between them and the majority of Israeli ḥilonim is the different balance they maintain between their Israeliness (that is, the product of the theopolitics of the state, on its appropriation of Jewish identity) and their Jewish traditions: This balance allows non-secular Israeli Jews to maintain and express non-Israeli identities (such as their intra-Jewish ethnicity) alongside their Israeliness.

The practical identification between Israeliness and Jewishness is thus strongest and most apparent among those "secular by default"[59] Israeli-Jews, namely those for whom their identification as secular holds no meaningful ideological agenda. Unlike ideologically driven secular Israeli-Jews, the secular-by-default Israeli Jews do not seek an explicit political/ideological identification as secularists, but rather seek to reside comfortably inside the confines of the dominant "taken-for-granted" identity of the Israeli mainstream. They do not wish to self-identify with a minority group, i.e., with those who lack symbolic and social capital, neither are they "anti-religion" (as some radical secularist are viewed).[60] As an oft-quoted series of surveys on Jewish practices among Israeli-Jews puts it, these Israeli Jews are "not religious but not anti-religion;"[61] that is, they are "simply Israelis"—Jewish, of course.

# 8

# Statist Jews

## *Secularity, Sovereignty, Zionism—and Judaism*

In the previous chapter I suggested the term "statist Jews" as capturing an important aspect of the ways in which the State of Israel and the political culture it propagates maintain and uphold the Jewish identity of the state's population (to be precise: the non-Arab majority of this population). The remainder of the book is dedicated to the exploration of the term and the phenomenon it entails. This will shed light on the ways in which the sovereignty of the Jewish nation-state redefines Jewish identity.

Statist Jews are individuals—and an identity group to which they belong—for whom the meaning of their Jewishness is constituted, defined, and maintained by the Zionist nation-state. These are people for whom Jewishness-Judaism, that is, their Jewish identity, their private and collective identity as Jews, is of evident importance. Yet at the same time they can view themselves as essentially liberated from the authority of a Jewish (supposedly "religious") tradition. They can believe themselves to be sovereign over and independent from such a tradition, and, most importantly, as implicitly ignorant of and explicitly indifferent to the contents and meaning of such a tradition. This is so since they, themselves, in their private and public lives, do not necessarily take an active, self-conscious part in the interpretation, maintenance, and expression of their Jewish identity. The state handles this for them, using all tools assigned to it by the fact of its being sovereign: the law, coercion, education, finance, the power to define and mark, and so on.

The phenomenon these Jews manifest—a statist Jewish identity, or statist Jewishness—is enabled, of course, by the success of Political-Zionism, which has been focused on the establishment of a nation-state and on the sovereignty of Jews as the expression of modern Jewish identity. The Political-Zionist idea (as opposed to, for example, the cultural Zionism propagated by Aḥad Ha'am, a harsh critic of Political-Zionism) redefined Jewish identity not "simply" in terms of a nation, but rather in terms of a nation-*state*. The realization of this political idea in the form of the Israeli nation-state is what enables, then, the constitution and maintenance of this new Jewishness-Judaism.

Statist Jewishness, in other words, is an outcome of Israeli *etatism* (or, to use David Ben-Gurion's preferred Hebrew them, *mamlachtiyut*[1]). As such, it embodies a development of Zionist ideology itself, highlighting a further shift from the national dimension of this ideology to its political one. Put differently, *national* Jews, those whose Jewishness is defined through the concept of nationalism, can, in principle, be nevertheless independent from the state in the articulation and manifestation of their Jewish identities. Indeed, this has been a central idea of Aḥad Ha'am and his successors, such as Mordecai Kaplan. Granted, these thinkers adopted, like their Political-Zionists counterparts, a Euro-Christian conceptual scheme and discourse, which, among other things, also involved the reinterpretation of Jewish identity in terms such as "culture," "secularism," and "nationalism." But their reading-construction of Jewishness in terms of nationalism has not been limited or subjected to the idea of a sovereign nation-state. It has been essentially liberated from political sovereignty.

Statist Jewishness, on the other hand, is a direct product of the sovereign state. Statist Jews' Jewish identity is embodied in and dependent on the sovereign state. As such, it can even remain indifferent to its nationalism. Statist Jews can be ignorant of the meaning of their national identity; they can remain passive and avoid partaking in the project of instilling their (Zionist) nationalism with meaning, be critical of certain expressions of its political manifestations, and even reject some of its central ideas (such a stance is rather prevalent among Liberal-Zionists).

The discursive gap, at least at the institutional level, between the political, statist realm and one's private, personal identity, is what enables these individuals and their group's spokespersons to ignore the role played by the state in the construction and maintenance of their Jewish identity. Thanks to the power of the state they can reside in the confines of the "taken-for-granted," the unmarked, which does not require one to self-identify, and is allegedly not attentive to identity politics—i.e., the "silent majority," the colorless, non-hyphenated Israeliness. The state, the sovereign, dictates the rules of the game, such as the hierarchy of identities, and these individuals, who clearly gain the upper hand thanks to these rules (they make them the majority, and the state *theirs*) can remain indifferent to the political context that endows them with this privilege. Moreover, they can oppose certain practices and institutions (usually titled the "status quo") that manifest the Jewishness maintained by the state, and even blame others (mostly the "Orthodox," "Ultra-Orthodox," or "religious" Israeli Jews) for enforcing Jewish "religion" upon them and coercing them to partake in the observance of defunct rituals—and still enjoy the privileges granted to them by their very identity as Jews in the nationstate of Jews, an identity that is maintained exactly by these practices and institutions.

Later on I shall elaborate the discussion on the set of meanings instilled in their identification as Jews in the Jewish nation-state. But already at this early point what often goes as obvious and takenfor-granted must be explicated: the Jewish identity of these Israelis is of high importance for them. Its implications are critical, even if these Israelis do not explicitly acknowledge them. This importance is a direct outcome of the state's identification as the state of the Jews or a Jewish state. Their being Jewish means that Israel is their state; that the "nationality of the state,"[2] that is, the identity bestowed upon them by the very fact of their nationality or citizenship is primarily *Jewish* (and only secondarily "Israeli"). The state maintains their Jewish identity for them. Doing so, it takes the place of preceding institutions, which Jewish traditions have developed as maintaining identity, primarily the community, Jewish law, habitus and custom.

## Israeli Secularism as a Key
## to Understanding Statist Jewishness

We may begin the explication of the term suggested here and the phenomenon it entails through one of the great enigmas of Jewish identity in Israel, namely Israeli secularity. As I mentioned earlier, this has to do with the tension between the preference of around half of Israeli Jews to self-identify[3] as *"ḥiloni"* (i.e., "secular"), and the fact that secularism, in its "thick" meaning commonly used in non-Israeli contexts is quite rare in Israel. The surveys, problematic as they are, render the meaning of Israeli secularism perplexing. They repeatedly suggest that a large group—at least a sizable minority—of Israeli Jews who identify as "*ḥilonim*" observes a lifestyle that is in part based on practices, which may be reasonably identified as traditionally Jewish, and upholds to certain beliefs which are commonly identified as "religious." As students of Israeli Judaism/Jewishness repeatedly note, it is quite apparent that inside the wide realm of what is labeled "*ḥiloni*" identity, or "*ḥiloniyut*," there is a noticeable, persistent presence of distinctly traditional stances.[4]

Another way to frame this "enigma" would be to wonder why do so many Israeli *ḥilonim* report to the surveyors that they, as a general matter, do not observe Jewish tradition *at all*, while this declaration directly contradicts what they themselves report on their behavior when asked regarding the observance of specific practices. How is it that they inform their surveyors that they view themselves primarily as "Israelis," and that "Judaism," as a "religion" and tradition, does not play any meaningful role in their life, while at the same time reporting on a noticeable presence of "religious" and traditional Jewish characteristics in their identity, practices, and beliefs?

As I suggested in the previous chapter, a central part of the solution to this puzzle has to do with the alternating ways in which these practices and beliefs are understood by both their practitioners and their surveyors. This is the result of an obvious overlap and "confusion" between the terms "Israeliness" and "Jewishness." For many Israeli Jews, who maintain this way of life, central parts of which are indeed rooted firmly in Jewish tradition (even if they are interpreted through the narrow lens of a Political-Zionist reading of these traditions), the meaning of their actions is not "Jewish" but "Israeli." When they report on their observance or belief—or, more importantly, when they actively maintain them—they do not think of them in terms of Judaism, but rather in terms of Israeliness. This, of course, would not be possible were it not for the de facto identification between the two terms, which is (as discussed earlier) a product of the Zionist state's sovereignty.

When these *ḥiloni* Israeli Jews light Shabbat candles, with or without reciting the traditional blessing, or fast during Yom Kippur, and surely when they build a sukkah, light Hanukkah candles, and celebrate the Passover *seder*, they think of themselves as carrying an Israeli practice more than they do Jewish—if, in the first place, the distinction between these two terms makes sense at all. This very distinction is problematic, since Israeli political culture, followed by

Israeli Jews as individuals, is "naturally" inclined to identify Israeliness with Jewishness. Moreover, the very fact that these Israelis—as well as some of the prominent intellectuals who express and interpret their identity (see my discussion below)—tend to view Israeliness *as* Jewishness (and often synonymize the names) serves this confusion or vagueness regarding their relation with Jewish tradition.

This merit reiteration: what I am presenting here is an interpretation of a main stream among Israeli seculars, or *hilonim*, according to which many of these Israelis' sense of commitment to Jewish tradition is indeed weak; I do not wish to claim that they "deceive" themselves when they view themselves, personally, as lacking an essential tie to what they would identify as "religious" Jewish tradition. At the same time, practically every reasonable observer will easily identify a rather central, distinctly "religious"-traditional Jewish element in these Israelis' identity. This schism between self-image and practice has to do with the role of the state, which dictates many of the rules of the games by which these individuals live. The state imposes the quasi-traditional practices, and enables these Israelis' self-image as indifferent to and liberated from tradition to endure.

These Israelis' "ambivalent," apparently self-contradictory stance toward their Jewish identity, that is, toward a certain interpretation of Jewish traditions, is constituted mainly through their ethno-national identification—i.e., their political identity, as members of the Jewish majority in the State of Israel (and not necessarily as Israeli citizens). What might be seen, in a "religious," "Orthodox," or even "traditionist" context mainly a matter of "religious" practice, of tradition-inspired observance, and ultimately, pertaining mainly to one's *Jewish* identity is understood and used in a *hiloni* context mainly as a matter of expressing one's political, *Israeli* ethno-national identity (which is not necessarily of a religious context; sometimes it can even carry an anti-religious sentiment). This political identification carries immediate, rather obvious implications in the context of nation-state that favors—either symbolically and ideologically or politically and materially—the members of the Jewish majority over the non-Jewish minorities, against the background of a continuing political-national conflict between (Jewish) Israelis and (non-Jewish) Arabs.

The celebration/observance of Jewish rituals (again, mostly in their narrow Zionist interpretation) is thus used to express one's identification with the majority, and to distance oneself from the weak and weakened minorities. According to this interpretation, "religion" is used as an instrument in a conflict-ridden political-national setting.

This way, a person can observe practices whose origins and contents are "clearly religious," and still view oneself as "secular," or *ḥiloni*, and as having no meaningful tie to "religious" Jewish tradition. After all, for this person, the matter at hand is primarily (even if this remains implicit) political, and not religious (assuming that this distinction holds in the first place. As I discussed in chapter 1, it does not).

The state's role is far from being limited to setting the rules of the decisive game, according to which Israel is a state of Jews. Following the ethos of *etatism*, which positions the state as the guarantor of the very existence of the Jewish People in its entirety, the state also formulates and maintains a worldview, accompanied by a whole system of values, symbols, rituals, myths, practices, norms, etc.—that manifests the state's "*Jewishness.*"

In other words, the rules of the game have to do with more than the State of Israel being a state of Jews; they also touch upon its being a "Jewish" state; they are (also) about the state's identity. This identity is expressed primarily in the (manipulative) manner in which the state interprets Jewish traditions that preceded it and enforces this interpretation on the public sphere and on its citizens and inhabitants. This is how the state creates statist Jews.

Statist Jewishness, then, has a theology, or better put: a theopolitics, a worldview or doctrine, and practice. The theopolitics is formulated by Zionist intellectuals, such as A. B. Yehoshua, whose ideas I shall discuss below. The worldview/doctrine is expressed in the ideational system of Zionist-Israeli statism. And the practice is embodied in the various arrangements (legal and others) held by the state (namely the "status quo"), which function as a primary mechanism for the construction of the very meaning of statist Jewishness as well as for the "maintenance" of the statist Jews. Given that the system of values, symbols, and rituals have gained extensive explication in the literature,[5] I shall focus my attention on the first and the third of these aspects of statist Jewishness. The remainder of this chapter discusses A. B. Yehoshua's construction of the theopolitics of statist Judaism. Chapter 9 will explore the meaning of the "status quo."

## A. B. Yehoshua and the Theopolitics of Statist Judaism

The author, essayist, and public intellectual A. B. Yehoshua is one of the more committed and outspoken spokespersons of the State of

Israel's political theology. As such, Yehoshua also functions as an influential formulator of the ideological bed upon which statist Jewishness is founded. Not coincidently, he is also considered one of the primary spokespersons of Israeli secularism, or *ḥiloniyut*. I would argue that he is channeling, formulating, and theorizing a largely inchoate, somewhat un-theorized—yet dominant—national sensibility.[6]

Yehoshua's political theology constructs a hierarchy of identities (whole, or total vs. partial Jews, majority vs. minority, strong vs. weak Jewish identity, natural vs. artificial identity, and so on). This is accompanied by concepts of sickness and health, pathology and rehabilitation (*tiqun*), contamination and purity, exile and redemption, etc., applicable to individuals and collectives alike. In this sense (as in many others), Yehoshua remains distinctly loyal to Zionist ideology's tendency to adopt traditional Jewish theological concepts, primarily those of exile and redemption, and reinterpret them so as to render them applicable to a political-national, supposedly secular, theology.[7]

A study of the theopolitics he formulates, as well as of the ways in which the intellectual of Zionist sovereignty understands and constructs Jewish identity can thus be helpful in understanding statist Judaism.[8]

## Israeli = (whole) Jewish

My comment above should be reiterated: Yehoshua is considered by many, himself surely included, as one of the primary spokespersons of Israeli *Jewishness*, or even Judaism. Moreover, his controversial comments regarding "diaspora" or "exilic" Jews (see below) make it quite apparent that he views himself as an authoritative spokesperson of the Jewish people and Judaism in their entirety. He is not "just" an Israeli or Zionist speaker, nor does he speak "only" for secular Israeliness, or *ḥiloniyut*: He speaks authoritatively for Judaism itself, for its very essence. It is not hard to see that he puts very high stakes in his identity as a *Jew*. He sees himself through this identity; it is what constitutes him as a person in the world. Moreover, Yehoshua makes sure to note that for him "Israeliness" and even "*ḥiloniyut*" are synonymous with "Jewishness," which is the foundation of his identity (or, as his style would prefer, of *our* identity).

In this context, it is interesting to note Yehoshua's continuous, relentless preoccupation with definitions. He describes himself as one of those "people who are attracted to dealing with definitions."[9] Accordingly, he repeatedly invests his intellectual prowess in the clarification of the meaning and definitions of foundational identity concepts: "Who is a Jew," "Who is an Israeli," and "Who is a Zionist."[10] This he explains, amounts to the purification of the terms involved, for "words are like coins, given to two processes: a process of erosion, and a process of contamination [. . .] There are words that have been soiled with mud, mortar and mire, and it is only proper that they shall be cleaned so as the reveal their original meaning."[11] And his "clean" definitions are what purify these words.

Yehoshua's persistent preoccupation with definitions and demarcations manifests, among other things, the statist-Jewish theologian's indebtedness to the narrative of modernization and secularization, on the various binaries it nourishes upon. Especially apparent, in the context of the current discussion, is Yehoshua's basic premise that "religion" and "nationalism" are two essentially separate organs, each an independent, "pure," universal, and acultural concept in for itself. In Yehoshua's reading, the Israeli (i.e., Jewish) case is characterized by a historical categorical mistake, in which the two categories/ organs have been "welded" to each other (and not "melted" together, as was the case with other, healthier nations), and continue to exist independently from each other while being tied to the same body.[12] This "welding" renders the Jewish-Israeli people an "androgynous"— a pathological disruption of the binary distinction—that desperately requires "healing":[13]

> The androgynous contains both the male and the female, but is neither a male nor a female. The Jewish people, too, is an androgynous. It is a people that contains in it elements of a nation and elements of religion, but in actuality is neither a nation nor a religion, but some problematic thing between them [. . .] We entered history, then, with a double identity fuse, the two entwined together, tangled in each other, both a religion and a nation.[14]

This tying together of Jewishness as a nationality and Judaism as a religion, a pathological sickness that is nevertheless at the root of "our essence," is "the reason for the Jews' fundamental, essential restlessness. This restlessness can be very creative spiritually, but it is also accompanied by severe existential problems." This combination is "paradoxical at root [. . .] and will continue to be paradoxical to the last Jew."[15] Nevertheless, it is quite apparent that Yehoshua does not view this sickness as incurable; as we shall see below, the remedy, or redemption, shall come from sovereignty.

Yehoshua is an enthusiastic spokesperson for Israeli *ḥiloniyut*, since he views it (through its ultimate embodiment in the "secular" nation-state) as the total, all-inclusive, supposedly neutral *Jewish* sum, in which there should be also found a certain, limited by definition, place for "religion" or "the Jewish concentrate[16] in its religious meaning."[17] This is so since "Jewish religion expresses only part (important in itself) of Jewish existence and behavior."[18] The secular nation-state should express all other aspects of Jewish existence.

In this sense, Yehoshua provides a rather loyal, straightforward articulation of the modern Protestant concept of religion, which is, in turn (to repeat a point elaborated on in chapter 1) a product of the interests of the nation-state's striving for exclusive and absolute sovereignty. His indebtedness to this definition can hardly be exaggerated. As he argues:

> We have to make a clear separation, that is, to call religion and belief for what they really are, clearly stressing the belief in God and everything that is demanded by this specific belief. The mixture of religion in concepts such as "Jewish consciousness" is very misleading. An Israeli may have a Jewish consciousness without believing in the existence of God, surely not a specific Jewish god.[19]

Such a definition of Judaism-as-religion, which ultimately reduces it to a matter of irrational and apolitical belief (in a certain God, at that, setting aside the understanding of Judaism as tradition, law, lifestyle, and so on) is necessary for the realization of the allegedly secular nation-state's sovereignty. Yehoshua views Zionist nationalism as plagued by the Jews' misguided tendency to understand Jewish "religion" in other, distinctly political terms—an obvious deviation from his clear, clean definition. This is a destructive tendency, since it does not allow for the essential separation and distinction between religion and nationalism. Yehoshua finds the culprit in, among others, the pathology of exile, for which "the identification Jew religion became absolute."[20]

He thus offers a process of healing (that includes, among other remedies, a purification of the meanings words carry), in which the identification between the Jew and Jewish religion can be untangled and replaced by another, i.e. the identification between Jewishness and Israeliness. In his understanding, the purification of the words' meanings makes it clear that "the word 'Israeli' is in actuality the original and authentic word for identifying the Jews."[21]

> The concept "Israeli" does not relate solely to the citizenship common to both Jews and Arabs in Israel, but is rather a self-containing concept of identity. Even if there were not a single Israeli Arab Palestinian in the state of Israel, the name of the state would be Israel, and its inhabitants—they would be Israelis and not Jewish; after all, "Israel" is the original name of the People of Israel.[22]

And so, Yehoshua repeatedly preaches a return to what he identifies as the original meaning of "Israel" and "Israeli" as synonymous with "Jewish." He repeatedly makes an essential, fundamental identification between the terms, striving to create a total identification *in practice* between Israeliness and Jewishness; he strives for "the understanding of Israeli identity as the whole[23] Jewish identity."[24] That is, for the identification between Jewish sovereignty and Jewish wholeness.[25]

This exercise demands careful attention, since it embodies an important element of the theopolitics Yehoshua preaches. Note the manner in which he presents the formula Israeli = Jewish:

> If I were required to present my identity card as a secular Jew, I would answer firstly that I do not use the concept "secular Jew" at all, but rather the concept "Israeli."
>
> I suggest nevertheless to simply return to the concept "Israeli" as the primary concept of identity, with no redundant additions. I am Israeli. And if the religious Israeli wishes to identify as religious, let him say, "I am a religious Israeli." I do ask this from him.[26]

A naïve reading of this text (slightly varying formulations of which, like Yehoshua's political theology as a whole, appear repeatedly throughout the many essays he has published on the matter) may bring about two immediate questions that touch upon the root of the Zionist tension. First, does Yehoshua deny the fact that there are "Israelis" (at least in the formal meaning of the term, that is, people constituting part of the State of Israel's population) who are not Jewish? How can he identify "Israeli" with "Jewish" without essentially excluding non-Jewish Israelis? Second, does he deny the fact that there are Jews—moreover, secular Jews—outside of the State of Israel? Does he reject the Jewish identity (a secular identity, which he himself celebrates as healthy and vital, as opposed to religious, pathological identity, at that) of those who are not part of the State of Israel's population?

Needless to say, Yehoshua does not ignore these two essential issues. His complex answer to the supposedly naïve questions above is to be found in the hierarchy constructed by his theology. This hierarchy renders these two entities (i.e., non-Jewish Israelis and non-Israeli Jews), together along with others (in effect, anyone identifying as Jewish or living in Israel, who does not fit into the Zionist-Israeli-Secular-Jewish model personified by Yehoshua himself), essentially missing. Yehoshua also suggests a treatment, aimed at making these missing, partial identities whole. To the first identity group, which Yehoshua identifies as a non-Jewish national minority, he offers the possibility of healing by sort-of-converting and joining the People of Israel (or the Israeli nation), in its *Jewish* meaning. To the second group, which Yehoshua identifies as composed of "partial," exilic Jews, he offers a remedy by means of joining statist Jewishness. I shall expand on these two issues below.

The simple formula Israeli = Jewish might be misleading, then, since it ignores the identity-hierarchy created by the statist-Jewish theopolitics. According to this theopolitics, it is the sovereignty of the nation-state that self-identifies as Jewish (or as belonging to the Jews) that renders Jewish existence whole or "total": "The word Israeli identifies the Jew (secular or religious) who lives in the *totality* of Jewish existence."[27] A more accurate formulation, then, would be Israeli = total (or whole) Jew.

## Whole Jew, Partial Jew

This is the background against which one of Yehoshua's favorite provocations should be understood: his public, aggressive declaration that diaspora (or exilic, *galuti*, as he would prefer) Jews "are partial Jews, while I [Yehoshua] am a whole Jew[28]:

> In no way are we the same thing—we are total and they are partial; we are Israeli and they are Jewish. In recent years, my fellows and I have needed to defend Israel vis-à-vis the

statist issue,[29] as if it were merely an issue of citizenship,
while Israel is the authentic, deep concept of the Jewish
people [. . .] [A]nd it is about this deep matter that we
must defend against the Jewish offensive.[30]

It is interesting to note how the latter part of this quote identifies,
almost unwittingly, between "Israel" or "the statist issue," that is, the
nation-state named Israel, and "Israel" as "the authentic, deep concept
of the Jewish people." As many texts by Yehoshua make clear, the latter refers to a certain community—the people or nation of Israel—and
not to a specific political organization. The "sliding" between these
two concepts—i.e., the nation-state and the national collective—is an
essential part of the statist-Jewish theopolitics. It identifies the sovereign state as the very foundation of the Jewish people's existence.
The state *is* the people/nation.

In any event, Yehoshua does not see his argument regarding the
wholeness or completeness of the Israelis' Jewish identity (a product of that same "statist issue") versus the partiality of the diaspora
Jews' Jewishness as judgmental. Rather, it is an objective assessment
of reality. He is "not judging who is a good Jew or a bad Jew [. . .]
the concept 'partial Jew' does not ascribe a certain moral appreciation
to diaspora Jews."[31] Moreover, it is this objective appreciation that
encourages him to compare himself to Maimonides and to arrive at
the conclusion that against the background of his own (Yehoshua's)
and other Israelis wholeness, Maimonides's partiality come to sharp
relief; "not in his feeling nor in his consciousness, but surely in his
reality."[32]

It is hard not to see through this rhetorical exercise, based as it is
firmly on the Zionist negation of exile. Like his terminological definitions and demarcations, so does Yehoshua's negation of exile embody
an exercise of purification and definition. He explains the controversy
surrounding his above-quoted comments as the result of his attempt
"to outline at least a fundamental boundary between Jewish identity
in Israel and Jewish identity in the Diaspora."[33] His words merit careful attention, since they betray the triple identification that lies at the
foundation of statist Jewishness: Real, authentic Judaism is Israeliness,
which in turn is statism, that is, the sovereignty of the nation-state of
Jews. And, as aforementioned, this triple identification negates all that
it is not: non-Jewish Israelis, non-Israeli Jews, and non-statist Jews.

Needless to say, Yehoshua is far from denying his explicit
empathy toward the negation of exile. It is as an adamant disciple

of democracy and tolerance that he notes that there is a limit to tolerance, stating: "I do not tolerate the exile [*golah*]."[34] Exile for him is a pathological, neurotic Jewish choice, emanating from "a very deep national deformity."[35] As such, it is a "very deep failure of the Jewish people."[36] See, for example, how he explains why Jewish life in exile should be considered missing or "partial," as expressing what he calls elsewhere "reduced nationalism:"[37]

> A jailed prisoner is a partial human being, in the sense that a considerable part of the horizon of human activity is blocked from him [. . .] In his feeling and consciousness he is surely a whole human being, but in his reality he is lacking, he is a deformed human being. The feeling and consciousness of the Jewish person in exile as a Jew is, no doubt, one and whole as a Jew, but in his *reality* as a Jew [. . .] he is limited, lacking and blocked. Exile is a partial, deformed and lacking situation, according to Judaism's very perception of itself.[38]

Not for nothing has Amnon Raz-Krakotzkin argued that beyond being a testimony of "the internalization of typical anti-Semitic imageries," Yehoshua's words quoted above, as well as similar expressions he has made, betray the manner in which statist Jewishness "radically negates" anything that does not fall under what Yehoshua identifies as "a total Jewish life," that is, life under the sovereignty of a modern nation-state ruled by Jews. Yehoshua thus refutes "an endless number of human experiences that were deemed Jewish by those experiencing them."[39]

Perhaps the most scathing of these negations, especially if we remember that Yehoshua has won the status of a public intellectual thanks to his profession as a novelist, is his aiming of what he calls "my Zionist Israeli fury"[40] at the cultural—specifically literary—creation of non-Israeli Jews. For Yehoshua, Jewish creation in exile is lacking, distorted by definition. As a member of Yehoshua's audience reported critically,

> [Yehoshua] sweepingly attacked [. . .] the non-Israeli Jewish literature; [He was] specifically furious at the greatest Jewish-American authors of the previous generation, Bernard Malamud, Philip Roth and Saul Bellow, from whom, he declared, he "is not impressed," since they have failed the

test and have not realized the greatness of Political-Zionism and have not accepted it as the one and only option of historical Jewish existence.[41]

In the same vein, Yehoshua repeatedly clarifies that the focus on culture, and especially the study of Jewish texts, is but an inferior substitution for political Jewish sovereignty. He refers to a figure of high Zionist authority to clarify his position:

> "A Jew in exile, even a Jew like you, who lives in his whole on Judaism and in Judaism, cannot be a whole Jew, and no Jewish public in exile can live a whole Jewish life. Only in the State of Israel is whole Jewish life possible. Only here would a culture worthy of its name flourish, such that would be fully Jewish and fully humane. The book is but a part, a segment of culture. A people's culture is composed of a field, a road, a house, a plane, a laboratory, a museum, an army, a school, self-rule, a homeland view, a theatre, music, language, memories, hopes and much more. A whole Jew and a whole human being [. . .] are not possible in exile."
>
> These profound words were written by the Prime Minister of Israel, David Ben-Gurion, to a Jew in exile named S. Rawidowicz. Similar things I said a few years ago [. . .] stirred a fierce controversy, since no one is happy to hear that his cherished identity is in actuality a partial identity. But when I found that in Israel, too, there were many who objected to what I said, I realized that some essential matter has gone wrong lately in the way people understand the fundamental change experienced by Jewish identity with the establishment of the State of Israel.[42]

Yehoshua blames primarily "the religious on their various kinds and schools"[43] for this "worrisome retreat" from the view of Israeli identity as (the only) whole Jewish identity. As we shall see below, Yehoshua acknowledges the fact that Israelis tend currently not to accept the principles of his sovereign utopia. He sees this as a testimony to the power of the pathology of exile, which keeps devastating the Jewish people, even in the framework of sovereignty.

The proper, exclusive remedy for the Jewish partiality in exile is clear: exilic, partial Jews must join the Israeli-Jewish sovereignty.

The nation-state is their redemption. It is interesting to note that this redemption is not dependent upon the "technicality" of Israeli citizenship. Yehoshua does acknowledge the "civilian" aspect of Israeliness (that is, Israeliness in the sense of having an Israeli citizenship), but for him this is a rather meaningless aspect. He is wholly focused on Israeliness as identity. In this dimension, where Israeliness is identical to Jewishness, or, to be precise, to *statist* Jewishness, it appears to be liberated from the civilian aspect. In this vein, Yehoshua even argues that Israel should "offer diaspora Jews to upgrade and deepen their Jewishness by adopting Israeliness,"[44] while still (physically) in exile.

One of the surprising aspects of this theopolitics is the complete reversal it finally makes between the idea of Jewish identity and the nation-state's sovereignty. Statist-Jewishness sees itself, its Jewishness, as protected, perpetuated by the state in an absolute, definitive manner. Thus, for example, Yehoshua claims that Israeli Jews are a priori immune to assimilation. Their "total" Jewishness is such that cannot be deformed, and shall remain absolute, whole, and full of meaning, as long as the infrastructure of the Israeli nation-state's sovereignty remains in place. Yehoshua clarifies, in emphasized letters: *A human being can never assimilate in his own land, but only to change.*"[45] Accordingly, all concerned talk regarding Israeli Jewish identity and the danger of assimilation (in the sense of losing Jewish identity) in Israel is "nothing but absurd;" "as long as a nation preserves its language and land, and the total framework of society, it changes, influenced, but not assimilated."[46]

Another notable expression of this inversion, in which political sovereignty guarantees Jewish identity, came to light in Yehoshua's correspondence with critics, who wondered how he can identify Israeli identity (and its cultural production) as "whole" or "total" Jewishness. One such criticism (from the eminent literary scholar, critic, and editor Menaḥem Peri) focused on Yehoshua's claim that he is a "whole" Jew, while diaspora Jews are "partial":

> There is no greater mockery. After all, we are talking about the same Israel that had risen by the great effort of the Zionist movement, which was focused in its entirety on the negation of exile and the negation of the Jew, on abhorrence from history and denial of large parts of its culture. This is the same Zionism whose "new" Jew, of which it dreamt, was supposed to see in the "old" Jew what the greatest

anti-Semites saw in him [. . .] We have sat in exile for two
thousand years and what did we bring from there? An
empty bag. The other, rich, non-Zionist options of cultural
Jewish life were erased in the educational brainwash in this
country even before the holocaust came and continued the
work. The cultural giants of the Jews in philosophy and
thought, in literature, in music, in painting, and in science,
are not part of us.[47]

Yehoshua's reply to this criticism repeats the claim that Jewish political sovereignty renders assimilation impossible and guarantees, no
matter what, that meaningful *Jewish* content is to be produced. For
him, "the cultural matter" is secondary, and as such not deserving
of judgment. Political sovereignty, on the other hand, is primary and
absolute:

Jewishness is not only culture and not only religion. These
are mere additives, necessary or unnecessary, to an existential being of human beings who view themselves in their
consciousness as belonging to the historical nation named
the People of Israel. No one can, nor is anyone allowed to
make a distinction, moral or otherwise, of who is Jewish
or who is not Jewish by cultural or religious criteria. But
it is *surely* possible to grade the level of legal and substantial commitment to this identity, and the degree of the
substantial sharing in it, not by speech or cultural action,
but by the substantial ingredients that create an identity,
primarily taking a demanding and complete responsibility
for the fate and life of other Jews in a defined territory, and
in the Zionist case also beyond it, as much as possible.[48]

## Sovereignty

The said "totality" of Jewish-Israeli identity has to do, then, with what
Yehoshua sees as the deeper meaning of sovereignty. It is hard to over-
state the importance of political sovereignty for his Zionist, Jewish-stat-
ist theology. Not for nothing, the very term is peppered throughout his
texts, leaving no doubt that it is sovereignty that captures the essence
of his theopolitics. It is sovereignty that renders the Israeli a whole

Jew; it separates the correct, pure, whole Jew from the wrong, polluted, lacking one. Thus, "while the Jew always signifies a partial form of existence [. . .] Israeli is a whole existence of Jewish being locked in a committing framework [. . .] The word Israeli denotes a total Jewish way of life [. . .] its totality results from the very framework in which [the Israeli] is given."[49] This framework is, of course, the sovereign nation-state: "To be Israeli means to be a total Jew."[50]

This totality, that Jewish wholeness, is exactly the "normality of sovereign life,"[51] to which Zionism has always aspired. For Yehoshua, the political sovereignty of Jews is the very essence of the Zionist project; it is this sovereignty that marks the distinction between whole-sovereign-Israelis and partial-exilic-Jews, which is so central to his theopolitics. The worship of sovereignty, in other words, is the mirror image of the negation of exile. As he clarifies:

> Jewish identity in Israel, which we call Israeli identity [. . .]
> contends with all the elements of life via the binding and
> sovereign framework of a territorially defined state [. . .]
> We in Israel live in a binding and inescapable relationship
> with one another, just as all members of a sovereign nation
> live together, for better or worse, in a binding relationship.
> We are governed by Jews. We pay taxes to Jews, are judged
> in Jewish courts, are called up to serve in the Jewish army,
> and compelled by Jews to defend settlements we didn't
> want or, alternatively, are forcibly expelled from settlements
> by Jews. Our economy is determined by Jews. Our social
> conditions are determined by Jews. And all the political,
> economic, cultural, and social decisions craft and shape our
> identity, which, although it contains some primary elements,
> is always in a dynamic process of changes and corrections.
> While this entails pain and frustration, there is also the
> pleasure of the freedom of being in your own home.[52]

This total relationship creates a system of identity that is far richer and more meaningful than the one existing in exile, where the arguments are only verbal, without a genuine ability to coerce.[53]

This should be emphasized: "sovereignty" means coercive, enforcing power; it is "Jewish" due to the fact that Jews are the coercers/enforcers. Note that Yehoshua does not mention at all positive, active aspects of common and independent Jewish creation; instead, he focuses exclusively on negative, passive aspects of obeying the law and power. "We" (that is, the "total Jews") are ruled over, judged, drafted to the army, sent by force, compelled, taxed; our economy is determined, our social conditions are dictated, and so on.

In the hierarchy of statist Jewishness' theology—the theology of sovereignty—sovereignty surely precedes all other human creations. As long as this hierarchy is clear, Yehoshua clarifies, his claim regarding "the difference between whole and partial" is clear and "acknowledged."

> But the moment that Jews insist that involvement in the study and interpretation of texts, or in the organized activity of Jewish institutions, are equal to the totality of the social and political and economic reality that we in Israel are contending with—not only does the moral significance of the historic Jewish grappling with a total reality lose its validity, there is also the easy and convenient option of a constant flow from the whole to the partial.[54]

The essential difference between the lacking, partial life of exile (which also consists of all the passive aspects of sovereignty; in exile, too, is the person given to power, coercion, enforcement, judgment, etc.) and the whole, total Israeli life, then, is the "identity"—or, more accurately, the ancestry, or origin—of the sovereign. In Israel, "Jews" rule the nation-state, which is the active agent who rules, legislates, enforces, coerces. This is what makes Jewish life in Israel whole. See, for example, how Yehoshua distinguishes the (Jewish-)Israeli from the American Jew:

> Jewish identity in Israel, which we call Israeli identity (as distinct from Israeli citizenship, which is shared by Arab citizens who also live in the shared homeland, though their national identity is Palestinian)—this Jewish-Israeli identity has to contend with all the elements of life via the binding and sovereign framework of a territorially defined state. And therefore the extent of its reach into life is immeasurably fuller and broader and more meaningful than the Jewishness of an American Jew, whose important and meaningful life decisions are made within the framework of his American nationality or citizenship. His Jewishness is voluntary and

deliberate, and he may calibrate its pitch in accordance with his needs.[55]

The American Jew is not "sovereign," since the state that forces its law over her is not ruled by Jews. The Israeli, on the other hand, is sovereign, since he is ruled by "Jews."

The description of those holding sovereignty as "Jews" must be put in quotation marks, since as Yehoshua's words mentioned earlier make clear, the Jew of sovereignty, the statist Jew, can, indeed, be *not* Jewish. Remember that assimilation is impossible in Israel: Once the rules of the game—according to which the nation-state, the sovereign, is ruled by Jews—have been dictated, these "Jews" are incapable of losing their Jewish identity. Anything they would do (as long as the state remains identified as the Jews' state, of course) will be considered "Jewish." As Yehoshua repeatedly clarifies: "Homeland and national language and a binding framework are fundamental components of any person's national identity. Thus, I cannot point to a single Israeli who is assimilated, just as there is no Frenchman in France who is an assimilated Frenchman—even if he has never heard of Molière and has never been to the Louvre."[56]

The absolute commitment to sovereignty brings to life, then, an interesting paradox: Yehoshua's concern for Jewish content and meaning disappears when the discussion shifts to the issue of the state's sovereignty. Thus, on the one hand, he dedicates considerable attention to the hierarchy of *Jewish* identities, designating "whole" and "partial" *Jews*. On the other hand, once the "Jewish" activity takes place in the framework of sovereignty, it no longer makes sense to judge it: anything done in this framework is essentially Jewish by definition, and there is no point in trying to measure its value (Jewish or otherwise). The paradox is allegedly solved by sovereignty itself, since it is sovereignty that neutralizes judgment regarding the Jewish value of things: sovereignty is a redemption that cannot be undone. Everything Israelis do in their state is "Jewish": "The constant distinction people try to make between authentic and inauthentic in Jewish life becomes irrelevant, when it is applied to total Jewish life. [In the State of Israel] everything becomes authentic [. . .] language, land, and a homogenous society sovereign over itself always create a solid and authentic anvil for every struggle and every change."[57]

The other side of the coin is, of course, the essential, fatalistic dependency of the statist-Jews' Jewish identity on the state. On the one hand, their Jewishness is a matter of high, essential importance: it is given to hierarchies, judgments, criticism, and so on; it justifies actions, even gruesomely violent; it demands certain behaviors; etc. At least in Yehoshua's theology, Jewishness is not pushed aside or negated (as done, for example, by the Young Hebrews), but rather focuses attention. Yehoshua speaks primarily for Jewishness, and only secondarily for other values he cherishes (such as justice, democracy, liberty, and other values of Liberal-Zionism). Yet this Jewishness is concentrated exclusively in the hands of someone else: the sovereign that is the State of Israel. The individual Israeli seems to lose, or give up on, the responsibility over the maintenance of her own Jewishness, which is transferred to the sovereign state. Without the state, the Jew is not only partial—she is lost as a Jew. In Yehoshua's words: "The more the Jew in Israel becomes Israeli [. . .] the lower is the chance that he shall emigrate from Israel [. . .] because this leaving means a substantial breaking of his identity."[58]

The state-as-sovereign's essential importance for the statist-Jewish theology can also be grasped by considering the "remedy" it is supposed to bring to what Yehoshua identifies as both the secret of the Jewish people's survival and its malaise.[59] This, of course, is the tie (as aforementioned, a "welding" and not "melting together") between the two binary organs of nationalism (which he identifies as essentially secular, as it is "not religion") and religion. A central notion of the statist-Jewish theology is that the nation-state, or sovereignty, would heal this sickness. The medical procedure Yehoshua suggests is one of amputation: Since the two organs are welded together, the now-redundant element of "religion" can be cut away. This is possible only in the nation-state; Jewishness can once again be purely expressed as nationalism under the sovereignty of Jews.

Yehoshua's emphasis on the sovereign state peaks when he considers the essence of Zionism. Here, too, does he focus his attention on the purification of terms and concepts, such that would bring about "the release of the Zionist concept from all derivatives and all redundant additions that had stuck to it." This exercise makes it clear that "the keyword in the definition [of who is a Zionist] is state." Moreover, "Zionism is not an ideology," but rather an "outlook" focused exclusively on the sovereign state. Loyal to the narrative of modernization and secularization, and especially to the nationalist ideology of the sovereign state, Yehoshua uses the term "state" as if it were free from historical-political context; he speaks of the modern nation-state, and sees the entire human history in light of this historically specific phenomenon.[60]

Zionism makes the sovereign state all the more important due to its focus on immigration and land (as opposed, for example, to culture[61]): "At the foundation of the Zionist outlook stood the aspiration to establish a state. And absolute sovereignty is needed for Zionism more than for any other nation, because Zionism demanded the right of unrestricted immigration and unrestricted colonization, which can be brought about only by complete sovereignty."[62] This move (in simple terms, the Zionist struggle against the non-Jewish Palestinian inhabitants of the land) would be impossible were it not for sovereignty. This renders Zionism's definition dependent on the negation of the Palestinians' political arguments: "A Zionist is a person who accepts the principle that the State of Israel does not belong only to its citizens, but to the Jewish people in its entirety."[63] And a state means absolute sovereignty: "Half sovereignty is impossible, and the only choice is between full sovereignty and no sovereignty."[64]

## Exile Within Sovereignty

And yet, even the spokesperson of this theology confesses the weakness of his belief. The relation to non-Jews betrays it: "Let's be honest with ourselves. [. . .] Every authentically secular position, which demands the legitimacy of the secular Jew, must acknowledge the fact that a Jew can also be Christian or Muslim." However, "I, too, confess, with all my dedication and loyalty to the secular-Jewish principle, with all my strong belief that at Mount Sinai only a welding, and no melting, between religion and nation had taken place, that I still cannot accept the permission of the Jew to convert his religion to Christianity or Islam, and remain Jewish, a member of the Jewish nation."[65]

This weakness of heart can be partially explained by the major difference between Yehoshua and his Zionist ideological forefathers, namely the context of state sovereignty. While for them the sovereign nation-state has been mostly an aspiration, Yehoshua writes from within the context of such sovereignty. And against all predictions, his included, it clearly fails to bring about the aspired redemption. This amounts to a theological schism. Israelis keep on pursuing Jewish content, of the nonpolitical nature, in their life. While a part of

Jewish sovereignty they are nevertheless not satisfied with this political fact, and remain invested in the study of texts, the practice of
rituals, and the overall search for (Jewish) meaning—what Yehoshua
would identify as simply "religion," a shell of a kind that blurs the
glow of redemption. This sad reality cannot be refuted:

> Israeliness is not viewed as the perfect, total, and fullest
> expression of being Jewish. The decisive fact, that we live
> in the land of Jews, speak the archetypal language of the
> Jewish people, live in a society composed of a decisive
> majority of Jews, ruled by Jewish institutions, run a Jew-
> ish educational system, hold an attachment to the Jewish
> people, fight over Jewish aims and identified by the whole
> world as Jewish—all this is not enough, so it appears, to
> determine that Israel is a Jewish state; something else is
> also needed.[66]

Jews in Israel, in other words, hold on to the notion that there is a
Jewish essence, which cannot be reduced to the political sovereignty
of a state ruled by people of Jewish descent. One of the fascinating
aspects of Yehoshua's statist-Jewish theology is his ignoring the fact
that that "something else" that appears to be needed for Israeli Jews
to feel authentically Jewish is provided to them by that very same
sovereign, in the form of laws, norms, practices, education and overall
"values," which are considered Jewish, and not (just) Israeli. In other
words, Yehoshua, a disciple of the sovereign state, ignores the ways in
which the state itself, as the sovereign, avoids the construction of an
Israeli national identity and instead interprets its Jewishness in light
of a narrow reading of Jewish traditions, which Yehoshua will identify
as "religious." The sovereign then imposes this *Jewish* identity on the
public sphere and on the individuals' lives, using that same enforcing power that coerces, judges, taxes, drafts, etc., which Yehoshua
celebrates as the essence of sovereignty. The sovereign, the nation-
state identified as the state of Jews, constructs its subjects as Jews,
not as Israelis. Later on I shall explore some of the ways in which
the sovereign does so (mainly through a study of the sociopolitical
meaning of the "status quo").

   Yehoshua, then, would have liked to see Israeliness, that "whole"
Jewishness which is guaranteed by the sovereign state, identified (or
"defined," as he seems to prefer), like other nations, by "life in a

defined territory [. . .] the language of the people, ways of life and a defined society, which is demanded to give answers to each individual in it."[67] Were it to answer this definition, Israeliness would have rendered any action done by an Israeli individual Jewish. Yet we face a "strange" reality:

> While in the exile a social worker, for example, who works in a Jewish community center, is considered to be doing a Jewish act, an Israeli social worker is not considered as such [. . .] While in the exile any dealing with a matter that relates to the life of Jews immediately becomes a Jewish act [. . .] in Israel, where all activities are done among Jews and about quintessentially Jewish matters, other criteria are presented in order to determine which is the prototypical Jewish act. As if the partiality, which is of the essence of the concept Jew, needs to prove its partiality in the Israeli reality, too.[68]

This brings about, in Israel, the distinction, which Yehoshua mourns, between "actions and contents" that are considered Jewish and those that are not considered Jewish (but rather "Israeli"). For Yehoshua, this amounts to a Zionist failure, as "Israeliness is not conceived of as the perfect, total and fullest expression of being Jewish."[69] Instead, exile endures: "The classic mold that existed in exile is repositioned: a distinction between the everyday flow of life and some Jewish concentrate in which these neutral water must be diluted, and be given their Jewish character."[70]

## Non-Jewish, Non-Israelis

Yehoshua does see that at least part of the problem lies in the simple fact that there are Israelis—Israeli citizens, at the very least—who do not self-identify, nor are they identified by others as Jews. In other words, the problem is in "the fact of the present existence of non-Jewish Israelis. Indeed, this novel fact of the existence of non-Jews as minorities inside the total Jewish frame disrupts the concepts a little."[71]

He sees this disruption as resulting from the complexity of the distinction between Israeli identity, which is for him quintessentially

Jewish, and "Israeli citizenship, which is shared by Arab citizens who also live in the shared homeland, though their national identity is Palestinian."[72] In other words, the gap between the utopia of Jewish sovereignty, or statist-Jewishness, and the reality of Israeliness and Jewishness that although entangled and confused nevertheless exist as distinct concepts, is the result of another pollution, which stains the aforementioned aspiration to create a "homogenous society,"[73] one in which every Israeli is, by the sovereign definition, Jewish.

According to Yehoshua, this disruption is the outcome of "the Middle-Eastern conflict"[74]; the resolution of this conflict will bring about the natural assimilation of non-Jews inside the Israeli majority, without this majority losing its identification between Israeliness and Jewishness. It appears that Yehoshua presents non-Jews with the option of forced conversion of sorts, which will be the result of sovereignty itself. As the conflict is resolved,

> Our relation to non-Jewish Israelis shall become normal. Their Israeliness does not need to reduce our Israeliness [. . .] They—and not us, the majority in the state of Israel—would have to live the schizophrenia of a double identity [. . .] If the conflict of their double identity shall be severe, they always have the option to solve it by leaving and joining a place where their specific national identity is upheld by a majority (a Palestinian-Jordanian state) or fully joining the Jewish totality (that is Israeliness), i.e., their transformation into members of the People of Israel.[75]

In other words, the disruption shall be solved by either amputation (the political separation between Israeliness and Palestinianess, the solution of "two states for two peoples"—in which, it should be emphasized, each state is exclusively for one people only), or the erasure of the Palestinians' distinct identity through national conversion. A shared society (or sovereignty) is out of the question, since it will result in the erasure of the Israelis' Jewishness.

# 9

# Who Needs the Status Quo?

*Statist Jews and "Religious Coercion"*

Needless to say, statist Jews do not have to know the theology offered by A. B. Yehoshua and others, nor should they be expected to necessarily agree with it. For these Israelis, the critical issue is one of practice, i.e., the manner in which the state maintains their identity as Jews. In this context, the arrangement commonly titled "the status quo" is one of the most important frameworks for the preservation and maintenance of the Israelis' Jewish identity; it is a central mechanism of the very constitution of statist Jewishness.

In order to better appreciate my argument, we must examine, initially, the way in which the status quo is constructed and understood in the statist-Jewish discourse itself. As I shall argue, this dominant understanding contains a large measure of repression and self-denial: statist Jewishness is dependent on the status quo, and at the same time tends to rhetorically reject it, or at least some of its manifestations, depicting it as "religious coercion." Statist Jews often view the status quo as a result of the Israeli majority's—i.e., the *ḥilonim's*—submission by the "religious minority," which, so the argument goes, manages to impose its particularistic interests on the wider public. This helps statist Jewishness preserve its self-image as secular and enlightened (while at the same time, of course, also Jewish). I shall elaborate on this later on.

The following shall be built, then, on a dual exercise. First, I shall briefly retrace the dominant narrative, which presents the status quo as an awkward compromise between two contradicting, opposing stances held by two sides of unequal political strength. Second, I shall offer a "deconstruction" of the arrangement, focusing on the ways in which it constructs, serves and maintains statist Jewishness.

## The Dominant "Cleavage" Narrative

"The status quo" (or, in a longer form: "the secular-religious status quo," and even "the status quo on matters of religion and politics") is the name commonly assigned to various arrangements, laws, practices, and political-cultural norms that touch upon the "unique" and controversial "combination" of "religion and politics" or even of "secularity and religiosity" practiced in Israel. This name comes up in academic and political discussions as epitomizing the very identity of the State of Israel as a Jewish state that is both and at the same time "not-religious." i.e., "secular," and, nevertheless, Jewish.

This commonly used term testifies to the ways in which these arrangements are usually understood by both academics and politicians: the status quo is viewed as a compromise, a truce between two quarreling parties, each of which aspires to institute a political, social, and cultural order, which is the direct opposition of the other side's aspirations; it is a zero-sum-game of sorts, that instead of being decided was put on hold, via a compromise, which entails that each side gives up on some of its aims and aspirations in the name of preserving national unity.

In other words: according to this dominant understanding, the status quo is an exercise of mutual concessions and coexistence between two partners who were not really meant to live together in the first place, but were forced to do so because of this or that historical reason (mainly, anti-Semitism).

In one formulation (important in itself, since it comes from a senior member of the Israeli judiciary, which often functions as the arbitrator in this relationship), the two quarreling sides are the nation-state's law (which is secular by definition), and "religion."[1] Another author even presents it as a compromise (or, given the totalistic nature and unequal political strength of the two sides, as a submission of one side by the other) between the rule of law and the rule of halacha.[2]

While such a "legalistic" conception of the arrangement prefers to view the two quarrelling sides, the opposition between which is "neutralized" by the status quo, as law vs. religion, political scientists prefer, not surprisingly, to view the two as "politics" or "state"[3] (i.e., the secular) and "religion." Moreover, in other formulations, which blindly apply the Christian model on the Jewish-Israeli case, the arrangement at hand is a compromise between "state and synagogue"[4] (i.e., a local, Jewish case of the wider issue of "church and state").

In any event, according to this understanding, the status quo is a mechanism pertaining to the "regulation of the legal status of religion;"[5] it deals with religion and the religious. It is an interesting mechanism in for itself, since it is apparently based on an a priori "decision not to decide—that is, on preserving an existing status quo that acknowledges the priority of religious demands in some areas in a way that reflects a social-political compromise rather than a principled decision-making."[6]

As any undergraduate student of Israeli politics is expected to know, the gist of the matter is rather straightforward: the status quo is a historical "compromise,"[7] which has developed over the years into a full-fledged sociopolitical practice, at the root of which is that essentially unbridgeable gap between the secular and the religious, or between politics/law and religion. The status quo is "the most familiar [. . .] conflict-neutralizing, consociational arrangement"[8] on these matters. It is a practical-political manifestation of the consociational model of accommodation,[9] which "enables the rivals to avoid a head-on clash on controversial issues while portraying themselves as continuing to adhere to their principles."[10]

According to this mainstream narrative, the status quo has become a paradigm of defusing the tension between the conflicting principles and aspirations of the two sides (secular Zionism and the not-necessarily-Zionist Orthodox, or religious Jews), without deciding their rivalry one way or another. This, of course, is based on mutual concessions. Put differently, in a principal and fundamental manner, the ultimate goals of the two sides are mutually exclusive, negating each other.

But what exactly are these supposed oppositional aspirations? Although academics usually refrain from stating this explicitly, their basic premise is rather apparent: The "compromise" is a mutual concession between, on one side, the ambition to enforce Jewish law on the State of Israel and to transform it into a theocracy, and on the other side, an aspiration to completely clean the politics of this state from any trace of Jewish "religion"—to implement, that is, a total separation of religion and politics. Both sides supposedly understand that they cannot achieve their ultimate goals, and they are willing to forego the complete realization of their guiding visions. The status quo, then, is an arrangement of mutual compromise, in which both sides concede some of their ideals. This arrangement thus "neutralize[s] the explosive political potential" built around the "religious cleavage" by "depoliticizing" the tension around the cleavage.[11]

In this framework, the status quo has won the ire of liberal-secular Zionist critics. These critics view the status quo as putting Israeli secularity, which composes the majority of Israel's Jews, in the bondage of the religious minority. The arrangement, in simple words, is an expression of "religious coercion." In this vein, Shulamit Aloni has identified the document commonly referred to as the constitutive text of the status quo, the "status quo letter" (see below) as having become "the document that most strongly shackles the hands of Knesset members from the ruling parties, preventing them from legislating in accordance with their conscience and understanding."[12]

According to Aloni, this document, and, more importantly, the practice it constitutes, pave the way for the transformation of Israel from a state ruled by (civil) law into a theocracy, ruled by *Jewish* law (that is, halacha).[13] As we have seen in the previous chapter, A. B. Yehoshua's statist-Jewish theopolitics shares this appreciation, as it views religion as awkwardly "welded" into the national body, mutating into a tumor-like outgrowth, that is forced on secular Israelis by "the religious on their various kinds and schools"[14]—via, among other things, the status quo arrangements.

## The Status Quo as Myth

As an idea, this dominant image of the status quo has a "mythic-like presence" in Israeli political culture. It is not just about an "arrangement" setting certain rules of the sociocultural-political game, but also "a sign of the complexity of the sovereign Jewish identity." Fulfilling this role of a mythic narrative or symbol, the status quo is, "in Roland Barthes's terminology, both 'meaning' and 'form'; it transforms the particular history of the term into one that carries meaning that exceeds its immediate denotation."[15]

Like other myths, the status quo also has a constitutive historical narrative. Indeed, "it does not have a starting point,"[16] but it does have an origin story. According to the mainstream narrative, the status quo was originally an outcome of a formative compromise between the Zionist (secular) leadership and representatives of the (non-Zionist) Jewish Orthodox parties in pre-statehood Palestine. This compromise, so the story goes, was meant to achieve intra-Jewish unity during a period of formidable struggle against non-Jews. As time progressed, what started as a tactical move in the strategic campaign for the establishment of a Jewish nation-state transformed into a foundational principle of the Jewish political community in pre-statehood Palestine and then in the State of Israel; it is a political principle of preferring intra-Jewish consensus (again, in the name of a struggle against non-Jewish enemies) over majoritarian rule.[17]

This origin story further highlights a certain event, a foundational moment, that marks the very a birth of the status quo: The sealing of the "original document"[18] of the status quo—a letter sent by three members of the Jewish Agency Executive (the overseeing body of the pre-statehood World Zionist Organization) to the leadership of the Orthodox party, Agudat Yisrael, on June 19, 1947. This letter allegedly sealed as official a practice already observed in the Jewish political community of Mandatory Palestine.

The letter "was intended to persuade Agudat Yisrael to support the WZO's campaign for acceptance of the partition plan for Palestine."[19] The UN was considering the establishment of a "Jewish state" in Palestine (alongside an "Arab state"), and the mere possibility that Jewish (Orthodox) representatives would oppose this partition plan— since they have been uncomfortable with the secular character of the Zionist movement—was seen as threatening the Zionist leadership. The latter, so goes the narrative, thus succumbed to the Orthodox pressure (in what would allegedly become a model for Orthodox "blackmail" of the secular majority) and promised, in the form of an official letter, that while "it is clear that the intention is not to establish a theocracy,"[20] the political principles of the Jewish-state-to-come would be attentive to four dimensions of Jewish "religion." These include: (1) the observance of Saturday, the Jewish Shabbat, as the official day of rest; (2) the observance of *kashrut* (Jewish dietary rules) in kitchens run by state agencies; (3) the legislation of rules concerning marriage and divorce that would prevent marriages between Jews and non-Jews[21]; and (4) securing the autonomy of the Orthodox educational system. We shall soon return to this letter.

The status quo went through further foundational transformations in the early years of Zionist statehood, and since then has become, so the narrative goes, the primary measuring rod—although not a set and determined one but rather changing and evolving—for regulating the relation between "religion" and "politics" in Israel.[22] It should be noted that this mythical "being" is not frozen in time; moreover, it is exactly its "ever-changing," evolving character that holds the key to understanding its endurance.[23] What might sound like an oxymoron—i.e., the dynamic nature of a status quo—is simply a manifestation of the understanding that like other political arrangements, so does "the status quo principle [. . .] not prevent changes in the existing situation; it merely limits them, restrains them, and prevents them from attaining public legitimacy and official validation by means of legislation."[24] As such, the status quo has become a paradigm of solving-without-deciding the essential tension between the contradicting principles of the two sides ("secular" Zionism and the non-Zionist "religious").

## Beyond the Cleavage—Statist Jewishness and the Status Quo

The epistemological distinction between religion and non-religion (the secular), followed by the opposition of "religious" and "secular" identities, are, then, a foundation of the very notion of the status quo. This idea assumes the prior existence of two separate, oppositional camps—concrete sociopolitical embodiments of universal concepts— each with its own clear ideology, aims and aspirations regarding the shaping of the Israeli polity. Needless to say, this notion also constructs, shapes and reifies these identities:

> The status quo is given to processes of reification [. . .] In order for it to function the status quo mechanism demands clear, defined and loyally represented identities. The status quo ideology promotes a symbolic imagery of well-entrenched camps facing each other. Sociological studies prove this to be a deceiving imagery; it turns out that reality is more complicated than the binary and dichotomous imagery [. . .] But as a tool in the service of the politics of accommodation, the status quo demands concrete essences in order to reconcile them. Who is religious? Who is secular? Who represents them? What represents them? These are questions that demand clarification for the mechanism of accommodation to work; These are questions that demand a reifying manipulation of social identities.[25]

In other words, the status quo, which is built on the cleavage discourse, also reifies this discourse, as it takes a central role in the construction of those same oppositional identities it identifies in the first place as mutual rivals. It thus tends to preserve and strengthen the "political institutionalization" of the social cleavages, and in effect plays a decisive role in their very creation and in the preservation of the same opposition it presumes to solve.[26]

In order to expose and critique the way in which the status quo is constructed we must transcend the limited notion of a compromise between two whole, concrete, mutually exclusive, polar-oppositional identities. This, indeed, is far from being a novel argument. The academic field has already explicated it quite clearly. Some, for example, see clearly the manner in which the status quo mechanism perpetuates not only identities, but also a political order that prefers a certain group over others, and sheds a critical light on the notion of compromise as explaining the status quo's endurance.[27]

More important than the issue of whether compromise can explain the status quo is the very agreement—which the critics seems to share—on identifying Israeli-Jewish identities as constructed mainly along the two opposing stances toward religion. In other words, while the mainstream proponents of the status quo and its critics disagree on its political merit, they nevertheless share the secular/secularist epistemological framework. Even when scholars manage to highlight the ways in which the status quo itself constructs the identity scheme of secular vs. religious (reifying the very "cleavage" these identities are supposedly built around) they still think of the status quo in/through the absolute concepts of "religion" and "secularity." Even if they understand that "religious" and "secular" are socially constructed categories, in the construction of which the status quo itself plays a central role, they still think of the status quo through the secularist epistemology, which is centered around the secular vs. religious and religion vs. politics dichotomies. Thus, they assume as given the universality and absolute relevance—indeed, the very reality—of the foundational concepts religion, secularity, etc.

## The Status Quo Beyond "Secularization"

What is required, then, is a new, critical thinking of the status quo as a central organ of the theopolitics of Zionist sovereignty, which self-identifies as "Jewish."

The "deconstruction" of the dominant narrative can begin with a careful consideration of the allegedly constitutive document of the status quo, the aforementioned "status quo letter." This will not be aimed at "proving" that the document does not constitute the arrangements that followed in practice (as some critics of "religious coercion" have done, trying to prove that the observed practices do not have their legal backing in the letter[28]). Rather, it will focus on problematizing the very basic assumptions regarding the involved ideologies and the compromises their adherents allegedly had to make. In this regard, the letter can be used not necessarily as a quasi-legal contract, but rather as an anecdote that captures a deeper essence.

Menachem Friedman's careful consideration of the letter's content offers illuminating insights, which re-mark and highlight what the correspondence at hand takes for granted—an essential context that tends to get blurred in the long political and public clashes surrounding the status quo. Two important aspects of these insights deserve careful attention in the context of the current discussion: One has to do with the non-committal, declarative, and overall "open" nature of the document. The second touches upon the basic issue of the ideologies, interests, and values of the two sides, especially those of the Jewish Agency (representing the Zionist movement, allegedly speaking for secular Jews). Friedman's comments regarding the Zionist commitment to observe Saturday as the future state's day of rest tackles the matter head on. As he notes, the clause stipulating this promise does not refer to the halachic, "religious" concept of Shabbat, but rather to the European notion of a day of rest as a legal right of laborers' welfare. And this is where the fundamental issue lies:

> One may ask: What is the novelty here? Would it be even conceivable that the weekly day of rest in the state of the Jews will not be Saturday? How is this "commitment" supposed to satisfy Agudat Yisrael?[29]

Friedman goes on the explain that this commitment must be understood against the background of accepted practices in the settlements belonging to the Kibbutz movement, where Socialist ideology was dominant, and in which a member of the commune could choose any day of the week as her weekly day of rest. The leadership of Agudat Yisrael was worried that this practice may be adopted by the state-to-be, and the Zionist leadership promised that this will not be the case.

In other words, the Zionist, secularist clarification regarding the "public character" of the Shabbat has very little, if anything, to do

with the halachic or "religious" notion of Shabbat; Instead, it entails a
commitment of a national nature, a "secular" symbolic matter (if we
insist on preserving these misleading dichotomies in the first place).
It is an early expression of the way in which the "political" (here
personified by the representative of the yet-to-come-state), which
considers itself secular, constitutes its identity as Jewish through a
certain interpretation of the traditional symbols system. Indeed, as
Friedman notes, it would be hard to even conceive of a state, which
identifies as the state of Jews, that does *not* mark the Shabbat as a
formal day of rest (the practical meaning of this is, of course, given
to various interpretations and understandings). On the other hand, it
is quite hard to see how this non-committing declaration regarding
the "character" of the Shabbat is supposed to appease those who are
allegedly aiming at the establishment of a Jewish theocracy, such that
would follow the dictates of the Orthodox interpretation of Jewish law
regarding the Shabbat prohibition, public and private alike.

Friedman also highlights the illusiveness of the letter's language,
stressing that the letter does not hold a promise to any of the rules that
would later on become the benchmarks of the status quo: the clarification on matters of marriage and divorce leaves the very concepts
of "personal matters" (*ishut*) ambiguous; the supposed commitment
to serve kosher foods in governmental institutions does not promise
that these institution will *not* serve non-kosher food alongside the
kosher option—it barely promises the availability of kosher food for
those interested, and so on. In short: "This letter was meant, then,
to ease suspicions and fears in the Agudat Yisrael camp. It holds no
commitment that might be understood as relating to the status quo
that was practiced in the [pre-state Jewish community of Palestine]."[30]

Friedman also addresses our attention to the compromised position of the "religious" side in this relationship. He identifies Agudat
Yisrael's supposed threat not to support the establishment of a state
for Jews as baseless. Especially after the Holocaust, was it even conceivable that Jewish representatives shall deny the Jews' right to build
a national safe haven?

## A Compromise Between What?

The importance of the "status quo letter" for the current discussion
exceeds, then, the historical-legal puzzle of whether this "original

document"[31] really constitutes the arrangements later enshrined in political practice as the status quo, and the ensuing "religious coercion." This letter, like a consideration of the status quo as a whole, forces one to ask the simple yet profound question: why, then, has the status quo been observed? Why has the Zionist, Socialist, allegedly vehemently secularist, and surely dominant[32] leadership insisted on instituting rules, laws, practices, and norms that bind the public sphere as well as highly sensitive aspects of the citizens' lives by certain prohibitions, which allude to "Jewish religion"? Who does the status quo serve? To answer this, we must first deconstruct the dominant narrative of the status quo myth.

Looked at closely, the common premise underlying the conception of the status quo as essentially a compromise seems dubious at best. How does the status quo serve the "religious" or "Orthodox"? The connection between the practices of the status quo and the Orthodox interpretation of Jewish law is remote and questionable. What meaning does a "partial observance" of the law have? Note that the status quo is based on an identification of certain aspects of the Shabbat prohibitions, to take one contested example, as more important than others: it forbids mass public transportation (i.e., busses run by corporate business) and allows public transportation of a "lesser size" (cabs and privately owned minibuses); and it does not have anything to say on the private use of cars during the Shabbat. Similarly, it prohibits the opening of businesses on Shabbat, unless these are "pleasure houses," such as cinemas, theaters, and restaurants. Needless to say, Jewish law in its Orthodox interpretation has nothing to do with such distinctions. It seeks to enforce the rules of Shabbat, as all other rules, on the private and public spheres equally, and it does not see a difference between a small cab and a corporate bus.

Now, note that the basic assumption of the "compromise" narrative is that the Orthodox side's ultimate goal has been the establishment of a Jewish theocracy—i.e., the constitution of (Orthodox) Jewish law as the law of the land—in Israel. While this is highly debatable, let us assume for the purpose of the discussion that this has indeed been the case. How, then, would a "fragment" of a theocracy, such that imposes Jewish law only "partially," be satisfactory to anyone interested in the complete and exclusive rule of the halacha? What sense does a partial and selective imposition of only certain rules make to anyone interested in the rule of Jewish law (not of Jewish "sentiment")? Would it make sense, to draw a rather crude example, to impose rules prohibiting stealing in a partial and selective manner, according to which only a certain kind of stealing is not allowed?

Indeed, Menachem Friedman gives ample examples to show that the status quo letter was not aimed at satisfying, even partially so, any potential theocratic aspirations of Agudat Yisrael. Instead, it was aimed to reassure the Orthodox leadership that the Zionist state-to-be, ruled by representative of an ideology that views itself as radically secular and Socialist, will not persecute them, the non-secular minority.

The letter—as an instance of the whole arrangement and not as a cause in itself—addresses our attention to even more difficult questions regarding the very nature of the status quo: Why would a non-Zionist party, which does not accept, at least formally, the idea of establishing a Jewish nation-state (we must keep in mind that the Agudat Yisrael leadership preferred the continuation of the British Mandate over the establishment of a "secular" state of Jews; this had to do not only with their fears from the Socialist-Zionist camp, but also with their interpretation of traditional theological notions of exile and redemption)—why would it worry about the role played by Jewish customs in the (secular) law of the land? After all, Orthodoxy has been at the time already constituted as a community of Jews who lack political sovereignty. And so, the question remains: Who does the status quo serve?

## The Status Quo and Statist Jewishness

It seems to me that the rather simple answer is unavoidable. Arrangements in the spirit of the status quo, which mainly impose (as an expression of sovereignty) traditional Jewish symbols (whose connection to Jewish law in its Orthodox interpretation is weak at best) on the public sphere, and bind individuals in matters of marriage and divorce to the authority of an Orthodox rabbinate (which is established, financed and authorized by the state as sovereign) serve primarily the newly crowned sovereign's (that is, the newly established state's) need to identify as Jewish and to preserve a Jewish majority (a precondition of its very sovereignty). I shall explain this below.

The status quo arrangements impose on the Israeli public sphere rituals, symbols, and meanings that are reserved for Jews only. ("Secular" and "religious" Jews alike, at that.) These arrangements do *not* serve an Orthodox or Ultra-Orthodox agenda, such that wishes to be almost un-self-reflexively loyal to a conservative Ashkenazi interpretation of Jewish law. (To begin with, the question whether the non-Zionist Orthodox camp is interested in political sovereignty remains open. We should keep in mind that the formal position of this Orthodox leadership opposed *theologically* the Zionist political project.) The status quo arrangements manifest an understanding of Jewishness that is "political" and "national"—indeed, statist—and not "religious" or "Orthodox."

The sovereign state's imposition of this understanding on the public sphere includes almost automatically those identified as "Jews" in the majority groups, and excludes, also by definition, the non-Jews, which are also marked as a minority. Similarly, the binding of Israeli Jews to the state-established, state-sponsored, and state-authorized rabbinical courts for conducting their personal matters effectively prevents inter-"religious" or inter-ethno-national marriages, guaranteeing at that the preservation of the essential demarcation between ethno-national majority and minority.

This, then, is the key to understanding the status quo. It is not a matter of "compromise" and "submission" of the "secular majority" to the whims of the "religious minority," but an expression—a crude expression at that, no doubt—of the state's reliance (a state, it must be kept in mind, ruled by the leadership of this alleged "secular majority") on a narrow "religious" interpretation of the meaning of Jewish traditions, for the regulation of the public sphere and for the conducting of "national" (supposedly secular) politics. And the state imposes this interpretation on the public sphere and on the private lives of the citizens using whatever tools it has as sovereign—mainly the law.

The state still espouses, of course, the notion of making a distinction between these two "welded" organs—Jewish "religion" and "nationalism"; but as the debates surrounding the alleged "paradoxes" created by this distinction exemplify rather straightforwardly, the state and the culture it has built remain loyal to the idea that these two categories are seen as essentially identical.[33] This notion underlies the "statist" (*mamlachti*, supposedly secular, and overtly dominant) educational system, and it feeds a long list of laws, practices, and norms that impose a certain, narrow interpretation of Jewish tradition on the public sphere.

This should be explicated: the "secular majority" needs the supposed "religious coercion" of the status quo more than any other side in this relationship. This coercion is the ultimate mechanism that preserves the Jewishness of the statist Jews. It is this coercion that guarantees their positioning as Jews in the state of Jews; it guarantees their position as those whose state Israel is. This coercion is that which enables the preservation and maintenance of the Jewish identity of the "secular majority" in the nation-state that identifies as belonging to the Jews.

It will not be redundant to remind the reader here of some of the most basic facts of political reality in Israel. Being Jewish in Israel means belonging to the majority, which enjoys a privileged position in every aspect of public life. Whoever is Jewish—or identified as belonging to this majority—enjoys a political, symbolic, and cultural capital that is reserved for Jews only. It is their state, and no one else's. And without the state's imposition—coercion, indeed—of its narrow interpretation of Jewishness or Judaism on the public sphere, many members of this majority—the statist Jews—would have lacked the possibility to positively identify the content of their Jewish identity. The state, in other words, imposes "religion" on the public sphere, and by doing so guarantees the distinction between Jews and non-Jews, and the preference of the former over the latter.

As I noted in the previous chapters, the state of Israel has never invested its resources in the construction of an *Israeli* national identity, such that would be allegedly liberated from Jewish "religion" and would naturally include also Israel's non-Jewish population. Instead, the state has focused on constructing a Jewish identity, which, while obviously self-contradicted is nevertheless focused on one primary meaning: it is a national identity reserved for Jews only. The state has viewed the multiplicity and diversity of Jewish traditions and identities as a threat to "national cohesion," and devoted its energy and resources for the "melting" and erasure of these traditions, under the banner of the aggressive project of "the melting pot." But it has not given up on the imposition of a certain, Zionist-statist interpretation of Jewish tradition on the public sphere and the private lives of the state's population.

Political culture in Israel broadcasts, even if only shallowly, confusingly, and inconsistently so, the simple message that Israelis must respect Jewish tradition and be committed to the Jewish People at large. The Israeli public sphere—and especially the realm of mass media where Israeliness has been continually constituted—services, upholds, and reaffirms this understanding. It does so most commonly through continuous marketing (usually as a tool for the construction of audiences and costumers) or imposition (through the state's agencies) of these notions.

The Shabbat and Jewish holidays, to give but one example, are "forced" into the Israeli public sphere by the mere fact that the state and its agencies cease their daily working, and the TV channels switch to a "festive" schedule; even if the programs broadcast in this context have only limited, if any, meaningful connection to the traditional context of the Jewish holiday, the fact remains that Israel is probably the only place where a Jew can refrain from taking an active part in marking the Jewish holidays and still "experience" them—if only for the mere fact that she, as individual in the privacy of her own home—is "shifted" into a distinct temporal sphere, separate from the daily flow of time. And this has the effect, among others, of reaffirming her Jewish identity.

Thus, somewhat paradoxically, what many identify as "religious coercion" fulfills an essential and fundamental need of the secular majority's—more so than it serves, if at all, a "religious" agenda. After all, it is this imposition that allows the Israeli ḥiloni the historically unique privilege of being Jewish while avoiding practical observance of this identity. Needless to say, non-Jews (such as Israel's Palestinian citizens), who would be hard pressed to identify with this symbolic system, are predestined not to find themselves and their identity being represented in this public sphere.

The primary group benefiting from this coercion—in effect, a group whose very existence is dependent upon this coercion—is that of the statist Jews, those who have deposited, either knowingly or unknowingly, the maintenance of their Jewish identity with the sovereign, the nation-state. Without it, they would lose the meaning of their identity. In this context, we might recall the rather well-known phenomenon of Israelis (Jews) who self-identity as "total seculars" (ḥiloni gamur in colloquial Hebrew), who find themselves joining a Jewish community/congregation, which is constituted around a synagogue, and take part in a "religious" celebration of the Jewish holidays when they emigrate from Israel—even while still self-identifying as wholly indifferent to matters of "religion." Without the statist imposition/ maintenance of their Jewishness, they now require a "religious" institutional framework for the preservation and manifestation of their Jewishness—and Israeliness.

Indeed, one of the interesting questions arising in the context of a discussion on the status quo—a question asked by almost all scholars who examine it closely—has to do with the very persistence of the myth surrounding it. How is it that the dominant narrative of the status quo endures and keeps on telling a story of an Orthodox extortion and coercion, in the name of theocratic aspirations, on the naïve, passive and overall unfortunate secular majority? The answer has to do with statist Jewishness' self-denial. This Jewishness wishes to view itself as loyal to universal principles of enlightenment and secularism, and to imagine itself as "not-religious" and not-theological. As we have seen above, the identity and theology of the statist Jewishness is based on the foundational dichotomy of religious vs. secular. It sees itself through the secularist epistemology, and cannot accept the notion that it, too, is at the end an embodiment of a theopolitics. More specifically, statist Jewishness is based on the Israeli opposition between *ḥiloni* and *dati*; as A. B. Yehoshua clearly demonstrates, it is based on the conception of the *dati* (religious) as the primary enemy of the Israeli *ḥiloni*. This identification through the negation of the *dati* and the Orthodox means, among other things, that statist Jewishness is threatened by the possibility that elements of "religiosity" are also apparent in it; that it is the party most reliant on the purported "religious coercion" for the very maintenance of its identity.

## Statist Jewishness, Its Alternatives, and the Possibility of Resisting Sovereignty

An understanding of statist Jewishness offers, then, a window to deciphering the paradox or enigma of secular Jewishness in Israel. It explains how it can be that a majority of Israeli Jews would conduct a lifestyle that is rooted in part, meaningfully so, in Jewish traditions and practices that are considered "religious," and still view itself, being "secular," as "indifferent" to Jewish religion and its tradition. In other words, an understanding of statist Jewishness enables us to see how the invention of a supposedly "secular" Israeliness is enabled, while denying or repressing its critical dependency on Jewish traditions; it is the nation-state who maintains the Israelis' Jewish identity, preserves their privileged position as members of the majority, and also enables them to view themselves as fundamentally liberated from the dictates of Jewish religion, hence as implicitly ignorant of and explicitly indifferent to the contents and meanings of Jewish traditions that preceded the Israeli nation-state.

The sovereign's power is far from being limited only to those identifying as *ḥilonim*. Statist Jewishness, or the nationalization of Jewish identity by the sovereign is also apparent among groups that do not identify as secular, such as the Orthodox and traditionists. It is hard not to see how these groups adopt the supposedly nonreligious nation-state's theopolitics.

But these groups also offer, even if only as a theoretical option, the possibility of resisting the political sovereign and devising alternatives to the statist Jewishness is promotes. These identity groups preserve, by the very lifestyle they maintain, the possibility of Jewish identities that are not dependent on the state. If the statist Jew faces an existential danger when emigrating from Israel (what would preserve her children's identity as secular Jews?), then the Jewishness of these non-secular, non-statist groups is supposed, at least in principle, to survive and be maintained also in contexts outside of the State of Israel. The individual, the family, the community, the law, custom, and tradition are what maintain and preserve this identity—not the political-statist mechanism. These non-secular Jews may feel politically lacking—in that the state in which they live is not "theirs"—but this does not pertain to their Jewishness, or it may pertain to it only remotely, eschatologically. These Jews present a different balance between the theology of the state and Jewish traditions, such that enables a meaningful expression of non-"Israeli" (that is, non-statist-Jewish) identities—primarily intra-Jewish ethnic identities and traditions.

But the sovereign's power is immense. The statist Jewishness it has been promoting has managed to rewrite the meaning of Jewish identity for many Jews, whether secular by their self-identification or not, whether living in Israel or abroad. Indeed, it has managed to bestow "Jewishness" on people explicitly identified as non-Jews.[34] One of the greatest successes of the State of Israel has been the almost immediate, taken-for-granted identifications made by many—Jews and non-Jews, supporters of Israel and those opposing it alike—between Jewishness and the politics of the State of Israel. Non-Israeli Jews do not readily accept, of course, A. B. Yehoshua's statement by which they are "partial," compared to the "total" Jewish identity of his and any Israeli's; yet the public discourse they share tends to accept the claim that their relation to the State of Israel embodies the gravitational core of modern Jewish identity.[35] Similarly, when individuals and groups seek to violently oppose the State of Israel they may tend to direct their violence against non-Israeli Jews to express their opposition to the state.

I would not pretend to offer here a viable, self-sufficient alternative to the comprehensive worldview propagated by the sovereign nation-state on its reinvention of the meaning of Jewish identity. Such an explication of an alternative meaning of Jewish identity requires a political-philosophical intervention, one of a wholly different sort than the sociopolitical interpretation I have outlined here.[36] It seems to me that for such an alternative to be successful, it must nourish on Jewish traditions. This, I suspect, would enable it to resist the influence of the state, which self-identifies as Jewish. At the very least, it would guarantee such an alternative's relevance for those who view their Jewishness as a central, valuable element of their identity. This, indeed, may amount to an attempt to think politically of an order beyond the dominant one today, namely that of the nation-state. Given this dominance, this must be a formidable task; it must, indeed, be left for future interventions.

# Notes

## Introduction

1. I am borrowing the term from Cavanaugh, *Theopolitical Imagination*.
2. Ketubot 110b–111a.
3. Raz-Krakotzkin, "Exile within Sovereignty pt. 1"; Raz-Krakotzkin, "Exile, History and the Nationalization of Jewish Memory"; Boyarin and Boyarin, *Powers of Diaspora*; Butler, *Parting Ways*.
4. Agamben, *State of Exception*.
5. There had been, of course, dissenting minority voices within the Zionist movement. I focus my discussion here on the triumphant Political-Zionism, which has become the dominant mainstream of Zionist ideology and practice.
6. Shenhav, "Reflections," 27.
7. Who, in turn, hold on to a proto-conservative misunderstanding of the notion of Jewish tradition, viewing it as sort of a sealed package handed to us from the past, the dictates of which we must blindly obey, foregoing any sense of dialogue or reflection. For a critical assessment of this conservative stance see: Sagi, *Tradition vs. Traditionalism*, 5–15; Sagi, *The Challenge of a Return to Tradition*, 15–26; Sagi, *The Jewish-Israeli Voyage*, 87–121.
8. Yadgar, "Traditionism"; Yadgar, "A Post-Secular Look at Tradition."
9. Satlow, "Defining Judaism," 843.
10. Neusner, *The Way of Torah*, 8.
11. Neusner, quoted in Faur, *The Horizontal Society*, xx.
12. Ibid.

## Chapter 1

1. Cavanaugh, *The Myth of Religious Violence*, 58.
2. Ibid., 59.
3. Asad, *Genealogies of Religion*.

4. Dubuisson, *The Western Construction of Religion.*

5. Masuzawa, *The Invention of World Religions.*

6. Smith, *Imagining Religion.*

7. A comprehensive review of the critical discussion of the term "religion" is found in: Cavanaugh, *The Myth of Religious Violence*, 57–122; the ensuing discussion herein is built primarily on Cavanaugh's review.

8. Dubuisson, *The Western Construction of Religion.*

9. Cavanaugh, *The Myth of Religious Violence*, 59.

10. Asad, "Reading a Modern Classic."

11. Smith, *The Meaning and End of Religion*, 54–55.

12. See: Cavanaugh, *The Myth of Religious Violence*, 61–62; Skinner, *The Foundations of Modern Political Thought*, 349–350.

13. Cavanaugh, *The Myth of Religious Violence*, 62.

14. Ibid., 63.

15. Smith, *The Meaning and End of Religion*, 32.

16. Thomas Aquinas, quoted by Cavanaugh, *The Myth of Religious Violence*, 65.

17. Asad, *Genealogies of Religion*, 134.

18. Cavanaugh, *The Myth of Religious Violence*, 68.

19. Ibid., 69.

20. Cavanaugh identifies two Platonic Christian scholars, Nicholas of Cusa and Marsilio Ficino, writing in the fifteenth century, as the firsts to formulate this new understanding of religion.

21. Nicholas of Cusa quoted in ibid., 70.

22. Marsilio Ficino quoted in ibid., 71.

23. Ibid., 73.

24. Asad, "Reading a Modern Classic," 221.

25. The literature here is immense, and continues to expand. For some of the major works in this field see: Asad, *Formations of the Secular*; Bhargava, *Secularism and Its Critics*; Casanova, *Public Religions in the Modern World*; Connolly, *Why I Am Not a Secularist*; Jakobsen and Pellegrini, *Secularisms*; Taylor, *A Secular Age*.

26. Cavanaugh, *The Myth of Religious Violence*, 79–80.

27. Ibid., 94.

28. Edward, Lord Herbert of Cherbury, quoted in ibid., 75.

29. Ibid., 76–77.

30. This suspicion receives its foundational formulation in Descartes, but it was predated by several thinkers, *conversos* or descendants of *conversos*; see: Faur, *In the Shadow of History*, 87–141.

31. Cavanaugh, *The Myth of Religious Violence*, 77.

32. Ibid., 78–79.

33. Ibid.

34. Ibid., 83.

35. Cavanaugh, *Migrations of the Holy.*

36. Arnal, "Definition," 31.

37. Ibid.; see also: Cavanaugh, *The Myth of Religious Violence*, 84.

38. Masuzawa, *The Invention of World Religions*; Dubuisson, *The Western Construction of Religion.*

39. Cavanaugh, *The Myth of Religious Violence*, 86.

40. For a detailed presentation of this argument see: Chidester, *Savage Systems*, 35–69; Cavanaugh, *The Myth of Religious Violence*, 85–101.

41. Cavanaugh, *The Myth of Religious Violence*, 101.

42. Smith, *The Meaning and End of Religion*, 19.

43. Cavanaugh, *The Myth of Religious Violence*, 119.

44. Ibid.

45. Marvin and Ingle, "Blood Sacrifice and the Nation," 770; Quoted in Cavanaugh, *The Myth of Religious Violence*, 119–120.

46. Cavanaugh, *The Myth of Religious Violence*, 125.

47. Ibid., 120.

# Chapter 2

1. Mostly, less successful. See my discussion below on the transformation of the English "religion" into the Hebrew *dat.*

2. This is true, of course, in Christian contexts, too. Faur gives as an example "modern secularists'" recurring surprise at learning that Francis Bacon, who is nowadays referred to as a founder of empiricism, "was a man of God, of the Judaic monotheistic persuasion, like Isaac Newton." Faur, *The Horizontal Society*, 10.

3. Ibid., 10 ff. 27.

4. Ibid., 47.

5. See: Benamozegh, *Jewish and Christian Ethics.*

6. Faur, *The Horizontal Society*, xx–xxi.

7. Ibid., xxi.

8. There is, indeed, also good reason to question the relevance of the usage of "mysticism" for the study of Jewish traditions. But this extends beyond the scope of the current discussion

9. Dan, "Religion Studies."

10. Dan's comments on the issue lack a critical organ, and the history of the term offered in his article is partial, at best.

11. Smith, "Religion, Religions, Religious."

12. Dan, "Religion Studies," 163.

13. Ibid., 166.

14. See: Yadgar, *Beyond Secularization*, chap. 3; Fischer, "The Concepts of 'Religion' and 'Secularism' in Hebrew."

15. This problematical usage of the term is further exasperated in Faur's contention that Sephardic Jewish tradition should be read in Vico's term of

"religious humanism." See Faur, "Vico, Religious Humanism and the Sephardic Tradition."

16. Batnitzky, *How Judaism Became a Religion*, 1.

17. Mine, like Batnitzky's, is a primarily intellectual analysis. Needless to say, such an analysis is far from exhaustive; Judaism's emphasis on practice should also address us to the social-historical realities carried by the categories discussed herein. For an analysis of modern Judaism through a focus on practice, see Eisen, *Rethinking Modern Judaism*.

18. Batnitzky, *How Judaism Became a Religion*, 1.

19. Ibid., 2.

20. Ibid., 18.

21. Ibid.

22. José Faur offers such a critical reading of this exercise, as well as a comprehensive traditionist Sephardic alternative to it. See esp. Faur, *The Horizontal Society*.

23. Especially Mendelssohn, *Jerusalem*.

24. Batnitzky, *How Judaism Became a Religion*, 21.

25. Ibid.

26. Ibid., 22, 27.

27. Ibid., 28.

28. Such, for example, was David Friedländer's rejection of Mendelssohn's distinction between the political and theological constructs of the Jewish community. Friedländer's solution to the tension was to deny any status—political or religious—to ceremonial Jewish law. Ibid., 22–28.

29. Ibid., 25.

30. Raz-Krakotzkin, "Exile within Sovereignty pt. 1," 30.

31. Batnitzky, *How Judaism Became a Religion*, 33.

32. Raz-Krakotzkin, "Exile within Sovereignty pt. 1," 30.

33. Ibid.

34. Batnitzky, *How Judaism Became a Religion*, 35.

35. Ibid., 36.

36. Geiger, *Abraham Geiger and Liberal Judaism*, 178; quoted in Batnitzky, *How Judaism Became a Religion*, 36.

37. José Faur's note on the matter is of value here: Faur identifies the failure of the "Jewish sciences" to aptly appreciate the book-oriented (alphabetical, in his terms) nature of Judaism as emanating from the doctrine according to which "to be legitimate, 'Jewish history' needs to have been first regurgitated by non-Jews." Faur, *The Horizontal Society*, 63.

38. Batnitzky, *How Judaism Became a Religion*, 37.

39. Ibid., 34.

40. Ibid.

41. Hirsch, *Judaism Eternal*, 103; quoted in Batnitzky, *How Judaism Became a Religion*, 41.

42. Batnitzky, *How Judaism Became a Religion*, 41.

43. Ibid., 41–42.

44. Ibid., 43.

45. Ibid.

46. Ibid.

47. Ibid., 45–46.

# Chapter 3

1. Shils, "Tradition and Liberty," 153.

2. Ibid., 156.

3. As he puts it: "It is now some years since I detected how many were the false beliefs that I had from my earliest youth admitted as true, and how doubtful was everything I had since constructed on this basis; and from that time I was convinced that I must once for all seriously undertake to rid myself of all the opinions which I had formerly accepted, and commence to build anew from the foundation, if I wanted to establish any firm and permanent structure in the sciences" (Descartes, *Meditations*, 18).

4. To use Richard Bernstein's term: Bernstein, *Beyond Objectivism and Relativism*, 16.

5. Taylor, *Philosophical Papers*, 2:4–6.

6. MacIntyre, *The Tasks of Philosophy*, 3–23; Taylor, *Philosophical Arguments*, 1–20, 34–60; Oakeshott, *Rationalism in Politics and Other Essays*, 6–42.

7. Rorty, *Philosophy and the Mirror of Nature*.

8. Polanyi, *Science, Faith and Society*; Polanyi, *Personal Knowledge*.

9. Kuhn, *The Structure of Scientific Revolutions*; Kuhn, *The Essential Tension*.

10. See esp.: Taylor, *Philosophical Arguments*, 61–78; Taylor, *Philosophical Papers*; MacIntyre, *The Tasks of Philosophy*, 3–23.

11. Douglas, *How Institutions Think*, 70.

12. Wittgenstein, *Philosophical Investigations*; Wittgenstein, *On Certainty*.

13. Esp. Geertz, *The Interpretation of Cultures*; Geertz, *Islam Observed*.

14. Polanyi, *Personal Knowledge*; Polanyi, *Science, Faith and Society*.

15. Kuhn, *The Structure of Scientific Revolutions*.

16. Oakeshott, *Rationalism in Politics and Other Essays*.

17. Esp. Taylor, *Human Agency and Language*; Taylor, "Interpretation and the Sciences of Man."

18. Gadamer, *Truth and Method*; Gadamer, "The Problem of Historical Consciousness"; Gadamer, *Philosophical Hermeneutics*.

19. MacIntyre, *After Virtue*; MacIntyre, *Whose Justice?*; MacIntyre, *Three Rival Versions of Moral Enquiry*.

20. Esp. Shils, *Tradition*.

21. Eisenstadt, "Intellectuals and Tradition"; Eisenstadt, *Tradition, Change, and Modernity*.

22. See: Taylor, *Philosophical Arguments*, 169–172.

23. As Wittgenstein comments on the (im)possibility of a private language (in MacIntyre's reading of it): "[O]n the best account of language that I can give and the best account of inner mental states that I can give, I can make nothing of the notion of a private language, I cannot render it adequately intelligible." MacIntyre, *After Virtue*, 101.

24. Cookery has been one of the oft-used examples in the ongoing intellectual discourse on tradition, mainly because it manages to capture nicely both the superiority of practice over intellectual knowledge (think of the cook who has learned to cook by standing next to—and accepting the authority of—an experienced master, versus the inexperienced "cook" who is trying to follow a cookbook's instructions). In a similar vein, cookery can also exemplify my point here: think of all the ways in which a certain cook, who is immersed in a certain culinary culture and practice—i.e., tradition—would never even think of cooking a certain dish, while those very same ways are the most obvious ways in which another cook, coming from another culinary tradition, would handle the same dish (preparing and serving raw meat dishes in certain kitchens versus the practical impossibility of doing the same in others is just one example that springs to mind in this regard). Needless to say, this is not limited to culinary traditions.

25. Rabinow, *Symbolic Domination*, 1.

26. Both are Taylor's "Interpretation and the Sciences of Man" phrases.

27. Oakeshott, *Rationalism in Politics and Other Essays*, 148.

28. Rabinow, *Symbolic Domination*, 1.

29. MacIntyre, *After Virtue*, 209, 216.

30. MacIntyre, *Whose Justice?*, 11.

31. Gadamer, *Truth and Method*, 103.

32. Ibid., 103, 105, 106.

33. Vattimo, "Democracy and Hermeneutics," 12.

34. Taylor, *The Ethics of Authenticity*.

35. Esp. MacIntyre, *The Tasks of Philosophy*, 15–23.

36. Ibid., 19; see also: MacIntyre, *Whose Justice?*, 354–5.

37. Oakeshott, *Rationalism in Politics and Other Essays*, 59.

38. Ibid.

39. MacIntyre, *Whose Justice?*, 353; Needless to say, MacIntyre's reading of Burke is not uncontested. See: Byrne, *Edmund Burke for Our Time*, 91–93; Baldacchino, "The Value-Centered Historicism of Edmund Burke."

40. As MacIntyre *Whose Justice?*, 12, puts it: "A tradition is an argument extended through time in which certain fundamental agreements are defined and redefined in terms of two kinds of conflict: those with critics and enemies external to the tradition who reject all or at least parts of those fundamental agreements, and those internal, interpretative debates through which the meaning and rationale of the fundamental agreements come to be expressed and by whose progress a tradition is constituted."

41. MacIntyre, *After Virtue*, 222.

42. At least according to MacIntyre's critical reading of Burke and Kuhn and to Gadamer's criticism of romanticism: MacIntyre, *The Tasks of Philosophy*, 2–23; MacIntyre, *After Virtue*, 221–22; Gadamer, *Truth and Method*, 282.

## Chapter 4

1. A most recent example of this is Walzer, *The Paradox of Liberation*, in which the eminent political philosopher aims to explain how it is that this "secular revolution" has been overtaken by a "religious counterrevolution."

2. Avineri, *Varieties of Zionist Thought*; an English iteration of this work was published as: Avineri, *The Making of Modern Zionism*; There are some differences between the two, and I will use both sources below.

3. This assessment is based on the academic prominence of the author, his role as a public intellectual and civil servant, and the tone of the book. Avineri's is not the first review of Zionist thought—Arthur Hertzberg's edited volume presenting the mainstays of the Zionist idea preceded it. Hertzberg's introduction to the volume remains one of the best assessments of Zionism's relation to Jewish concepts that preceded it. Hertzberg, *The Zionist Idea*.

4. Avineri, *The Making of Modern Zionism*, 217.

5. Avineri, *Varieties of Zionist Thought*, 21.

6. Avineri, *The Making of Modern Zionism*, 13.

7. Avineri, *Varieties of Zionist Thought*, 21.

8. Ibid., 16.

9. Ibid.

10. Avineri, *The Making of Modern Zionism*, 4.

11. Stark, "Secularization, R.I.P.," 255.

12. As Rodney Stark puts it in his devastating critique of this myth: "Everyone 'knows' that once upon a time the world was pious—that in olden days most people exhibited levels of religious practice and concern that today linger only in isolated social subcultures." Ibid.

13. Avineri, *The Making of Modern Zionism*, 3.

14. Ibid., 219.

15. Ibid., 218.

16. Avineri, *Varieties of Zionist Thought*, 248.

17. Ibid., 249.

18. Ibid.; the English version is slightly less determined: "The State of Israel put the public, normative dimension back into Jewish life. Without this having ever been defined or decided upon, it is a fact that to be Jewish today means, in one way or another, feeling some link with Israel"; Avineri, *The Making of Modern Zionism*, 219.

19. Avineri, *The Making of Modern Zionism*, 220.

20. Avineri, *Varieties of Zionist Thought*, 250.

21. Avineri, *The Making of Modern Zionism*, 221.

22. Ibid.

23. Avineri, *Varieties of Zionist Thought*, 251.

24. Ibid., 252.

25. Ibid., 21.

26. The study of Zionism and Israel has produced numerous attempts at capturing the nuanced relationship between what one scholar describes as the (oxymoronic) meeting of parallels. See Luz, *Parallels Meet*; Luz, *Wrestling with an Angel:*; Liebman and Don-Yehiya, *Civil Religion in Israel*.

27. Salmon, *Religion and Zionism*; Salmon, "Religion and Nationalism."

28. Salmon, "Religion and Nationalism," 115.

29. Ibid., 115–116.

30. Ibid., 116.

31. David Vital, quoted in ibid., 117.

32. Ibid.

33. Ibid.

34. Ibid., 118.

35. Avineri, "Zionism and the Jewish Religious Tradition," 1, emphasis added.

36. Ibid., 2.

37. Almog, Reinharz, and Shapira, *Zionism and Religion*.

38. Taylor, "Two Theories of Modernity."

39. Salmon also contributed to the discussed edited volume. See Salmon, "Zionism and Anti-Zionism in Traditional Judaism in Eastern Europe."

40. Salmon, "Religion and Secularism in the Zionist National Movement," 1.

41. Editors' Preface, Almog, Reinharz, and Shapira, *Zionism and Religion*, xi.

42. Shimoni, *The Zionist Ideology*, 269.

43. Ibid.

44. Ibid.

45. Ibid.

46. Ibid.

47. Ibid.

48. Ibid., 269–270.

49. Needless to say, this viewpoint on Zionism is far from exhaustive; it diverts our attention (for the sake of focus) away from other powerful motives of the Zionist project, such as the Jewish-European revolt against what some viewed as a pathological Jewish passivity and, maybe most importantly, the attempt to liberate Jews from the political authority of non-Jews. I should also stress that my argument here is focused on the mainstream of Zionist ideology, which viewed itself as "secular."

50. Voices coming from the margins of the Zionist movement exemplified the possibility of detaching these two sides of the mainstream Zionist

idea (which, in modern Israel, seem to be synonymous and identical). See Myers, "Rethinking the Jewish Nation"; Myers, *Between Jew and Arab*.

51. As Yosef Salmon puts it, the driving force propelling Zionism in the 1860s and 1870s was "the opposition to the new Jewish perceptions—the reformists and culturalist—that draw a distinction in Judaism between nationality and religion." Salmon, "Religion and Nationalism," 119.

52. In this vein, they often preferred to identify this nationalism (and themselves) as Hebrew, not Jewish. While the former name carried the aura of a healthy, modern-yet-ancient (indeed: "secular") national identity, the latter was marked by the stain of *"galut"* (Hebrew for exile), and the accompanying negative traits of passivity, immaterialism (that is, an unbalanced tilt toward the spiritual, on expense of a natural connection to the material, political world), archaism, and overall negativity. This lingual/nominal maneuver was thus expressing a sometimes implicit, often explicit sense of Zionists that their identity—a Hebrew *national* identity, then still lacking a state to carry it—is distanced, if not outright separate, from the *religious* identity of those other, "exilic" Jews. On Hebrewism as a "native culture" or "traditional Israeliness," see Even-Zohar, "The Emergence of a Native Hebrew Culture in Palestine: 1882–1948"; Regev and Seroussi, *Popular Music and National Culture in Israel*, 17.

53. Salmon, "Religion and Nationalism," 116.

54. Latour, *We Have Never Been Modern*.

55. Shenhav, "Modernity and the Hybridization of Nationalism and Religion," 1.

# Chapter 5

1. Moreover, a German-speaking state at that, as can be referred from the Herzlian utopia in *Altneuland*.

2. Aḥad Ha'am, "Altneuland."

3. Ibid.

4. Shimoni, *The Zionist Ideology*, 270.

5. See chapter 1.

6. Ghosh, *In an Antique Land*, 273.

7. "Secular" was often translated as *"hofshi"* (liberated). The term common in contemporary Hebrew, *"hiloni"* (derived from *hol*, as in profane, the opposite of *kodesh*, the sacred) seems to have been rarely in use by early Zionist ideologues. Zvi Zameret found one of the earliest uses of *hiloni* in an essay by Ḥeruti (a pen name of Moshe Smilansky) from 1909. The author predicted that it would be "A disaster! disaster if the religious [*dati*] force inserts itself inside the secular [*hilonainim* in the original; this is an unfamiliar use of the root in contemporary Hebrew] life—this is a hybridization of two separate kinds [. . .] it will slow down the natural development of society."

Heruti (Moshe Smilansky), "Michtavin El Aḥot" (Letters to a sister) *Hapoel Hatzair*, third year, no. 2, 20 Ḥeshvan 5670 (4 November 1909); Quoted in a letter from Zvi Zameret to Yesha'ayahu (Charles) Liebman, June 20, 2003.

8. For a comprehensive review of this argument see: Smith, *The Nation in History*.

9. The modern challenge against tradition and rabbinical authority begins, of course, with the *haskala* movement. All Zionist ideologues nourish, in this regard, from a preliminary Jewish-European adoption of the ideas of (Christian) European Enlightenment, on its "secularity."

10. This can be learned, for example, from Gideon Shimoni's work on the subject (mainly the section of his book dedicated to a study of "Zionism as Secular Jewish Identity")—out of ostensible disloyalty to the terminology and conceptual toolkit used by Shimoni himself. Shimoni also locates David Ben-Gurion as occupying a middle position between these two pillars. Shimoni, *The Zionist Ideology*, 269–332.

11. As we shall see herein, it gains some of its most striking formulations from Socialist Zionist ideologues who combine their readings of the Nietzschean philosophy with a Socialist/Marxist ideology.

12. Best represented by Shimoni's comprehensive analysis; Ibid.

13. For a review of the controversy, see Ibid., 391 onward.

14. See, for example, how Shimoni concludes his discussion of Aḥad Ha'am's "secular" doctrine: "it may be said that the nationalist ideology of Aḥad Ha'am was an attempt to synthesize deeply ingrained traditional Jewish cultural elements with an enlightened modernism"; Ibid., 277.

15. Ibid., 277–278; emphasis added.

16. The literature on Aḥad Ha'am is immense, and commonly deals with his understanding of Judaism as culture or his relation to Jewish religion. For a comprehensive intellectual biography of his see Zipperstein, *Elusive Prophet*. On Aḥad Ha'am's relation to "Jewish religion," see Ḥevlin, *Double Loyalty*.

17. As Shimoni notes, Aḥad Ha'am is not the first to formulate this stance. Phenomenologically (although not personally: Aḥad Ha'am denied being so indebted), he is the direct successor of Peretz Smolenskin; Shimoni, *The Zionist Ideology*, 270.

18. In Baruch Kurzweil's biting formulation, "Aḥad Ha'am's core belief was that of Spencer, J. S. Mill, and Darwin. The foundation of his approach is materialist-psychological, and his idol—the belief in Evolution." Kurzweil, *Our New Literature*, 191; See also: Shimoni, *The Zionist Ideology*, 270; Simon and Heller, *Aḥad Ha'am*, 139–148.

19. See: Stark, "Atheism, Faith, and the Social Scientific Study of Religion."

20. Or, in Kurzweil's critical formulation: "Aḥad Ha'am has taught the young generation that it must accept a Judaism without the living God. Moreover, this "Guide for the Perplexed" has shown that the belief in the

living God was sort of an earlier, more primitive incarnation of the national will of life. The concept *"ḥefetz haqiyoum"* [the will to life], which is one of the pillars of his doctrine originates in the philosophy of the Will, without the depth and consistency that characterize Schopenhauer's philosophy of the Will." Kurzweil, *Our New Literature*, 200.

21. Shimoni, *The Zionist Ideology*, 270.

22. Kurzweil, *Our new literature*, 201.

23. Aḥad Ha'am, *'Al Parashat Derachim*, 2:79.

24. Ibid.

25. Ibid., 2:80.

26. Kurzweil rightly identifies Aḥad Ha'am as striving to "transform his essays into a productive push [. . .] beyond the 'crossroad' to which his generation, the intellectual *maskilim*, has arrived." He notes that Aḥad Ha'am's view of secularization should be understood in the context of the late nineteenth century, "after a naïve period of *haskala*, which had fooled itself [. . .] and had not yet realized the meaning of its own secularity." Kurzweil, *Our New Literature*, 194–195.

27. Aḥad Ha'am, *'Al Parashat Derachim*, 2:80.

28. Both critical and approving readers of Aḥad Ha'am make this point. See Shimoni, *The Zionist Ideology*, 270–271; Kurzweil, *Our New Literature*, 190–224.

29. Or, in Shimoni's terminology, "purely idealistic" arguments, which follow Hegel's metaphysical abstractions; Shimoni, *The Zionist Ideology*, 271.

30. As done, for example, by Yitzḥak El'azari-Volcani; see below.

31. Kurzweil, *Our New Literature*, 219.

32. Ibid., 190.

33. Shimoni, *The Zionist Ideology*, 271.

34. Baruch Kurzweil, offers a consideration of the danger inherent in this double standard: "People often quote the sentence from [Aḥad Ha'am's] letter to the editor of *Haaretz* in [8 Elul] 5682 [September 22, 1922], in reaction to the murder of an innocent Arab boy, an act of revenge by Jews: 'If this be the Messiah, then I do not wish to see his coming!' But the one who has sanctified as supreme value the 'will to life' and the modern national idea, must have seen this [the murder] as a logical act. It is not in vein that people identify 'the will to life' with 'the Guardian of Israel.' It seems that Aḥad Ha'am was not able to see the connection between this deed and similar acts and his 'doctrine of continuation.' But the connection is viable." Kurzweil, *Our New Literature*, 219.

35. The essay was originally published in the volume *Revivim*, edited by Brenner: A. Tzioni (Yitzḥak Wilkanski), "Hateologia Haleumit (The National Theology)." It is reprinted in his collected writings: El'azari-Volcani, *Sefirot*, 13–68.

36. Shimoni, *The Zionist Ideology*, 295, describes El'azari-Volcani's arguments against Aḥad Ha'am as "one of the most potent and unequivocal affirmations of secular Jewish identity in the entire corpus of Zionist literature."

37. El'azari-Volcani, *Sefirot*, 48.

38. As Shimoni puts it: "For [Aḥad Ha'am] the question Why be a Jew? was quite as senseless and unnecessary as it was for the most orthodox of Jews, although his reasoning was on secular lines. One was a Jew as naturally, immutably, and unquestionably, as one was a child of one's natural parents. Any attempt of a born Jew to pass as a member of any other nation was as self-abasing as it was self-defeating." This merits a reiteration: Shimoni accepts that these evidently mythic reasoning is "secular." It is so, so it would appear, since it differs from the reasoning of "the most orthodox of Jews," that is: it is not "religious." Shimoni, *The Zionist Ideology*, 272.

39. Aḥad Ha'am describes the rabbi's words as "fiery words, the echo of the authentic sentiment existing among the people." He finds them "very important, as a fine sign of the future." Aḥad Ha'am, *'Al Parashat Derachim*, 2:60.

40. "A Western Rabbi," quoted in ibid., 2:61.

41. As Shimoni notes: "These are not Aḥad Ha'am's own words but a quotation from an article by an unnamed Western rabbi whose views in this regard Aḥad Ha'am wholeheartedly commended." Shimoni, *The Zionist Ideology*, 429 ff.6. Aḥad Ha'am references his quote as: "Warum sind wir Juden?" *Brull's Monatshefte* 1 (1898).

42. "A Western rabbi," quoted in Aḥad Ha'am, *'Al Parashat Derachim*, 2:60–61.

43. Walzer, "On the Role of Symbolism in Political Thought."

44. Aḥad Ha'am, *'Al Parashat Derachim*, 1:169–177; An English translation is available at: Aḥad Ha'am, *Selected Essays*, 107–124.

45. Aḥad Ha'am, quoted in Shimoni, *The Zionist Ideology*, 273.

46. Lilla, *The Stillborn God* offers the common "Enlightened" narrative positing the development of the atheistic premise as the basis of modern political philosophy, in which Hobbes's ideas hold a prominent role.

47. Hume, *An Enquiry Concerning Human Understanding*; see also Buzaglo, *A Language for the Faithful*, 33–35.

48. This is certainly how Berdyczewski demands we read Aḥad Ha'am. Berdyczewski, *Maamarim*, 23–40.

49. Aḥad Ha'am, *Selected Essays*, 92–93.

50. Ibid., 91–106.

51. Ibid., 97.

52. Berdyczewski, *Maamarim*, 31.

53. Aḥad Ha'am, *'Al Parashat Derachim*, 1:93.

54. Ibid., 1:213.

55. Shimoni, *The Zionist Ideology*, 273.

56. Aḥad Ha'am in a letter to Judah Magnes, Oct. 18, 1919, quoted in ibid.

57. Aḥad Ha'am in a letter to MKB, Apr. 4, 1899, quoted in ibid.

58. Ibid.

59. Berdyczewski, *Maamarim*, 38; Or, as Shimoni summarizes this, in a distinctively less cynical language: "The national morals were a faithful reflection of the national spirit no less than was the national language. On these lines Aḥad Ha'am proceeded to argue that it behooved the national Jew to uphold the unique moral values of the Jewish people, rooted particularly in the biblical prophets, even if he had ceased to observe the laws and rituals of the Jewish religion. Not to do so would be to deprive the national Jewish culture of its essence." Shimoni, *The Zionist Ideology*, 274.

60. Berdyczewski, *Maamarim*, 39.

61. Aḥad Ha'am, *Kol Kitvey*, 121.

62. Shimoni, *The Zionist Ideology*, 276.

63. The image of childhood is indeed central to understanding Berdyczewski's Nietzschean position. He himself summarizes his criticism of Aḥad Ha'am with the vision: "The clouds of old age are clearing, and childhood dew is falling upon us!" Berdyczewski, *Maamarim*, 24.

64. Aḥad Ha'am, *Selected Essays*, 89–90.

65. Aḥad Ha'am, *Kol Kitvey*, 440.

66. See: Zipperstein, *Elusive Prophet*.

67. Such, for example, was his argument against the importation of what he viewed as Christian morality into the Jewish world: He bases his argument against such "moral Christianization" on a re-reading of an argument detailed in the Talmud (an argument between Ben Petora and Rabbi Aqiva, which appears in Baba-Metzi'a 62). Aḥad Ha'am, *Kol Kitvey*, 383.

68. Berdyczewski, *Maamarim*, 33.

69. Shimoni, *The Zionist Ideology*, 284–285.

70. Ibid., 279.

71. This was most vividly expressed by Yehiel Michel Pines in an open letter to Aḥad Ha'am, in which Pines protested against what he viewed as an enforcement of secular values in the Beni Moshe society. This society, Pines argued, failed to provide common ground for "the two types of Jews," i.e., secular and religious. Y. M. Pines, quoted in ibid., 280.

72. It is also worth noting how indebted this view is to the contemporaneous Ashkenazi understandings of Jewish identity; it is wholly indifferent to alternative, non-Ashkenazi conceptions.

73. In other words, he outlines the basic scheme of the "statue quo"; see chapter 9.

74. This quote appears in a correspondence between Aḥad Ha'am and the educator Menachem Sheinkin (Feb. 14, 1908), following a controversy whether the (male) students at the Hebrew Gymnasium should be forced to cover their heads during their studies of the Hebrew Bible (the Zionist inclination was to categorically negate the covering of the head, which it viewed as a "religious" act. Aḥad Ha'am believed a compromise on this issue could

be justified, if the covering of the head promotes the actual study of the text.) The Hebrew text appears in Aḥad Ha'am, *Igrot*, vol. 4, p. 7. This English translation is taken from Shimoni, *The Zionist Ideology*, 277.

75. Shimoni, *The Zionist Ideology*, 278.

76. For an overview of Berdyczewski's life work, see Holtzman, *Micha Joseph Berdyczewski*; Holtzman, *Literature and Life*.

77. See Anidjar, *Blood*.

78. Shimoni, *The Zionist Ideology*, 288; Note the ethno-national, taken-for-granted presupposition assuming ethnicity as "normal" and "natural."

79. Ibid., 286.

80. Ibid.

81. Ibid., 287.

82. Berdyczewski, *Maamarim*, 23.

83. See, for example, how Shimoni—who ties the discussion on Aḥad Ha'am, Berdyczewski and others under the unifying title of "Zionism as Secular Jewish Identity"—describes the difference between the two rebels, Aḥad Ha'am and Berdyczewski:

> There was [. . .] a major difference between the lines of *haskala* revolt followed by these two pivotal personalities. Aḥad Ha'am took up the cudgels from those *maskilim* [. . .] who had attacked the established authorities of Jewish religion but at the same time nurtured some hope for internal reform of the religion. They had also evinced growing concern about the void that was being created by what they assumed to be the irreversible decline of religion in Jewish life. Since Aḥad Ha'am shared this concern, he labored to formulate an alternative national Jewish identity bound by norms that would constitute a surrogate of sorts for the eclipsed religious authority and precepts. By contrast, in Berdyczewski's eyes religious authority was still a ubiquitous power, an unrestrained threat to free self-expression of the individual Jew in the present, no less than in the past. His concern was neither to reform the religion—a futile exercise, in his view—nor to fabricate a surrogate national Judaism lest the entire edifice of Jewish identity collapse but rather to break away completely from all religious authority and from all established norms.
>
> Shimoni, *The Zionist Ideology*, 287–288

84. In Shimoni's dichotomous terminology, the matter at hand is not dialogue or reinterpretation, but "compromise": they "tended to seek compromise with traditionalism in the interests of national integrity"; Ibid., 288.

85. Ibid.

86. Shils, "Tradition and Liberty."

87. Berdyczewski, *Maamarim*, 25.

88. Ibid., 31.

89. Ibid., 22.

90. Ibid., 20.

91. Ibid.

92. Ibid., 32.

93. Shimoni, *The Zionist Ideology*, 288.

94. Berdyczewski, *Maamarim*, 31.

95. This English translation of Nietzsche's quote is taken from: Nietzsche, *Untimely Meditations*, 62. Berdyczewski's translation of the German text is more forceful, and can be translated as "the inherited sense of regurgitation of memories from ancient times." Berdyczewski, *Maamarim*, 31.

96. Berdyczewski, *Maamarim*, 36.

97. Ibid.

98. Ibid., 25.

99. Ibid., 26.

100. Berdyczewski is here paraphrasing Numbers 25, 5: "How goodly are thy tents, O Jacob, thy dwellings, O Israel!"

101. Ibid., 13.

102. Ibid., 28.

103. Ibid., 28–29.

104. Ibid., 33, 34.

105. Ibid., 18.

106. Ibid., 33.

107. Ibid., 20.

108. Aḥad Ha'am, *'Al Parashat Derachim*, 1:161.

109. Berdyczewski, *Maamarim*, 35.

110. Ibid., 20.

111. Shimoni, *The Zionist Ideology*, 288.

112. Berdyczewski, *Maamarim*, 31.

113. Ibid., 26.

114. Ibid.

115. Ibid., 39.

116. The "Young Hebrews" (or "Canaanites") movement developed this notion into a full fledge ideology. See Kurzweil, "The New Canaanites in Israel"; Shavit, *The New Hebrew Nation*; Porath, *The Life of Uriel Shelah*.

117. Berdyczewski, *Maamarim*, 40.

118. Ibid., 37.

119. Berdyczewski refers here to the lack of a political expression of Jewish nationalism, that would by definition carry implications of the cultural, social, etc,. kind; the problem, at root, is that "we do not have a home"; Ibid., 38.

120. Ibid.

121. MacIntyre, *The Task of Philosophy*, 2–23.

122. Berdyczewski, *Maamarim*, 40.

123. Berdyczewski paraphrases here Moses's call, facing the unruly worshipers of the golden calf, *Exodus* 32, 26: "Whoso is on the LORD'S side, let him come unto me."

124. Shimoni, *The Zionist Ideology*, 286.

125. Berdyczewski, *Maamarim*, 25.

126. Shimoni, *The Zionist Ideology*, 290–291.

127. Berdyczewski, *Maamarim*, 42–43.

128. Ibid., 46.

129. Ibid., 52.

# Chapter 6

1. I am borrowing the terms "crypto-religious" and "crypto-secular" from Hamid Dabashi's discussion of the ideological sources of the Iranian Revolution. Dabashi, *Theology of Discontent*, 10.

2. Shimoni, *The Zionist Ideology*, 269–332.

3. Ibid., 293.

4. As Cavanaugh shows (see the extended discussion in chapter 1 of this book), this is a prevalent exercise among academics.

5. Ibid.

6. Socialist-Zionist ideology, which has clearly preferred the dictates of Nationalism over Socialism, argues that the two are in effect complimentary, not contradictory. See Sternhell, *The Founding Myths of Israel*.

7. In this, Socialist-Zionism is indeed different from the ideologies propagated by Liberal or Nietzschean Zionists, who lacked a totalistic ideological infrastructure similar to Socialism.

8. Yosef Salmon identifies this as the "atheistic model" of Zionism's relation to Jewish religion. As mentioned earlier, Salmon, too, remains chained to the conceptual framework of the secularization discourse, even when he sheds light on the invalidity of its basic premise and arguments, and offers a far more nuanced description of the relationship between Zionist nationalism and Jewish tradition. Salmon, *Religion and Zionism*; Salmon, "Religion and Secularism in the Zionist National Movement."

9. As Shimoni notes, the Hebrew phrase used by Syrkin, "*dat yehudit ma'asit,*" (which Shimoni translates as "Jewish religion in practice") might alternatively be translated as "religious praxis." Shimoni, *The Zionist Ideology*, 294 ff. 64.

10. Syrkin, *Kitvei*, 68–69.

11. Ibid., 104; Shimoni, *The Zionist Ideology*, p. 294 ff. 65, in an apparent *pilpul*, interprets this as a parody. He writes: "That secular Zionists desecrate the sancta of Israel was a typical accusation made by orthodox rabbis. By quoting it thus, Syrkin was declaring provocatively that his policy was indeed to debunk

certain orthodox religious beliefs." It is easy to see why Zionist apologetics would demand such a *pilpul*. I do not see it as demanded by the text.

12. Syrkin, *Kitvei*, 169–170.

13. Shimoni, *The Zionist Ideology*, 295; This statement is a summation of the data offered by Gorni, "Changes in the Social and Political Sturcture of the Second 'Aliyah, 1904–1914"; and compare: Alroey, "The Demographic Composition of the 'Second 'Aliyah.' "

14. Shimoni, *The Zionist Ideology*, 295.

15. Ibid., 296.

16. As he states: "The doctrine of morals and ethics, on which countries and people fight, has been nothing but a bifurcation of the self." El'azari-Volcani, *Sefirot*, 34.

17. For a debunking of this narrative, see Cavanaugh, *The Myth of Religious Violence*, chap. 4.

18. El'azari-Volcani, *Sefirot*, 34, 36.

19. Ibid., 35–37.

20. Ibid., 37.

21. Ibid.

22. Ibid.

23. Ibid., 37–38.

24. El'azari-Volcani's' biological imagery merits extended quotation: "In the whole field of creation, and in all professions of our life; in poetry, in art, in concepts of ethics, in simple bargaining, in relationships between man and his God and between man and his fellow men, in practices, and in norms,—in everything there is some special essence ['*etzem meyuḥad*] in us, remnants of generations that have been absorbed in our blood and milk, which are not absorbed in the organism of the masters of the land, who dictate our life." Ibid., 39.

25. After having described the "abnormal" existence of the "Hebrew soul" in exile, El'azari-Volcani concludes: "Anti-Semitism is not a psychosis, it is not a sickness, nor is it a lie. Liberalism is a sickness and lie, as it burdens the soul with the empty declarations [of] equality and progress [. . .] Anti-Semitism is a necessary outcome of a collision between two kinds of selfhood [or 'essence']. Each people and its selfhood [. . .] Hate is dependent upon the amount of 'agents of fermentation' that are pushed into the general organism [i.e., the non-Jewish group], whether they are active in it and irritate it, or are neutralized in it—and the 'fermenting agents' are in the blood, not in dress and belief." Ibid., 39–40.

26. Ibid., 40.

27. Ibid., 43.

28. Shimoni, *The Zionist Ideology*, 297.

29. On Brenner see: Shapira, *Yosef Haim Brenner*; Brinker, "Brenner's Jewishness"; Sagi, *To Be a Jew*.

30. Shimoni, *The Zionist Ideology*, 297.

31. See also: Zameret, "Berdyczewski, Brenner and Gordon on the Sabbath."

32. Brenner, "Leverur Ha'inyan," 15.

33. Brenner; signed as Yosef Ḥaver, "Ba'itunot Uvasifrut," 7.

34. Ibid.

35. In Brenner's own words: "As for myself, for me the Old Testament, too, does not have the value that everyone calls clamorously as 'Holly Texts,' 'The Book of Books,' 'The Eternal Book,' and so on and so forth. I have long ago already been released from the hypnotization of the twenty-four books of the Bible [*biblia* in the Hebrew original] . . .—Many secular books [*sifrei ḥol*] from the last generations are closer to me, [and are] greater and deeper in my eyes. But the same importance I do find in the Hebrew Bible [*tanach* in the original], as remnants of memories of distant days and as the embodiment of the spirit of our people and the human spirit inside us during many generations and eras—this importance I also find and acknowledge in the books of the New Testament." Ibid.

36. Brenner, "Leverur Ha'inyan," 13.

37. Ibid.

38. Ibid.

39. Shimoni, *The Zionist Ideology*, 299.

40. Brenner, "Leverur Ha'inyan," 16.

41. Ibid.

42. Ibid., 13.

43. Sagi, *To Be a Jew*, 111.

44. Brenner, "Avi Hapublitzistiqa."

45. Brenner; signed as Yosef Ḥaver, "Ba'itunot Uvasifrut," 8.

46. Brenner, "Avi Hapublitzistiqa."

47. Sagi, *To Be a Jew*, 111–112.

48. Ibid., 112.

49. Brenner; signed as Yosef Ḥaver, "Ba'itunot Uvasifrut," 8.

50. Ibid.

51. Brenner, "Leverur Ha'inyan," 16.

52. Brenner; signed as Yosef Ḥaver, "Ba'itunot Uvasifrut," 7.

53. Ibid.

54. Brenner, "Leverur Ha'inyan," 13; or, in Shimoni's formulation, "the new national Hebrews"; Shimoni, *The Zionist Ideology*, 299.

55. Brenner, "Leverur Ha'inyan," 16.

56. Shimoni, *The Zionist Ideology*, 299.

57. Brenner, *Ketavim*, vol. 4, p. 1296; in Shimoni's translation this reads as: "How can we, as ourselves, become other than ourselves"; Shimoni, *The Zionist Ideology*, 300.

58. Brenner, *Ketavim*, vol. 4, pp. 1295–1296.

59. Ibid., vol. 4, p. 1296.

60. Shimoni, *The Zionist Ideology*, 300.

61. Berdyczewski, who dealt with the meaning of Jewish identity inside a Liberal framework, one that views Judaism as an idea, as philosophy, could not "skip outside" of the tension: Liberalism does not offer a similar totalistic surrogate to tradition, as does Socialism. For a comparison between the two see: Brinker, "Brenner's Jewishness"; Shimoni, *The Zionist Ideology*, 300.

62. Brenner; signed as Yosef Ḥaver, "Ba'itunot Uvasifrut," 8.

63. Ibid., 6.

64. Ibid.

65. Ibid., 8.

66. Brenner uses the term "the history of beliefs and religions," and clarifies that he uses this term "intentionally." Ibid., 7.

67. Ibid.

68. Ibid.

69. Ibid., 6.

70. Ibid.

71. Ibid.

72. Ibid.

73. Alcalay, *After Jews and Arabs*, 52.

74. Ibid.

75. Ben-Ezer, "Tzel"; see also: Ben-Ezer, *Sleep Walkers and Other Stories*; Ben-Ezer, "Brenner and the 'Arab Question.' "

76. Brenner, *Mikan Umikan*, third notebook, 71; My translation is based on Ben-Ezer, "Brenner and the 'Arab Question,' " 20.

77. Ben-Ezer, "Tzel" notes that this probably refers to Zichron Ya'aqov.

78. Brenner, *Mikan Umikan*, third notebook, 71–72; Ben-Ezer, "Tzel,"—comments on this: "[Brenner's] protagonists [in this book] are all Jews. And through this hard cruelty towards us, to ourselves, one can also understand Brenner's expressions regarding the danger of assimilating among the Arabs, which he calls, with a kind of maliciousness, "the natives of the land," as we, the readers, do not exactly know if the natives of the land are only the colony's Arabs, or also the first Sabra generation who was born in it, and is already so similar to the Arabs, so much so that it is impossible to distinguish between the dependents of the two peoples [. . .] This is a horrible description of a young boy, probably Arab, who already speaks the Romanian-Yiddish of Zichron's farmers, and tells about bestiality."

79. Ben-Ezer, "Tzel."

80. Alcalay, *After Jews and Arabs*, 52–53.

81. Brenner, *Shechol Vekishalon*; in Englsh: Brenner, *Breakdown and Bereavement*.

82. Ben-Ezer, "Tzel."

83. Ibid.

84. Brenner, *Shechol Vekishalon*, 98.

85. Ben-Ezer, "Tzel."

86. As Alcalay sums this: "Haifa, Jaffa, the Arabs, and even the Arab Jews simply become a backdrop for superimposed images from another world: the Cossacks, Poles, and Russians of the Ukraine. The space is transparent: for all their professed but idealized 'love of the land,' many of the early European settlers had x-ray vision, seeing through things without recognizing them." Alcalay, *After Jews and Arabs*, 53.

87. Brenner, "Leverur Ha'inyan," 16.

88. Shimoni, *The Zionist Ideology*, 298.

89. Ibid.

90. Hertzberg, *The Zionist Idea*, 315.

91. Shimoni, *The Zionist Ideology*, 321.

92. Hertzberg, *The Zionist Idea*, 315.

93. Shimoni, *The Zionist Ideology*, 322.

94. Klatzkin, *Teḥumim*, 18; I am using here Shimoni's translation: *The Zionist Ideology*, 323.

95. Klatzkin, *Teḥumim*, 18.

96. Ibid.

97. Shimoni, *The Zionist Ideology*, 324.

98. Klatzkin, *Teḥumim*, 64.

99. Ibid., 76–77.

100. Luz, *Parallels Meet*.

101. Zeira, *We Are Torn Apart*.

102. Liebman and Don-Yehiya, *Civil Religion in Israel*; Don-Yehiya and Liebman, "The Symbol System of Zionist-Socialism"; Don-Yehiya, "Secularization, Negation and Accommodation."

103. Tsur, "Pesach in the Land of Israel."

104. Zerubavel, *Recovered Roots*.

105. Don-Yehiya and Liebman, "The Symbol System of Zionist-Socialism," 121.

106. Almog, "Secular religion in Israel."

107. Don-Yehiya, "Secularization, Negation and Accommodation," 29.

108. Don-Yehiya and Liebman, "The Symbol System of Zionist-Socialism," 121.

109. Don-Yehiya, "Secularization, Negation and Accommodation," 30.

110. As was done by the "Young Hebrews" or "Canaanite" movement (see chapter 7), or by its ideological successors, who reject Judaism as a derivative of their rejection of Zionism, such as Sand, *How I Stopped Being a Jew*.

111. Liebman and Don-Yehiya, *Civil Religion in Israel*.

112. Don-Yehiya, "Secularization, Negation and Accommodation," 30.

113. *Masortiyut*, or "traditionism" was originally conceptualized through the dichotomy "religious vs. secular" as a residual category of those neither secular nor religious. Later on it has been positively instilled with meaning

that aims to transcend the dichotomy. See Yadgar, *Secularism and Religion in Jewish-Israeli Politics*; Yadgar, "Traditionism."

114. Liebman and Don-Yehiya, in *Civil Religion in Israel*, 30, label the Socialist-Zionist stance toward tradition as "confrontation."

115. Shoham, *Let's Celebrate* offers a comprehensive discussion on the Israeli "civil holidays" and their relation to Jewish tradition; see also his work on the Zionist rewriting of Purim: Shoham, *Carnival in Tel Aviv*.

116. Thus, for example, in the case of the Socialist-Zionist rewriting of the message of Hanukkah, in which the declaration "A miracle did not happen to us, we did not find a cruse of oil" became a central notion of a holiday traditionally celebrated to mark these miracles. See Don-Yehiya, "Hanukkah and the Myth of the Maccabees in Ideology and in Society."

117. My discussion on Religious-Zionism draws substantially on the work of Noam Hadad, who has written his PhD dissertation on the subject under my supervision. Hadad, "Religious Zionism." For a comprehensive review of the history and ideology of Religious-Zionism, see Schwartz, *Religious Zionism*.

118. Salmon, "Religion and Nationalism," 117.

119. Esp. Marty and Appleby, *Fundamentalisms Observed*; Marty and Appleby, *Fundamentalisms and Society*; Marty and Appleby, *Fundamentalisms and the State*. Peter Berger's biting criticism of the Fundamentalism Project is worth repeating here: "So-called fundamentalism was assumed to be a strange, difficult-to-understand phenomenon; the purpose of the Project was to delve into this alien world and make it more understandable. But here came another question: Who finds this world strange, and to whom must it be made understandable? The answer to that question was easy: people to whom the officials of the MacArthur Foundation [who funded the Project] normally talk, such as professors at American elite universities. And with this came the Aha! experience: The concern that must have led to this Project was based on an upside-down perception of the world. The notion here was that so-called fundamentalism (which, when all is said and done, usually refers to any sort of passionate religious movement) is a rare, hard-to-explain thing. But in fact it is not rare at all, neither if one looks at history, nor if one looks around the contemporary world. On the contrary, what is rare is people who think otherwise. Put simply: The difficult-to-understand phenomenon is not Iranian mullahs but American university professors. (Would it, perhaps, be worth a multi-million-dollar project to try to explain the latter group?) The point of this little story is that the assumption that we live in a secularized world is false." Berger, "Secularism in Retreat," 3.

120. Aran, "A Mystic-Messianic Interpretation of Modern Israeli History"; Aran, "From Religious Zionism to Zionist Religion."

121. Liebman, "Extremism as a Religious Norm."

122. Cavanaugh, *The Myth of Religious Violence*.

123. Cohen, "Changes in the Orthodox Camp and Their Influence on the Deepening Religious-Secular Schism at the Outset of the Twenty-First Century."

124. Inbari, *Messianic Religious Zionism Confronts Israeli Territorial Compromises*; see also Ravitzky, *Messianism, Zionism, and Jewish Religious Radicalism*.

125. Cohen, "Patriotism and religion."

126. On Kook see: Schwartz, *The Religious Genius in Rabbi Kook's Thought*; Mirsky, *Rav Kook*.

127. See: Batnitzky, *How Judaism Became a Religion*, 95; Ravitzky, *Messianism, Zionism, and Jewish Religious Radicalism*, 34.

128. Leibowitz, *Judaism, Human Values, and the Jewish State*.

129. Hadad, "Religious Zionism."

130. Ibid.

131. For a careful historical, political and ideological assessment of Revisionist-Zionism, see Kaplan, *The Jewish Radical Right*.

132. For a comprehensive list of the relevant literature see: Naor, "Epicureans Also Have a Share in Sinai," 131 ff. 1. My discussion herein is based primarily on the works by Don-Yehiya, "Between Nationalism and Religion"; Naor, "Epicureans Also Have a Share in Sinai"; Ratzabi, "Jabotinsky and Religion."

133. Jabotinsky, *My Father, Zeev Jabotinsky*, 95.

134. The other Zionist leader he is referring to is Theodor Herzl, whose anti-religious stance had been allegedly censored by his successors.

135. Ibid.

136. Don-Yehiya, "Between Nationalism and Religion," 161.

137. Jabotinsky, *Ketavim*, 116.

138. Ibid., 119.

139. Don-Yehiya, "Between Nationalism and Religion," 166.

140. Ibid., 161.

141. What Liebman and Don-Yehiya call in the 1983 "the new civil religion," propagated by Menachem Begin. Liebman and Don-Yehiya, *Civil Religion in Israel*, chap. 5.

142. Naor, "Epicureans Also Have a Share in Sinai," 131–133.

143. Jabotinsky, *My Father, Zeev Jabotinsky*, 106.

144. Ratzabi, "Jabotinsky and Religion."

145. Naor, "Epicureans Also Have a Share in Sinai," 134.

146. Liebman and Don-Yehiya, *Civil Religion in Israel*, chap. 4.

# Chapter 7

1. This self-identification is proclaimed in the "purpose clauses" of certain Basic Laws, which determine the State of Israel's identity as a "Jew-

ish and Democratic State." See, for example, clause 1 of *Basic Law: Human Dignity and Liberty.*

2. This was indeed forecasted by Klatzkin; see pp. 141–144 above.

3. This, of course, is in part what led students of Israeli politics to limit the sense in which the democratic principles are seen as applicable to understanding Israeli politics, identifying it instead as an "ethnic democracy." See Peled, "Ethnic Democracy"; Peled, *The Challenge of Ethnic Democracy*; Smooha, "The Model of Ethnic Democracy"; Smooha, "Ethnic Democracy." See also, Gavison, "Jewish and Democratic?" More profoundly, Israel has been identified as an "ethnocracy." See: Yiftachel, " 'Ethnocracy,' "; Yiftachel, *Ethnocracy.*

4. Taylor, "Interpretation and the Sciences of Man," 27.

5. Baruch Kurzweil's work is one of the more poignant criticisms in this regard. See: Kurzweil, "The New Canaanites in Israel"; Kurzweil, *In the Struggle Over the Values of Judaism*; Kurzweil, *Our New Literature.*

6. On the political importance of the nomenclature distinguishing Hebrew from Jew see page 81, ff. 52 in this book.

7. On the "Young Hebrews" see: Shavit, *The New Hebrew Nation*; Porath, *The Life of Uriel Shelah.*

8. Porath, *The Life of Uriel Shelah*, 397, gives a personal account of this.

9. For a historical-legal review of the "who is a Jew" controversy, see Gavison, *The Law of Return.*

10. The legal procedure, on its varying appeals, lasted until 2013.

11. Solberg, HP (Jerusalem) 6092/07 *Ornan, et al. v. Interior Ministry*, 6 (2008).

12. Ornan, "Haleum sheli: Yisraeli."

13. Ibid.

14. Agranat, CA 630/70 *Tamarin v. The State of Israel* (1972).

15. Ibid.

16. Quoted in ibid.

17. Quoted in ibid.

18. Ibid.

19. Ibid.

20. Ibid.

21. As put by the concurring judge, Zvi Berenson ibid.

22. Solberg, HP (Jerusalem) 6092/07 *Ornan, et al. v. Interior Ministry*, 60 (2008).

23. As summarized by the Supreme Court; Vogelman, CA 8573/08 *Ornan, et al. v. Interior Ministry*, 2 (2013).

24. Solberg, HP (Jerusalem) 6092/07 *Ornan, et al. v. Interior Ministry*, 59 (2008).

25. Quoted in Vogelman, CA 8573/08 Ornan, *et al. v. Interior Ministry*, 18 (2013).

26. Ibid.

27. Judge Hanan Melcer in ibid.

28. For the English rendition of this see: Yakobson and Rubinstein, *Israel and the Family of Nations*.

29. "Arab," in their formulation.

30. Ibid., 184; the Hebrew original is quoted in Vogelman, CA 8573/08 *Ornan, et al. v. Interior Ministry*, 19 (2013).

31. Vogelman, CA 8573/08 *Ornan, et al. v. Interior Ministry*, 20 (2013).

32. Ibid.

33. Ibid.

34. Ibid.

35. As summarized by the court: Ibid.

36. Solberg, HP (Jerusalem) 6092/07 *Ornan, et al. v. Interior Ministry*, 8 (2008).

37. For a critical, Liberal-Zionist assessment of the proposed Basic Law: Israel—the Nation State of the Jewish People see: Gavison, *A Constitutional anchoring*. At the time of the publication of the editorial, as well as of the writing of this book, the measure has yet to be approved by the Knesset, the Israeli parliament.

38. *Haaretz*, May 5, 2014; the English translation is taken from *Haaretz'* English website: *Haaretz* Editorial, "There Is Such a Thing as 'Israeli'–Opinion."

39. Needless to say, the founders' preference to name the newly established state "Israel" (and not, for example, Yehouda, or Judea, Zion, The Jews' State, etc.,) holds a key to the way they perceived some of the matters discussed herein. For a historical testimony and assessment of the matter see: Reouveni, "Hamedina, Ma Shema?"

40. This is the point to mention that, to the best of my knowledge, Israel is the only state in the world that makes it its own business to determine one's Jewish identity.

41. On Druze and the State of Israel, see Yiftachel and Segal, "Jews and Druze in Israel"; Firro, "Reshaping Druze Particularism in Israel"; Firro, *The Druzes in the Jewish State*; Oppenheimer, "The Druze in Israel."

42. For some of the reports on this controversy, see Nesher, "Education Ministry Suspends Dismissal of Civics Supervisor"; Nesher, "Israel Education Ministry Fires Civics Studies Coordinator Attacked by Right–News"; *Haaretz* Editorial, "Stop Politicization of the Education System."

43. Shafir and Peled, *Being Israeli*.

44. On the Jewish Israeli conception of a "demographic threat," see Yonah, "Israel's Immigration Policies"; Melamed, "Motherhood, Fertility, and the Construction of the 'demographic Threat' in the Marital Age Law."

45. One quasi-encyclopedic attempt at indexing the meaning of Israeliness culminated in a two-volume monograph that exceeds 1400 pages. See Almog, *Farewell to Srulik*.

46. On Zionist-Israeli nationalism's uses of traditional Judaism, see Liebman and Don-Yehiya, *Civil Religion in Israel*.

47. Shoham, *Let's celebrate*, 9.

48. Ibid., 10.

49. Needless to say, the Israeli scene at large also hosts what may be seen as "exceptions" to the "rule" of identification between Israeliness and Jewishness I am discussing here. These would include, for example, Palestinian-Arab writers who write in Hebrew, and partake in the mainstream cultural scene. These cases merit a careful consideration that is beyond the scope of the current discussion. Yet it is interesting to note that a recent report on probably the most famous and successful contemporary Palestinian-Arab Hebrew writer, Sayed Kashua, reveals this exception to the rule to be overwhelmed by the exclusionary logic of the rule itself: "[Kashua] is openly undergoing an identity crisis [. . .] Kashua says that he was a 'hostage' who lived in 'fear' when he was in Israel; all his efforts to fit in and change Israeli society by making jokes to Jewish Israelis did nothing to change the balance of power; he feels he took the 'wrong paths' in language and work. He said he had been trying to quit his *Haaretz* column for over a year, and did so again just last week [. . .]; he does not know why he writes in Hebrew, the language of the 'enemy' or the 'oppressor.' [Kashua:] 'The only reason I'm there [in the U.S., having left Israel in 2014] is the political situation, the racism and the despair. I think that I couldn't handle it any more back in the summer of 2014. [. . .] I think that I'm still suffering some kind of traumatic situation. I didn't recover yet from that traumatic period [. . .] I had a very strong feeling that I took the wrong paths in my life. And all the decisions [. . .] writing for TV, and choosing the wrong language, and living in the wrong place—I very much hope that I will gain some powers and recover [. . . .]' " Weiss, "Sayed Kashua Doesn't Want to Write in Hebrew for 'Haaretz' Anymore."

50. Gans, "Symbolic Ethnicity and Symbolic Religiosity," 577.

51. Ibid.

52. On Israeli Jews in the U.S., see Gold and Phillips, "Israelis in the United States"; Mittelberg and Waters, "The Process of Ethnogenesis."

53. Triandafyllidou, "National Identity and the 'Other' "; Yadgar, "Between 'the Arab' and 'the Religious Rightist.' "

54. The terms are Asher Cohen's *Non-Jewish Jews in Israel*; Cohen views these "non-Jewish Jews" as a central answer to "the challenge of expanding the Jewish nation" (as attested to by the very subtitle of his Hebrew book).

55. Lustick, "Israel as a Non-Arab State."

56. See, for example, Segev, "Mihu ḥiloni?," and compare with Inbari, "The End of the Secular Majority."

57. Yadgar, *Beyond Secularization*.

58. Having concluded that the term *"ḥiloni,"* or "secular" lacks any coherent meaning (due to the fact that the vast majority of those self-identified as seculars is also at least "partially observant" of certain religious traditions), the scholars overseeing the largest surveys of "religious" observance and beliefs among Israeli Jews had decided to replace *"ḥiloni"* with *"lo-dati,"*

that is "not-religious" in their questionnaires. See Levy, Levinsohn, and Katz, *Beliefs, Observances, and Social Interaction Among Israeli Jews*; Levy, Levinsohn, and Katz, *A Portrait of Israeli Jews*; Arian and Keissar-Sugarmen, *A Portrait of Israeli Jews*.

59. Liebman and Yadgar, "Secular-Jewish Identity and the Condition of Secular Judaism in Israel," 156.

60. The abovementioned surveys introduced *"ḥiloni anti-dati"*—that is, anti-religion secular—as an optional category of self-identification in their questionnaires, and concluded that roughly 5 percent of Israeli Jews do so self-identify: Levy, Levinsohn, and Katz, *Beliefs, Observances, and Social Interaction Among Israeli Jews*; Levy, Levinsohn, and Katz, *A Portrait of Israeli Jews*; Arian and Keissar-Sugarmen, *A Portrait of Israeli Jews*.

61. Levy, Levinsohn, and Katz, *Beliefs, Observances, and Social Interaction Among Israeli Jews*; Levy, Levinsohn, and Katz, *A Portrait of Israeli Jews*; Arian and Keissar-Sugarmen, *A Portrait of Israeli Jews*.

# Chapter 8

1. There is somewhat of a disagreement regarding the proper translation of the Hebrew term. I am following Liebman and Don-Yehiya, *Civil Religion in Israel*, chap. 4, in reading it as akin to statism. See also Kedar, *Mamlachtiyut*; Kedar, "Ben-Gurion's Mamlachtiyut"; Ohana, *Messianism and Mamlachtiyut*.

2. To borrow Ornan's term (see page 169) and reverse the meaning intended in its coinage.

3. It should be noted that they choose to identify through this or other categories of Jewish identity when asked to do by surveyors, whose questionnaires often demand that respondents choose one of the "common" labels/categories, i.e., *"dati," "ḥiloni," "masorti,"* and the like: the large, oft-quoted surveys do not even offer their respondents the "none of the above" option. See, for example, Levy, Levinsohn, and Katz, *A Portrait of Israeli Jews*. For a general critique of surveys dealing with Israeli Jews' Jewish identities and practices, see Yadgar, *Beyond Secularization*, 73.

4. For a review of these see: Yadgar, *Beyond Secularization*, chap. 3.

5. See note 1.

6. Needless to say, Yehoshua, who as the succeeding discussion shall show tends to prefer the use of provocative language to stir debate as a public intellectual, cannot be taken as wholly representative of the wider phenomenon at hand. Indeed, no single person can; sociopolitics is always larger and more diverse than the intellectual biography of a single person, no matter how influential she may be. Yet I would claim that Yehoshua captures certain essential aspects of the statist-Jewish theopolitics. The public attention he manages to instigate (see the various texts referenced below, and specifi-

cally, Yehoshua and Others, *The A. B. Yehoshua Controversy*) testify to the fact that his "provocations" are taken to be serious interventions that merit a careful consideration in the public sphere at large.

7. See chapters 4 through 6 above.

8. My discussion here is limited to Yehoshua's essays, and does not deal with his fiction.

9. Yehoshua, *Bizchut Hanormaliyut*, 108.

10. These are the titles of three essays by Yehoshua, published in *Haaretz*'s celebratory issues of the Israeli Independence Day, Rosh Hashanah and Yom Kippur: Yehoshua, "Mihu Yisraeli"; Yehoshua, "Mihu Yehudi"; Yehoshua, "Mihu Tziyoni." Yehoshua has repeatedly addressed these issues, in varying formulations, in many of his Zionist essays.

11. Yehoshua, *Bizchut Hanormaliyut*, 108.

12. Yehoshua, *Haqir Vehahar*, 207.

13. Yehoshua, "Lehavri Et Haandrogynous"; Yehoshua, "Hapetil Hakaful."

14. Yehoshua, "Hapetil Hakaful."

15. Ibid.

16. *Tarkiz* in the Hebrew original.

17. Yehoshua, *Bizchut Hanormaliyut*, 129.

18. Ibid., 135.

19. Ibid., 129.

20. Ibid.

21. Ibid., 125.

22. Yehoshua, "Mihu Yisraeli."

23. *Shelema* in the Hebrew original.

24. Ibid.

25. It is interesting to note that Yehoshua nevertheless understands Jewish identity through Jewish law. For him, a Jew is primarily someone born to a Jewish mother. He clarifies that "this is not a racial definition" (Yehoshua, *Bizchut Hanormaliyut*, 111), and makes sure to add to this halachic definition a dimension of "liberty," according to which "a Jew is one who identifies oneself as Jewish" (Ibid., 112). But his real interest lies in Jewishness, in Jewish identity, which is, according to his Zionist understanding, a matter of nationalism: "Being Jewish means belonging to a national group, which can be left or joined" (Ibid., 108).

26. Yehoshua, "Hahayim Beparadox," 19.

27. Yehoshua, *Bizchut Hanormaliyut*, 126.

28. The full Hebrew presentation of Yehoshua's argument is found in Yehoshua, *Ahizat Moledet*, 60–67. Published in English as: Yehoshua, "The Meaning of Homeland."

29. *ha'inyan hamedinati* in the Hebrew original.

30. Quoted in Blumenfeld, "A. B. Yehoshua: Hashoah."

31. Quoted in ibid.

32. Yehoshua, *Bizchut Hanormaliyut*, 131.

33. Yehoshua, "The Meaning of Homeland," 8.

34. Yehoshua, *Haqir Vehahar*, 209.

35. Yehoshua, *Bizchut Hanormaliyut*, 27.

36. Quoted in Blumenfeld, "A. B. Yehoshua: Hashoah."

37. Yehoshua, "Mihu Yisraeli."

38. Yehoshua, *Bizchut Hanormaliyut*, 132.

39. Raz-Krakotzkin, "Exile within Sovereignty pt. 1," 32.

40. Yehoshua, *Ahizat Moledet*, 62.

41. Namdar, "Mofa' Haeimim."

42. Yehoshua, "Mihu Yisraeli"; on Rawidowicz see: Myers, *Between Jew and Arab*.

43. Yehoshua, "Mihu Yisraeli."

44. Ibid.

45. Yehoshua, *Bizchut Hanormaliyut*, 132.

46. Ibid.

47. Peri, "Afillu Lo Reva' Yehudi."

48. Yehoshua, "Ma Ze Yehudi Shalem."

49. Yehoshua, *Bizchut Hanormaliyut*, 126.

50. Ibid., 133.

51. Yehoshua, "The Meaning of Homeland," 8.

52. Ibid., 9.

53. Yehoshua, "Mihu Yisraeli."

54. Yehoshua, "The Meaning of Homeland," 10.

55. Ibid., 9.

56. Ibid., 9–10.

57. Yehoshua, *Bizchut Hanormaliyut*, 133–4.

58. Ibid., 131.

59. Yehoshua, "Hapetil Hakaful."

60. Yehoshua, "Mihu Tziyoni."

61. Against the potential counter arguments, according to which there were/are formulations of Zionist ideology which are not identical to Political-Zionism, that is "Zionists [. . .] who had not thought necessarily of a Jewish state," Yehoshua argues: "At the end of the process, all Zionists aimed at achieving political and social independence, which could be organized only in the form of a state." Moreover, even Ahad Ha'am's cultural Zionism had to acknowledge its submission to this principle: "a spiritual center could not have been formed as a minority community of Jews inside another nation [. . .] rather, this community would have to be sovereign in order to become a spiritual center." Yehoshua, *Bizchut Hanormaliyut*, 117–18.

62. Ibid., 118.

63. Yehoshua, "Mihu tziyoni." Elsewhere (Yehoshua, *Bizchut Hanormaliyut*, 116.) Yehoshua clarifies that the word "person" may be replaced by "Jew" (that is, a Zionist is a Jew who accepts the principle . . . etc.). Yet he prefers to keep open the option of including non-Jews under this definition.

64. Yehoshua, *Bizchut Hanormaliyut*, 117.

65. Yehoshua, *Haqir Vehahar*, 207–08.

66. Yehoshua, *Bizchut Hanormaliyut*, 129.

67. Ibid., 126.

68. Ibid., 126, 128.

69. Ibid., 127.

70. Ibid., 128.

71. Ibid., 129–30.

72. Yehoshua, "The Meaning of Homeland," 9.

73. Yehoshua, *Bizchut Hanormaliyut*, 134.

74. Ibid., 130.

75. Ibid.

# Chapter 9

1. Barak-Erez, "Law and Religion," 2495.

2. Aloni, *The Arrangement*.

3. Hebrew plays a double game here, which serves the vagueness: *medina* denotes both politics and state.

4. See Ben-Porat, *Between State and Synagogue*.

5. Barak-Erez, "Law and Religion," 2495.

6. Ibid.

7. Ibid.

8. Cohen and Susser, *Israel and the Politics of Jewish Identity*, 18.

9. Lijphart, *The Politics of Accommodation*.

10. Don-Yehiya, *Religion and Political Accommodation in Israel*, 35.

11. Ibid., 34, 35, 54.

12. Aloni, *The Arrangement*, 70. I am using here the translation offered by Don-Yehiya, *Religion and Political Accommodation in Israel*, 43.

13. Aloni, *The Arrangement*.

14. Yehoshua, "Mihu yisraeli."

15. Boaz, "The Religious 'Status Quo,'" 107.

16. Ibid.

17. For an explication of this narrative see Horowitz and Lissak, *Trouble in Utopia*.

18. Aloni, *The Arrangement*, 90.

19. Don-Yehiya, *Religion and Political Accommodation in Israel*, 42.

20. The "status quo" letter, quoted in Ibid. The letter is quoted in full in Friedman, "Status quo," 66–67.

21. My formulation here is more straightforward than the convoluted language of the letter: "All the members of the Executive appreciate the seriousness of the problem and the major difficulties involved, and all those represented by the Jewish Agency will do everything possible to meet the profound need of the religious in this regard, so as to prevent the division

of the Jewish people into two." Quoted in: Don-Yehiya, *Religion and Political Accommodation in Israel*, 42.

22. For a concise retelling of this story see Ben-Porat, *Between State and Synagogue*, 32.

23. Barak-Erez, "Law and Religion," 2495.

24. Don-Yehiya, *Religion and Political Accommodation in Israel*, 38.

25. Boaz, "The Religious 'Status Quo,'" 112.

26. Don-Yehiya, *Religion and Political Accommodation in Israel*, 15.

27. For example: Levy, "Secularism, Religion and the Status Quo"; Boaz, "The Religious 'Status Quo.'"

28. Menachem Friedman renders the matter quite clear when he concludes that "no one had viewed the letter [during the period immediately following the establishment of the State of Israel] as a commitment to observe the status quo on matters of religion in the State of Israel." Friedman, "Status quo," 48.

29. Ibid., 51.

30. Ibid., 52.

31. Aloni, *The Arrangement*, 90.

32. We must bear in mind that the foundational framework of the status quo arrangements was formed during a period of time in which the Socialist-Zionist camp, headed by the Mapai party, enjoyed a dominant stance that guaranteed its rule over the state, and enabled it to replace its coalition partners at will. The Orthodox or religious parties surely had not have the political power to "extort concessions" in these or other matters during the era of Mapai's dominance.

33. The history of the legislative and judicial debates and decisions on the Law of Return and the derived matter of "who is a Jew" reflect this identification quite clearly. Indeed, as we saw in chapter 8, even a secular Zionist believer such as A. B. Yehoshua is reluctant to accept, for example, the viability of a national Jew of the Christian faith.

34. See my discussion in page 183–184.

35. Myers, "Rethinking the Jewish Nation" offers a rare formulation of an American-Jewish position that seeks a release from the state's gravitational core.

36. Julie E. Cooper, who offers a comprehensive review of the attempts to formulate a (modern) reading of Jewish political thought, both stresses the essential dependency of most of these attempts on the sovereignty of the nation-state, and calls for an exploration of the meaning of Jewish political tradition outside and beyond the framework of state's sovereignty. Cooper, "The Turn to Tradition in the Study of Jewish Politics."

# Bibliography

Agamben, Giorgio. *State of Exception*. Translated by Kevin Attell. Chicago: University of Chicago Press, 2005.

Agranat, Shimon. CA 630/70 *Tamarin v. The State of Israel* (1972). (Hebrew)

Aḥad Ha'am (Asher Ginzburg). *'Al Parashat Derachim (On a Crossroad)*. 2 vols. Berlin: Judischer Verlag, 5690. (Hebrew)

———. "Altneuland." *Hashiloaḥ* 10, no. 6 (December 1902). (Hebrew)

———. *Igrot Aḥad Ha'am (Letters of Aḥad Ha'am)*. 6 vols. Jerusalem and Berlin: Yavneh and Moriah, 1923. (Hebrew)

———. *Kol Kitvey Aḥad Ha'am (The Collected Writings of Aḥad Ha'am)*. Tel-Aviv and Jeruslaem: Dvir, 5707. (Hebrew)

———. *Selected Essays*. Translated by Leon Simon. Philadelphia: The Jewish Publication Society of America, 1912.

Alcalay, Ammiel. *After Jews and Arabs: Remaking Levantine Culture*. Minneapolis: University of Minnesota Press, 1992.

Almog, Oz. *Farewell to Srulik: Changing Values among the Israeli Elite*. 2 vols. Haifa: Haifa University Press, 2004. (Hebrew)

———. "Secular Religion in Israel." *Megamot* 37, no. 3 (5756): 314–39. (Hebrew)

Almog, Samuel, Jehuda Reinharz, and Anita Shapira, eds. *Zionism and Religion*. Boston: University Press of New England, 1998.

Aloni, Shulamit. *The Arrangement: From a State of Law to a State of Halacha*. Tel-Aviv: Otpaz, 1970. (Hebrew)

Alroey, Gur. "The Demographic Composition of the 'Second 'Aliyah.'" *Israel: Studies in Zionism and the State of Israel* 2 (2002): 33–55. (Hebrew)

Anidjar, Gil. *Blood: A Critique of Christianity*. New York: Columbia University Press, 2014.

Aran, Gideon. "A Mystic-Messianic Interpretation of Modern Israeli History: The Six-Day War in the Religious Culture of Gush Emunim." In *Israeli Judaism, Studies of Israeli Society 7*, edited by Shlomo Deshen, Charles S Liebman, and Moshe Shokeid, 197–212. New Brunswick: Transaction Publishers, 1995.

———. "From Religious Zionism to Zionist Religion: The Roots of Gush Emunim." *Studies in Contemporary Jewry* 2 (1986): 116–43.

Arian, Asher, and Ayala Keissar-Sugarmen. *A Portrait of Israeli Jews: Beliefs, Observance, and Values of Israeli Jews, 2009.* Jerusalem: Israel Democracy Institute and Avi Chai Foundation, 2011. (Hebrew)

Arnal, William E. "Definition." In *Guide to the Study of Religion,* edited by Willi Braun, and Russell T. McCutcheon, 21–34. London: Cassell, 2000.

Asad, Talal. *Formations of the Secular: Christianity, Islam, Modernity.* Stanford, CA: Stanford University Press, 2003.

———. *Genealogies of Religion: Discipline and Reasons of Power in Christianity and Islam.* Baltimore: Johns Hopkins University Press, 1993.

———. "Reading a Modern Classic: W. C. Smith's The Meaning and End of Religion." *History of Religions* 40, no. 3 (2001): 205–22.

A. Tzioni (Yitzhak Wilkanski). "Hateologia Haleumit (The National Theology)." In *Revivim 3–4,* edited by Y. H. Brenner, 115. Jerusalem, 5683. (Hebrew)

Avineri, Shlomo. *The Making of Modern Zionism: Intellectual Origins of the Jewish State.* New York: Basic Books, 1981.

———. *Varieties of Zionist Thought.* Tel-Aviv: Am-Oved, 1980. (Hebrew)

———. "Zionism and the Jewish Religious Tradition: The Dialectics of Redemption and Secularization." In *Zionism and Religion,* edited by Shlomo Almog, Jehuda Reinharz, and Anita Shapira, 1–12. Boston: University Press of New England, 1998.

Baldacchino, Joseph. "The Value-Centered Historicism of Edmund Burke." *Modern Age* 27, no. 2 (1983): 139–45.

Barak-Erez, Daphne. "Law and Religion Under the Status Quo Model: Between Past Compromises and Constant Change." *Cardozo Law Review* 30 (2008): 2495–2508.

Batnitzky, Leora Faye. *How Judaism Became a Religion: An Introduction to Modern Jewish Thought.* Princeton, NJ: Princeton University Press, 2011.

Benamozegh, Elia. *Jewish and Christian Ethics.* Jerusalem: Kest-Lebovits Jewish Heritage and Roots Library, 2000.

Ben-Ezer, Ehud. "Brenner and the 'Arab Question.'" *Modern Hebrew Literature* 12, no. 3–4 (1987): 20–22.

———, ed. *Sleep Walkers and Other Stories: The Arab in Hebrew Fiction.* Boulder, CO: Three Continents Press, 1998.

———. "Tzel Hapardesim Vehar Haga'ash—Sihot 'al Hishtaqfut Hasheela Ha'aravit Vedmut Ha'aravi Basifrut Ha'ivrit Beertz Yisrael Misof Hameah Haqodemet 'ad Yamenu: Siha Revi'it, Merirut Hametziout," 1997. https://library.osu.edu/projects/hebrew-lexicon/hbe/hbe00492.php#6. (Hebrew)

Ben-Porat, Guy. *Between State and Synagogue.* Cambridge, MA: Cambridge University Press, 2013.

Berdyczewski, Micha Yosef. *Maamarim, Baderech: Part 2. Shinui Arachin (Articles, on the Way: Part 2 Transvaluation).* Lipsia: Stiebel, 5682. (Hebrew)

Berger, Peter L. "Secularism in Retreat." *The National Interest* 46 (1996): 3–12.

Bernstein, Richard J. *Beyond Objectivism and Relativism: Science, Hermeneutics, and Praxis.* Oxford: B. Blackwell, 1983.

Bhargava, Rajeev, ed. *Secularism and Its Critics.* New York: Oxford University Press, 2005.

Blumenfeld, Revital. "A. B. Yehoshua: Hashoah Hie Kishalon Shel Ha'm Hayehudi." *Haaretz,* March 18, 2012. (Hebrew)

Boaz, Hagai. "The Religious 'Status Quo' and the Generation of Social Categories: The Struggle for Female Suffrage in the Pre-State Period." *Theory and Criticism* 21 (2002): 107–32. (Hebrew)

Boyarin, Jonathan, and Daniel Boyarin. *Powers of Diaspora: Two Essays on the Relevance of Jewish Culture.* Minneapolis: University of Minnesota Press, 2002.

Brenner, Yosef Haim; signed as Yosef Haver. "Ba'itunot Uvasifrut: He'arot Ve-tziyunim) (In the newspapers and literature: Comments and notes)." *Hapo'el Hatza'ir* 4th year, no. 3 (November 24, 1910): 6–8. (Hebrew)

Brenner, Yosef Ḥaim. "Avi Hapublitzistiqa Shelanu ('Al Ḥayei M. L. Lilienblum)," 5674. http://benyehuda.org/brenner/brenner_140.html. (Hebrew)

———. *Breakdown on Bereavement.* Translated by Hillel Halkin. Ithaca, NY: Cornell University Press, 1971.

———. *Ketavim (Writings).* Tel-Aviv: Sifriyat Po'alim and Haqibutz Hameuḥad, 5738. (Hebrew)

———. "Leverur Ha'inyan (Clarifying the matter)." *Hapo'el Hatza'ir* 4th year, no. 12 (March 31, 1911): 13–17. (Hebrew)

———. *Mikan Umikan (From Here and Here).* Warsaw: Sifrut, 5671. (Hebrew)

———. *Shechol Vekishalon (Breakdown and Bereavement).* Tel-Aviv: Am-Oved, 1972. (Hebrew)

Brinker, Menahem. "Brenner's Jewishness." *Studies in Contemporary Jewry,* 4 (1988): 232–50.

Butler, Judith. *Parting Ways: Jewishness and the Critique of Zionism.* New York: Columbia University Press, 2012.

Buzaglo, Meir. *A Language for the Faithful: Reflections on Tradition.* Jerusalem: Keter and the Mandel Foundation, 2008. (Hebrew)

Byrne, William F. *Edmund Burke for Our Time: Moral Imagination, Meaning, and Politics.* DeKalb: Northern Illinois University Press, 2011.

Casanova, José. *Public Religions in the Modern World.* Chicago: University of Chicago Press, 1994.

Cavanaugh, William T. *Migrations of the Holy: God, State, and the Political Meaning of the Church.* Grand Rapids: Wm. B. Eerdmans Publishing Company, 2011.

———. *The Myth of Religious Violence: Secular Ideology and the Roots of Modern Conflict.* New York: Oxford University Press, 2009.

———. *Theopolitical Imagination: Christian Practices of Space and Time.* London and New York: Bloomsbury T&T Clark, 2003.

Chidester, David. *Savage Systems: Colonialism and Comparative Religion in Southern Africa*. Charlottesville: University Press of Virginia, 1996.

Cohen, Asher. "Changes in the Orthodox Camp and Their Influence on the Deepening Religious-Secular Schism at the Outset of the Twenty-First Century." In *Critical Issues in Israeli Society*, edited by Allan Dowty, 71–94. Westport, CT, and London: Greenwood Press, 2004.

———. *Non-Jewish Jews in Israel*. Jerusalem and Ramat-Gan: The Shalom Hartman Institute; The Faculty of Law, Bar-Ilan University; Keter Publishing House, 2006. (Hebrew)

———. "Patriotism and Religion: Between Coexistence and Confrontation." In *Patriotism: Homeland Love*, edited by Avenr Ben-Amos, and Daniel Bar-Tal, 453–78. Tel-Aviv: Haqibutz Hameuḥad and Dyonon, 2004. (Hebrew)

Cohen, Asher, and Bernard Susser. *Israel and the Politics of Jewish Identity: The Secular-Religious Impasse*. Baltimore: Johns Hopkins University Press, 2000.

Connolly, William E. *Why I Am Not a Secularist*. Minneapolis: University of Minnesota Press, 1999.

Cooper, Julie E. "The Turn to Tradition in the Study of Jewish Politics." *Annual Review of Political Science* 19 (2016): 5.1–5.21.

Dabashi, Hamid. *Theology of Discontent: The Ideological Foundation of the Islamic Revolution in Iran*. New York: NYU Press, 1993.

Dan, Joseph. "Religion Studies and the Concept of Religion: On the Verge of a New Era)." In *Bekhur Hayetzira (The Cradle of Creativity: Shlomo Giora Shoham Jubilee)*, edited by Chemi Ben-Noon, 139–66. Hod-Hasharon: Shaarei Mishpat, 2004. (Hebrew)

Descartes, Rene. *Meditations on First Philosophy*. Translated by Haldane, Elizabeth S. Forgotten Books, 2008.

Don-Yehiya, Eliezer. "Hanukkah and the Myth of the Maccabees in Ideology and in Society." In *Israeli Judaism, Studies of Israeli Society 7*, edited by Shlomo Deshen, Charles S. Liebman, and Moshe Shokeid, 303–21. New Brunswick: Transaction Publishers, 1995.

———. "Between Nationalism and Religion: The Transformation of Jabotinsky's Attitude toward the Religious Tradition." In *In the Eye of the Storm: Essays on Zeev Jabotinsky*, edited by Avi Bareli and Pinhas Ginossar, 159–86. Sede Boqer: The Ben-Gurion Institute, 2004. (Hebrew)

———. *Religion and Political Accommodation in Israel*. Translated by Deborah Lemmer. Jerusalem: The Floersheimer Institute for Policy Studies, 1999.

———. "Secularization, Negation and Accommodation of Conceptions of Traditional Judaism and Its Terms in Socialist Zionism." *Kivunim* 8 (1980): 29–46. (Hebrew)

——— and Charles S. Liebman. "The Symbol System of Zionist-Socialism: An Aspect of Israeli Civil Religion." *Modern Judaism* 1, no. 2 (1981): 121–48.

Douglas, Mary. *How Institutions Think*. Syracuse, NY: Syracuse University Press, 1986.

Dubuisson, Daniel. *The Western Construction of Religion: Myths, Knowledge, and Ideology*. Baltimore: Johns Hopkins University Press, 2007.

Eisen, Arnold M. *Rethinking Modern Judaism: Ritual, Commandment, Community*. Chicago: University of Chicago Press, 1998.

Eisenstadt, S. N. "Intellectuals and Tradition." *Daedalus* 101, no. 2 (1972): 1–19.

———. *Tradition, Change, and Modernity*. New York: Wiley, 1973.

El'azari-Volcani, Yitzḥak. *Kitvey Yitzḥak El'azari-Volcani. Volume 2: Sefirot (El'azari-Volcani's writings, Vol. 2)*. Tel-Aviv: N. Taberski, 5710. (Hebrew)

Even-Zohar, Itamar. "The Emergence of a Native Hebrew Culture in Palestine: 1882–1948." *Journal of Israeli History* 2, no. 2 (1981): 167–84.

Faur, José. *In the Shadow of History: Jews and Conversos at the Dawn of Modernity*. Albany, NY: State University of New York Press, 1992.

———. *The Horizontal Society: Understanding the Covenant and Alphabetic Judaism*. 2 vols. Boston: Academic Studies Press, 2008.

———. "Vico, Religious Humanism and the Sephardic Tradition." *Judaism* 27 (1978): 63–71.

Firro, Kais M. *The Druzes in the Jewish State: A Brief History*. Leiden: Brill Publishing, 1999.

———. "Reshaping Druze Particularism in Israel." *Journal of Palestine Studies* 30, no. 3 (2001): 40–53.

Fischer, Yochi. "The Concepts of 'Religion' and 'Secularism' in Hebrew Language and Their Manifestations in Israel's Socio-Political Dynamics." In *Religion and Secularity: Transformations and Transfers of Religous Discourses in Europe and Asia*, edited by Marion Eggert and Lucian Hölscher, 109–30. Leiden: Brill Publishing, 2013.

Friedman, Menachem. "And This is the History of the Status Quo." In *Hama'var Miyeshuv Limdina (The Transition from Yishuv to Statehood 1947–1949: Continuity and Changes)*, edited by Varda Pilovsky, 47–79. Haifa: Herzl Institute, 1990. (Hebrew)

Gadamer, Hans-Georg. *Philosophical Hermeneutics*. Translated and Edited by David E. Linge. Berkeley: University of California Press, 1976.

———. "The Problem of Historical Consciousness." In *Interpretive Social Science: A Reader*, edited by Paul Rabinow and William M. Sullivan, 103–62. Berkeley: University of California Press, 1979.

———. *Truth and Method*. Translated by J. Winsheimer, and D. G. Marshall. 2nd ed. New York: Crossroad, 1989.

Gans, Herbert J. "Symbolic Ethnicity and Symbolic Religiosity: Towards a Comparison of Ethnic and Religious Acculturation." *Ethnic and Racial Studies* 17, no. 4 (1994): 577–92.

Gavison, Ruth. *A Constitutional Anchoring of the State's Vision: Recommendations to the Justice Minister)*. Jerusalem: The Metzilah Center for Zionist, Jewish, Liberal and Humanist Thought, 2014. (Hebrew)

———. "Jewish and Democratic? A Rejoinder to the 'Ethnic Democracy' Debate." *Israel Studies* 4, no. 1 (1999): 44–72.

————. *The Law of Return at Sixty Years: History, Ideology, Justification*. Jerusalem: The Metzilah Center for Zionist, Jewish, Liberal and Humanist Thought, 2010.

Geertz, Clifford. *Islam Observed: Religious Development in Morocco and Indonesia*. The Terry Lectures, v. 37. New Haven, CT: Yale University Press, 1968.

————. *The Interpretation of Cultures: Selected Essays*. New York: Basic Books, 1973.

Geiger, Abraham. *Abraham Geiger and Liberal Judaism*. Edited by Max Wiener. Philadelphia: Jewish Publication Society, 1962.

Ghosh, Amitav. *In an Antique Land: History in the Guise of a Traveler's Tale*. New York: Vintage, 1994.

Gold, Steven J, and Bruce A Phillips. "Israelis in the United States." *The American Jewish Year Book* 96 (1996): 51–101.

Gorni, Yosef. "Changes in the Social and Political Sturcture of the Second 'Aliyah, 1904–1914." *HaTziyonut* 1 (1970): 204–46. (Hebrew)

Haaretz Editorial. "Stop Politicization of the Education System." *Haaretz.com*, July 25, 2012. http://www.haaretz.com/opinion/stop-politicization-of-the-education-system-1.453427.

————. "There Is Such a Thing as 'Israeli'—Opinion." *Haaretz.com*, May 5, 2014. http://www.haaretz.com/opinion/1.588976.

Hadad, Noam. "Religious Zionism:Theo-politics and Nationalism; A Renewed Examination of Theology, Politics and Nationalism within the Ideology and Practice of Religious Zionism, and Their Implications for the Issue of Religion-State in Israel." PhD dissertation, Bar-Ilan Univerity, 2016.

Hertzberg, Arthur. *The Zionist Idea; a Historical Analysis and Reader*. Westport, CT: Greenwood Press, 1970.

Ḥevlin, Rinah. *Double Loyalty: Jewish Identity between Tradition and Secularization in Aḥad Ha'am's Thought*. Tel-Aviv: Hakibutz Hameuchad, 2001. (Hebrew)

Hirsch, Samson Raphael. *Judaism Eternal: Selected Essays from the Writings of Samson Raphael Hirsch*. Edited by Isadore Grunfeld. London: Soncino Press, 1956.

Holtzman, Avner. *Literature and life: Essays on M. J. Berdyczewski*. Jerusalem: Karmel, 2003. (Hebrew)

————. *Micha Joseph Berdyczewski*. Jerusalem: Zalman Shazar Center for Jewish History, 2011. (Hebrew)

Horowitz, Dan, and Moshe Lissak. *Trouble in Utopia: The Overburdened Polity of Israel*. Albany, NY: State University of New York Press, 1989.

Hume, David. *An Enquiry Concerning Human Understanding*. Hollywood, FL: Simon & Brown, 2011.

Inbari, Assaf. "The End of the Secular Majority." *Haaretz.com*, February 3, 2012. http://www.haaretz.com/weekend/magazine/the-end-of-the-secular-majority-1.410880.

Inbari, Motti. *Messianic Religious Zionism Confronts Israeli Territorial Compromises*. Cambridge, MA: Cambridge University Press, 2012.

Jabotinsky, Eri. *My Father, Zeev Jabotinsky.* Tel-Aviv: Steimatzky, 1980. (Hebrew)

Jabotinsky, Zeev. *Ketavim Tziyoniyim Rishonim (Early Zionist writings).* Jerusalem: The Jabotinsky Institute, 5709. (Hebrew)

Jakobsen, Janet, and Ann Pellegrini, eds. *Secularisms.* Durham, NC: Duke University Press, 2008.

Kaplan, Eran. *The Jewish Radical Right: Revisionist Zionism and Its Ideological Legacy.* Madison, WI: University of Wisconsin Press, 2005.

Kedar, Nir. "Ben-Gurion's Mamlachtiyut: Etymological and Theoretical Roots." *Israel Studies* 7, no. 3 (2002): 117–33.

———. *Mamlachtiyut: Ben-Burion's Civilian Conception.* Sede Boqer and Jerusalmem: Ben-Gurion University Press; The Ben-Gurion Institute for the Study of Israel and Zionism; Yad Yitshaq Ben Zvi, 2009. (Hebrew)

Klatzkin, Jacob. *Tehumim: Ketavim (Spheres: Essays).* Berlin: Devir, 1925. (Hebrew)

Kuhn, Thomas S. *The Essential Tension: Selected Studies in Scientific Tradition and Change.* Chicago: University of Chicago Press, 1977.

———. *The Structure of Scientific Revolutions.* Chicago: University of Chicago Press, 1962.

Kurzweil, Baruch. *In the Struggle over the Values of Judaism.* Tel-Aviv: Schocken, 1969. (Hebrew)

———. *Our New Literature: Continuation of Revolution?* Tel-Aviv: Schocken, 1971. (Hebrew)

———. "The New Canaanites in Israel." *Judaism* 2 (1953): 3–15.

Latour, Bruno. *We Have Never Been Modern.* Cambridge, MA: Harvard University Press, 1993.

Leibowitz, Yeshayahu. *Judaism, Human Values, and the Jewish State.* Edited by Eliezer Goldman. Translated by Yoram Navon, Zvi Jacobson, Gershon Levi, and Raphael Levy. Cambridge, MA: Harvard University Press, 1995.

Levy, Gal. "Secularism, Religion and the Status Quo." In *Religion and the State: A Comparative Sociology,* edited by Jack Barbalet, Adam Possamai, and Bryan S. Turner, 93–119. London: Anthem Press, 2011.

Levy, Shlomit, Hanna Levinsohn, and Elihu Katz. *A Portrait of Israeli Jews: Beliefs, Observance, and Values of Israeli Jews, 2000.* Jerusalem: Avi Chai and the Israel Democracy Institute, 2002. (Hebrew)

———. *Beliefs, Observances, and Social Interaction Among Israeli Jews.* Jerusalem: Louis Guttman Israel Institute of Applied Social Research, 1993. (Hebrew)

Liebman, Charles S. "Extremism as a Religious Norm." *Journal for the Scientific Study of Religion* 22, no. 1 (1983): 75–86.

Liebman, Charles S., and Eliezer Don-Yehiya. *Civil Religion in Israel: Traditional Judaism and Political Culture in the Jewish State.* Berkeley: University of California Press, 1983.

Liebman, Charles S., and Yaacov Yadgar. "Secular-Jewish Identity and the Condition of Secular Judaism in Israel." In *Religion or Ethnicity? Jewish*

*Identities in Evolution*, edited by Zvi Gitelman, 149–70. New Brunswick, NJ: Rutgers University Press, 2009.

Lijphart, Arend. *The Politics of Accommodation: Pluralism and Democracy in the Netherlands*. Berkeley: University of California Press, 1975.

Lilla, Mark. *The Stillborn God: Religion, Politics, and the Modern West*. New York: Alfred A. Knopf, 2007.

Lustick, Ian S. "Israel as a Non-Arab State: The Political Implications of Mass Immigration of Non-Jews." *Middle East Journal* 53, no. 3 (1999): 417–33.

Luz, Ehud. *Parallels Meet: Religion and Nationalism in the Early Zionist Movement (1882–1904)*. Philadelphia: Jewish Publication Society, 1988.

———. *Wrestling with an Angel: Power, Morality, and Jewish Identity*. New Haven, CT: Yale University Press, 2003.

MacIntyre, Alasdair. *After Virtue: A Study in Moral Theory*. 2nd ed. Notre Dame, IN: University of Notre Dame Press, 1984.

———. *The Tasks of Philosophy: Volume 1: Selected Essays*. Cambridge, MA: Cambridge University Press, 2006.

———. *Three Rival Versions of Moral Enquiry: Encyclopaedia, Genealogy, and Tradition*. Notre Dame, IN: University of Notre Dame Press, 1991.

———. *Whose Justice? Which Rationality?* Notre Dame, Ind.: University of Notre Dame Press, 1988.

Marty, Martin E., and R. Scott Appleby. *Fundamentalisms and Society: Reclaiming the Sciences, the Family, and Education*. Chicago: University of Chicago Press, 1993.

Marty, Martin E., and R. Scott Appleby, eds. *Fundamentalisms Observed*. Chicago: University of Chicago Press, 1992.

Marty, Martin E., and Scott R. Appleby, eds. *Fundamentalisms and the State: Remaking Polities, Economies, and Militance*. Chicago: University of Chicago Press, 1996.

Marvin, Carolyn, and David W. Ingle. "Blood Sacrifice and the Nation: Revisiting Civil Religion." *Journal of the American Academy of Religion* 64, no. 4 (1996): 767–80.

Masuzawa, Tomoko. *The Invention of World Religions: Or, How European Universalism Was Preserved in the Language of Pluralism*. Chicago: University of Chicago Press, 2005.

Melamed, Shoham. "Motherhood, Fertility, and the Construction of the 'Demographic Threat' in the Marital Age Law." *Theory and Criticism* 25 (2004): 69–96. (Hebrew)

Mendelssohn, Moses. *Jerusalem: Or on Religious Power and Judaism*. Translated by Allan Arkush. Hanover, NH: Brandeis, 1983.

Mirsky, Yehudah. *Rav Kook: Mystic in a Time of Revolution*. New Haven, CT: Yale University Press, 2014.

Mittelberg, David, and Mary C. Waters. "The Process of Ethnogenesis among Haitian and Israeli Immigrants in the United States." *Ethnic and Racial Studies* 15, no. 3 (1992): 412–35.

Myers, David N. *Between Jew and Arab: The Lost Voice of Simon Rawidowicz.* Hanover, NH; London: Brandeis, 2009.

———. "Rethinking the Jewish Nation." *Hevruta* Winter (2011): 26–33.

Namdar, Reuven. "Mofa' Haeimim Shel A. B. Yehoshua (A. B. Yehoshua's Horror Show)." *Haaretz*, May 29, 2014. (Hebrew)

Naor, Arye. "'Epicureans Also Have a Share in Sinai': On Jabotinsky's Approach to Jewish Legacy." *Iyunim Bitkumat Israel—Annual Collection* 6 (2006): 131–70. (Hebrew)

Nesher, Talila. "Education Ministry Suspends Dismissal of Civics Supervisor." *Haaretz.com*, August 23, 2012. http://www.haaretz.com/news/national/education-ministry-suspends-dismissal-of-civics-supervisor-1.460132.

———. "Israel Education Ministry Fires Civics Studies Coordinator Attacked by Right—News." *Haaretz.com*, August 6, 2012. http://www.haaretz.com/print-edition/news/israel-education-ministry-fires-civics-studies-coordinator-attacked-by-right-1.456182.

Neusner, Jacob. *The Way of Torah: An Introduction to Judaism.* 7th ed. Albany, NY: Cengage Learning, 2003.

Nietzsche, Friedrich. *Untimely Meditations.* Edited by Daniel Breazeale. Translated by R. J. Hollingdale. Cambridge Texts in the History of Philosophy. Cambridge, MA: Cambridge University Press, 1997.

Oakeshott, Michael. *Rationalism in Politics and Other Essays.* New York: Basic Books, 1962.

Ohana, David. *Messianism and Mamlachtiyut: Ben Gurion and the Intellectuals between Political Vision and Political Theory.* Sede Boqer: Ben-Gurion University Press; The Ben-Gurion Institute for the Study of Israel and Zionism, 2003. (Hebrew)

Oppenheimer, Jonathan. "The Druze in Israel as Arabs and Non-Arabs: Manipulation of Categories of Identity in a Non-Civil State." In *Studies in Israeli Ethnicity: After the Ingathering*, edited by Alex Weingrod, 259–80. New York: Gordon and Breach, 1985.

Ornan, Uzi. "Haleum Sheli: Yisraeli (My Nationality: Israeli)." *ynet*, September 3, 2008. http://www.ynet.co.il/articles/0,7340,L-3591497,00.html. (Hebrew)

Peled, Yoav. "Ethnic Democracy and the Legal Construction of Citizenship: Arab Citizens of the Jewish State." *American Political Science Review* 86, no. 02 (1992): 432–43.

———. *The Challenge of Ethnic Democracy: The State and Minority Groups in Israel, Poland and Northern Ireland.* London; New York: Routledge, 2013.

Peri, Menaḥem. "Afillu Lo Reva' Yehudi (Not even a quarter Jewish)." Accessed August 4, 2015. http://www.newlibrary.co.il/page_1463. (Hebrew)

Polanyi, Michael. *Personal Knowledge: Towards a Post-Critical Philosophy.* Chicago: University of Chicago Press, 1958.

———. *Science, Faith and Society.* London: Oxford University Press, 1946.

Porath, Yehoshua. *The Life of Uriel Shelah*. Tel-Aviv: Maḥbarot Lesifrut, 1989. (Hebrew)

Rabinow, Paul. *Symbolic Domination: Cultural Form and Historical Change in Morocco*. Chicago and London: University of Chicago Press, 1975.

Ratzabi, Shalom. "Jabotinsky and Religion." *Isreal—Studies in Zionism and the State of Israel—History, Society, Culture* 5 (2004): 1–30. (Hebrew)

Ravitzky, Aviezer. *Messianism, Zionism, and Jewish Religious Radicalism*. Chicago: University of Chicago Press, 1996.

Raz-Krakotzkin, Amnon. "Exile, History and the Nationalization of Jewish Memory: Some Reflections on the Zionist Notion of History and Return." *Journal of Levantine Studies* 3, no. 2 (2013): 37–70.

———. "Exile within Sovereignty: Toward a Critique of the 'Negation of Exile' in Israeli Culture. Part 1." *Theory and Criticism* 4 (1993): 23–55. (Hebrew)

Regev, Motti, and Edwin Seroussi. *Popular Music and National Culture in Israel*. Berkeley: University of California Press, 2004.

Reouveni, Aharon. "Hamedina, Ma Shema? Mi Qara Lah Kach, Lama, Umatai? (The State, What is its name? Who Named it, Why and When?)." *Haaretz*, April 30, 2006. http://www.haaretz.co.il/news/education/1.1102064. (Hebrew)

Rorty, Richard. *Philosophy and the Mirror of Nature*. Princeton, NJ: Princeton University Press, 1979.

Sagi, Avi. *The Challenge of a Return to Tradition*. Jerusalem and Ramat-Gan: Hartman Institute/Bar-Ilan University, Faculty of Law/Keter, 2003. (Hebrew)

———. *The Jewish-Israeli Voyage: Culture and Identity*. Jerusalem: Shalom Hartman Institute, 2006. (Hebrew)

———. *To Be a Jew: Joseph Chayim Brenner as a Jewish Existentialist*. London; New York, NY: Continuum, 2011.

———. *Tradition vs. Traditionalism: Contemporary Perspectives in Jewish Thought*. Amsterdam and New York: Rodopi, 2008.

Salmon, Yosef. "Religion and Nationalism in the early Zionist Movement." In *Jewish Nationalism and Politics: New Perspectives*, edited by Jehuda Reinharz, Yosef Salmon, and Gideon Shimoni, 115–40. Jerusalem and Boston: The Zalman Shazar Center for Jewish History and the Tuaber Institute, Brandeis University, 1996. (Hebrew)

———. "Religion and Secularism in the Zionist National Movement." *Israel: Studies in Zionism and the State of Israel* 2 (2002): 1–14. (Hebrew)

———. *Religion and Zionism: First Encounters*. Jerusalem: Hebrew University Magnes Press, 2002. (Hebrew)

———. "Zionism and Anti-Zionism in Traditional Judaism in Eastern Europe." In *Zionism and Religion*, edited by Samuel Almog, Jehuda Reinharz, and Anita Shapira, 25–43. Boston: University Press of New England, 1998.

Sand, Shlomo. *How I Stopped Being a Jew*. Translated by David Fernbach. London; New York: Verso, 2014.

Satlow, Michael L. "Defining Judaism: Accounting for 'Religions' in the Study of Religion." *Journal of the American Academy of Religion* 74, no. 4 (2006): 837–60.

Schwartz, Dov. *Religious Zionism: History and Ideology*. Translated by Batya Stein. Boston: Academic Studies Press, 2008.

———. *The Religious Genius in Rabbi Kook's Thought: National Saint?* Translated by Edward Levin. Boston: Academic Studies Press, 2015.

Segev, Tom. "Mihu ḥiloni? (Who is a secular?)." *Haaretz*, September 25, 1996. (Hebrew)

Shafir, Gershon, and Yoav Peled. *Being Israeli: The Dynamics of Multiple Citizenship*. Cambridge, MA; New York: Cambridge University Press, 2002.

Shapira, Anita. *Yosef Haim Brenner: A Life*. Stanford, CA: Stanford University Press, 2014.

Shavit, Jacob. *The New Hebrew Nation: A Study in Israeli Heresy and Fantasy*. London: Frank Cass, 1987.

Shenhav, Yehouda. "Modernity and the Hybridization of Nationalism and Religion: Zionism and the Jews of the Middle East as a Heuristic Case." *Theory and Society: Renewal and Critique in Social Theory* 36, no. 1 (2007): 1–30.

———. "Reflections on a post-Westfalian Sovereignty." In *Four lectures on Critical Theory*, edited by Gil Eyal, 24–50. Jerusalem: Van-Leer Jerusalem Institute, 2012. (Hebrew)

Shils, Edward. *Tradition*. Chicago: University of Chicago Press, 1981.

———. "Tradition and Liberty: Antinomy and Interdependence." *Ethics* 68, no. 3 (1958): 153–65.

Shimoni, Gideon. *The Zionist Ideology*. Hanover, NH, and London: Brandeis University Press. Published by University Press of New England, 1995.

Shoham, Hizky. *Carnival in Tel Aviv: Purim and the Celebration of Urban Zionism*. Boston: Academic Studies Press, 2014.

———. *Let's Celebrate! Festivals and Civic Culture in Israel*. Jerusalem: The Israel Democracy Institute, 2014. (Hebrew)

Simon, Aryeh, and Yosef Eliyahu Heller. *Aḥad Ha'am: The Man and His Life-work*. Jerusalem: Magnes Press, 1954. (Hebrew)

Skinner, Quentin. *The Foundations of Modern Political Thought*. 2 vols. Cambridge, MA; New York: Cambridge University Press, 1978.

Smith, Anthony D. *The Nation in History: Historiographical Debates about Ethnicity and Nationalism*. Boston: University Press of New England, 2000.

Smith, Jonathan Z. *Imagining Religion: From Babylon to Jonestown*. Chicago: University of Chicago Press, 1982.

———. "Religion, Religions, Religious." In *Critical Terms for Religious Studies*, edited by Mark C. Taylor, 269–84. Chicago and London: University of Chicago Press, 1998.

Smith, Wilfred Cantwell. *The Meaning and End of Religion: A New Approach to the Religious Traditions of Mankind*. New York: Macmillan, 1963.

Smooha, Sammy. "Ethnic Democracy: Israel as an Archetype." *Israel Studies* 2, no. 2 (1997): 198–241.

———. "The Model of Ethnic Democracy: Israel as a Jewish and Democratic State." *Nations and Nationalism* 8, no. 4 (2002): 475–503.

Solberg, Noam. HP (Jerusalem) 6092/07 *Ornan, et al. v. Interior Ministry* (2008). (Hebrew)

Stark, Rodney. "Atheism, Faith, and the Social Scientific Study of Religion." *Journal of Contemporary Religion* 14, no. 1 (1999): 41–62.

———. "Secularization, R.I.P." *Sociology of Religion* 60, no. 3 (1999): 249–73.

Sternhell, Zeev. *The Founding Myths of Israel: Nationalism, Socialism, and the Making of the Jewish State*. Princeton, NJ: Princeton University Press, 1998.

Syrkin, Naḥman. *Kitvei Naḥman Syrkin (Naḥman Syrkin's Writings)*. Edited by Berl Katznelson and Yehouda Kaufman. Tel-Aviv: Dvir, 1939. (Hebrew)

Taylor, Charles. *A Secular Age*. Cambridge, MA: Belknap Press of Harvard University Press, 2007.

———. *Human Agency and Language*. Vol. 1. Philosophical Papers. Cambridge, MA: Cambridge University Press, 1985.

———. "Interpretation and the Sciences of Man." *The Review of Metaphysics* 25, no. 1 (1971): 3–51.

———. *Philosophical Arguments*. Cambridge, MA: Harvard University Press, 1995.

———. *Philosophy and the Human Sciences*. Vol. 2. Philosophical Papers. Cambridge, MA: Cambridge University Press, 1985.

———. *The Ethics of Authenticity*. Cambridge, MA: Harvard University Press, 1992.

———. "Two Theories of Modernity." *Public Culture* 11, no. 1 (1999): 153–74.

Triandafyllidou, Anna. "National Identity and the 'Other.'" *Ethnic and Racial Studies* 21, no. 4 (1998): 593–612.

Tsur, Muky. "Pesach in the Land of Israel: Kibbutz Haggadot." *Israel Studies* 12, no. 2 (2007): 74–103.

Vattimo, Gianni. "Democracy and Hermeneutics." *Telos* 2012, no. 161 (2012): 9–15.

Vogelman, Uzi. CA 8573/08 *Ornan, et al. v. Interior Ministry* (2013). (Hebrew)

Walzer, Michael. "On the Role of Symbolism in Political Thought." *Political Science Quarterly* 82, no. 2 (1967): 191–204.

———. *The Paradox of Liberation: Secular Revolutions and Religious Counterrevolutions*. New Haven, CT: Yale University Press, 2015.

Weiss, Phillip. "Sayed Kashua Doesn't Want to Write in Hebrew for 'Haaretz' Anymore." *Mondoweiss*, March 15, 2016. http://mondoweiss.net/2016/03/sayed-kashua-doesnt-want-to-write-in-hebrew-for-haaretz-anymore/.

Wittgenstein, Ludwig. *On Certainty*. New York: Harper, 1969.

———. *Philosophical Investigations*. 3rd ed. New York: Macmillan, 1968.

Yadgar, Yaacov. "A Post-Secular Look at Tradition: Toward a Definition of Traditionism." *Telos* 156 (2011): 77–98.

———. "Between 'the Arab' and 'the Religious Rightist': 'Significant Others' in the Construction of Jewish-Israeli National Identity." *Nationalism and Ethnic Politics* 9, no. 1 (2003): 52–74.

———. *Beyond Secularization: Traditionists and the Critique of Israeli Secularism.* Jerusalem: The Van-Leer Institute/Haqibutz Hameuḥad, 2012. (Hebrew)

———. *Secularism and Religion in Jewish-Israeli Politics: Traditionists and Modernity.* London: Routledge, 2011.

———. "Traditionism." *Cogent Social Sciences* 1, no. 1061734 (2015): 1–17. http://dx.doi.org/10.1080/23311886.2015.1061734.

Yakobson, Alexander, and Amnon Rubinstein. *Israel and the Family of Nations: The Jewish Nation-State and Human Rights.* New York: Routledge, 2009.

Yehoshua, A. B. *Aḥizat Moledet (Homeland Grasp: 20 Articles and One Story).* Edited by Avner Holtzman. Tel-Aviv: Haqibutz Hameuḥad, 2008. (Hebrew)

———. *Bizchut Hanormaliyut: Ḥamesh Masot Bishelot Hatziyonut (For Normality: Five Essays on the Questions of Zionism).* Jerusalem: Shoken, 1980. (Hebrew)

———. "Haḥayim Beparadox (Life in a paradox)." In *Anu Hayehudim Haḥilonim*, edited by Dedi Zucker, 13–22. Tel-Aviv: Yedi'ot Aḥaronot, 1999. (Hebrew)

———. "Hapetil Hakaful Shel Hayisraelim (The Israelis' Double Fuse)." *Haaretz*, September 29, 1988. (Hebrew)

———. *Haqir Vehahar: Metziuto Halo-Sifrutit Shel Hasofer Bisrael (The Wall and the Mountain: The Non-Literary Reality of the Author in Israel).* Tel-Aviv: Zemora Bitan, 5749. (Hebrew)

———. "Lehavri Et Haandrogynous (To Heal the Androgynous)." In *'Osim Ḥoshvim: 'Imutim Bamaḥashava Hatziburit Bisrael*, by Yonah Hadari-Ramaj, 264–89. Yad Ṭabenqin and Yedi'ot Aḥaronot, 5755. (Hebrew)

———. "Ma ZeYehudi Shalem (What Is a Whole Jew)." Accessed August 5, 2015. http://www.newlibrary.co.il/page_1469.aspx?c0=16602&bss53= 13176. (Hebrew)

———. "Mihu Tziyoni (Who Is a Zionist)." *Haaretz*, May 14, 2013. (Hebrew)

———. "Mihu Yehudi (Who Is a Jew)." *Haaretz*, September 5, 2013. (Hebrew)

———. "The Meaning of Homeland." In *The A. B. Yehoshua Controversy: An Israel-Diaspora Dialogue on Jewishness, Israeliness, and Identity*, 7–13. New York: Dorothy and Julius Koppelman Institute on American Jewish-Israeli Relations, American Jewish Committee, 2006.

———. "Mihu Yisraeli (Who is an Israeli)." *Haaretz*, September 13, 2013. (Hebrew)

Yehoshua, A. B. and others. *The A. B. Yehoshua Controversy: An Israel-Diaspora Dialogue on Jewishness, Israeliness, and Identity.* New York: Dorothy and Julius Koppelman Institute On American Jewish-Israeli Relations, American Jewish Committee, 2006.

Yiftachel, Oren. *Ethnocracy: Land and Identity Politics in Israel/Palestine.* Philadelphia: University of Pennsylvania Press, 2006.

———. "'Ethnocracy': The Politics of Judaizing Israel/Palestine." *Constellations* 6, no. 3 (2002): 364–90.

Yiftachel, Oren, and Michaly D. Segal. "Jews and Druze in Israel: State Control and Ethnic Resistance." *Ethnic and Racial Studies* 21, no. 3 (1998): 476–506.

Yonah, Yossi. "Israel's Immigration Policies: The Twofold Face of the 'Demographic Threat.'" *Social Identities* 10, no. 2 (2004): 195–218.

Zameret, Zvi. "Berdyczewski, Brenner and Gordon on the Sabbath." In *Around the Dot: Studies on M. Y. Berdichevsky, Y. H. Brenner and A. D. Gordon: Iyunim Bitkumat Israel: Thematic Series*, edited by Avner Holtzman, Gideon Katz, and Shalom Ratzabi, 451–68. Sede Boqer: Ben-Gurion University Press; The Ben-Gurion Institute for the Study of Israel and Zionism, 2008. (Hebrew)

Zeira, Moti. *We Are Torn Apart.* Jerusalem: Yad Yitzhak Ben Zvi, 2002. (Hebrew)

Zerubavel, Yael. *Recovered Roots: Collective Memory and the Making of Israeli National Tradition.* Chicago: University of Chicago Press, 1995.

Zipperstein, Steven J. *Elusive Prophet: Ahad Ha'am and the Origins of Zionism.* Berkeley: University of California Press, 1993.

# Index

www.ingramcontent.com/pod-product-compliance
Lightning Source LLC
Chambersburg PA
CBHW030343270326
41926CB00009B/939